W9-CKH-942

FOR
THOSE
STILL
AT
SEA

Simas Kudirka
& Larry Eichel

FOR THOSE STILL AT SEA

THE DIAL PRESS · NEW YORK

Published by
The Dial Press
1 Dag Hammarskjold Plaza
New York, New York   10017

Copyright © 1978 by Simas Kudirka and Lawrence E. Eichel

All rights reserved. No part of this book may be reproduced in any form or by any means without the prior written permission of the Publisher, excepting brief quotes used in connection with reviews written specifically for inclusion in a magazine or newspaper.

Manufactured in the United States of America
First printing

Library of Congress Cataloging in Publication Data

Kudirka, Simas.
    For those still at sea

    1. Kudirka, Simas.   2. Defectors—Russia—Biography.
3. Political Prisoners—Russia—Biography.
    I. Eichel, Lawrence E., joint author.   II. Title.
DK511. L28K   874.   323.6'4'0924[B]   78-5699
ISBN 0-8037-2684-8

TO THE POLITICAL PRISONERS,
THEN AND NOW

With best wishes

Simas Kudirka –

Acknowledgments

Simas Kudirka has the extraordinary good fortune to be surrounded by three women who care deeply about both the struggle he represents and the man he is. Since 1974, Rima Mironas has played the supporting roles of big sister, confessor, teacher, public relations woman, and translator to Simas's lead. Rima did nothing more than make it possible for Simas and me to talk to each other. She converted my questions into his Lithuanian and his answers into my English. Without her energy and endurance, this book would not have been possible. Daiva Kezys, who has worked for Simas's cause since the first day there was a cause to work for, provided documents, insight, guidance, and always hope. Gene Kudirka, Simas's wife, attended to the family business while her husband was off with Rima and me, telling his life story. Gene had the courage to allow the truth to be written, even though she knew that some readers might not approve.

Many of the characters in this story talked to me about their parts in it, some eagerly, others reluctantly. I thank them all, particularly Mary Achenbach, Dr. C. Kazys Bobelis, Betty Burger, William Dyess, Ralph Eustis, James Fowlie, S. Algimantas Gecys, Shimon Grilius, Robert Hanrahan, David Ilchert, Robert McFadden, Grazina Paegle, Roland Paegle, Marija Sulskis, Leonard Willems, and Ausra Zerr. The U.S. State Department and U.S. Coast Guard provided documents that aided my research. The officers and crew of the Coast Guard cutter *Vigilant* welcomed us, fed us, and gave us the run of their ship one cold February afternoon. Their hospitality allowed Simas to reenact for me the seven hours on November 23, 1970, that form the base of this story. Thanks to them.

Despite all the help, this book would not have been completed had it not been for the support of three other people. John Sterling, our agent, got me into this project, helped shape it, and kept working to see it through despite disheartening setbacks. Nancy van Itallie, our editor, got excited about the book when no one else could.

And Barbara Beck, my wife, allowed me to sacrifice much of the first year of our marriage to this book. She left me alone just long enough to get the work done and bothered me enough to remind me that she missed me. For that reminder, I thank her.

L.E.

ACKNOWLEDGMENTS

FOR
THOSE
STILL
AT
SEA

One

The short, husky man in the brown windbreaker stood on the third deck of his ship and stared out over the rail. The gray skies were low and thick. The air was unseasonably mild, the winds gentle, and the sea almost calm.

For weeks, Simas Kudirka had eagerly anticipated this day—November 23, 1970. His ship, the *Sovetskaya Litva,* a floating factory that processed the catch of the Soviet fishing fleet, was at anchor one-half mile off the island of Martha's Vineyard in a gentle curve of American water called Menemsha Bight. There the Soviet ship and her crew of 160 awaited the arrival of an American Coast Guard cutter. The American ship would be carrying a special delegation of angry Massachusetts fishermen who wanted to protest that the Soviets were harvesting too many fish from New England waters. But Simas did not care about the substance of the meeting. He was a radio operator, not a fisherman. He just wanted to see the Americans close up and maybe talk to them for a few minutes. As a child growing up in Lithuania, he had dreamed of visiting America, as his grandfather had done so long ago. Now, as a man entering middle age, he felt certain that this brief encounter would be as close to America as he would ever get.

He turned his head and watched the chalky white American cutter, so tiny in comparison to his own ship, approach from astern. As the cutter drew closer, he could make out its name—*Vigilant.*

3

Soon the men on both ships began mooring them together with thick sea line. They rocked back and forth in the gentle swells, six feet apart one moment, ten feet apart the next.

The smiling American seamen waved wildly and shouted their greetings. Simas looked below him down to the main deck of the *Sovetskaya Litva*. There the Soviet sailors stood in silence, their teeth clenched, their arms folded in front of them, lining the deck like robots. He had feared it would be this way. Soviet sailors were always rude and aloof to Westerners, not because they liked being rude but because they valued their careers. Only a fleet officer could safely offer an American a smile and a handshake and only in a situation staged for a photographer's benefit.

Yet when the lines were secured and the two ships linked, the atmosphere changed. The American good cheer proved irresistible. As the American fishermen were hoisted across from the *Vigilant* to the *Sovetskaya Litva* for the meeting itself, the American sailors bombarded the Soviet ship with gifts in a spontaneous cultural exchange. They hurled boxes of cigarettes, cans of beer and soda, belts, pennies, and dark blue baseball caps with VIG for *Vigilant* sewn across the front in gold letters. The Soviet sailors caught the gifts, waved in thanks, and threw their own belts, caps, and cigarettes in return.

"Come on aboard!" one American shouted to a Soviet seaman.

The smile on the Soviet seaman's face disappeared, and he quickly drew his finger across his Adam's apple, as if slitting his throat. There was a moment of uneasy silence. Then he burst into laughter, and the relieved American laughed with him.

Soon the deck of the *Sovetskaya Litva* was littered with debris, mostly magazines; and the magazines just lay there, their pages riffled by the breeze. The Soviet sailors were in no hurry to pick them up. Smoking an American cigarette or wearing an American baseball cap was one thing. Reading a piece of capitalist propaganda was quite another.

On the third deck, about four feet down the railing from Simas, Emilius Gruzauskas, the ship's first mate and chief political officer, was watching the exchange with professional interest. It was his job to vaccinate the men of his ship with constant doses of Soviet ideology, to immunize them against the Western ideas they would encounter on their voyages. He had been enjoying himself until the Americans started throwing magazines. Those glossy magazines, so full of dangerous ideas, were a threat to him and his work. He knew that he was about to find out how effective his vaccinations had been. He anxiously surveyed the main deck. Suddenly, his eyes locked into a cold, hard stare.

"Look," he said to another officer. "Watch this."

Simas, overhearing the conversation, looked too.

Two young crew members, a man and a woman, had stooped to the deck in an area that was covered with magazines. They slipped a few under their jackets and hurried below to hide their treasures. The vaccinations had not taken on everyone.

Grusauskas turned to the officer. "Those two will never go to sea again," he said.

I heard those words and inside I blew up. "I'm finished," I said to myself. "I've had it." I wanted to turn around and really let Gruzauskas have it. Those two poor kids! You walk a tightrope between staying alive and dying and then one careless, meaningless gesture can throw you off. One wrong word, and it's all gone for the rest of your life. I knew. I had fallen off the tightrope once long ago. And I had paid for it dearly. Wasn't that slip the real reason I had still not received a seaman's passport? Wasn't that the reason I had had to wait thirteen years to get an apartment big enough for myself, my wife, my daughter, and my son? Now this pair would have to endure the same suffering I had endured. They would be booked on voyages and then taken off at the last minute by the border police without ever knowing why. They would always be threatened with the loss of their right to work. And for what? In the instant they picked up those magazines, their lives melted into mine and mine melted into meaninglessness. We were victims—all of us. We were trapped on a floating jail.

I had to do something to break out of it. The idea of jumping to the American ship flashed into my mind out of nowhere. The idea felt right, and I never questioned it. I guess I had a rocket inside me just waiting for the right spark to light the fuse. No salary, no feeble promise of getting a passport someday was going to stop me. I was going to jump. I was going to defect to the United States of America. I didn't know much about American law or American society. I didn't know a soul in the whole country. I knew only what my grandfather had told me, and that was sixty years out of date. I knew only a few words of English. But I had a clear conscience. I would find someone who would listen to my sorrows, someone who would understand me and give me a job. I would work hard. I would get my family out of the Soviet Union. It wouldn't be easy—I knew that—but in three or four years I could do it. I could pull them out into freedom, and any wound I had caused them would be healed.

My mind was set. I was going to jump.

Simas walked to the far end of the third deck and looked straight across at a tall, red-headed American sailor who was standing outside the *Vigilant*'s pilothouse.

"Hello," Simas said in English.

The American returned the greeting.

"I am radio operator," Simas continued, straining his command of the language. He wanted to explain his problems, but his English would not allow it. He would have to keep it simple.

"I want asylum," he said.

The American, Seaman John Fowlie, thought the Soviet sailor had made a joke. "You think your ship is an asylum," he laughed. "You should spend a few days on this boat, baby. Whew! It's a real nuthouse."

Simas knew he was not getting through. "I from Lithuania, not Russia. I not like Russians." He paused. "Gestapo! Gestapo!"

Now Fowlie was staring at him.

"I will go to you," Simas said. "I want asylum."

Lieutenant Junior Grade Douglas Lundberg, operations officer of the *Vigilant,* had heard Fowlie's laughter and came outside the pilothouse to find out what was going on. Fowlie told Lundberg he thought the earnest-looking man on the Soviet ship wanted to defect.

Lundberg took a look at Simas, then ducked inside the pilothouse and found Paul Pakos, a short, boyish-looking lieutenant commander who was the ship's second-ranking officer. The skipper of the *Vigilant,* Commander Ralph Eustis, had accompanied the American fishermen to the *Sovetskaya Litva.* In his absence, Pakos was in command of the ship.

"Mr. Pakos, you aren't going to believe this, but this guy says he wants political asylum," Lundberg said.

Pakos followed Lundberg back outside. Simas was still there, looking over his shoulder to make sure his fellow crew members were not watching. When he saw the Americans, he put up his hand, as if asking them to wait.

"I will check," he said, then disappeared. He raced down into the bowels of the Soviet ship to check the sea water temperature. "Not too cold," he said on his return. "I swim." With his hands, he made swimming motions.

Without giving the man an answer, Pakos and Lundberg walked back inside. Pakos, like the others, was convinced the man was serious, and he was eager to help him succeed. He ordered that a rope ladder be lowered into the sea on the side of the *Vigilant* out of the view of the Soviet ship. If the man did jump into the water, he could swim to the ladder and climb up. Then Pakos hurried down one flight of stairs to the cutter's radio room, and, at 12:43 P.M., sent out a secret message to Coast Guard District Headquarters in Boston:

ESTIMATE WITH EIGHTY PERCENT PROBABILITY THAT ONE CREWMAN FROM SOVIET MOTHER SHIP WILL ATTEMPT DEFECTION TO VIGILANT. DEFECTION WAS NOT ENTICED. CREWMAN SPOKE IN BROKEN ENGLISH TO OPERATIONS OFFICER [Lundberg] THAT HE WISHED ASYLUM. SAME MAN LATER INDICATED TO EXECUTIVE OFFICER [Pakos] THAT WATER NOT TOO COLD AND THAT HE WOULD SWIM. COMMANDING OFFICER [Eustis] AND OTHER VISITORS STILL ABOARD [*Sovetskaya Litva*] AND UNAWARE OF SITUATION. WILL ATTEMPT TO ADVISE COMMANDING OFFICER.

IF ESCAPE IS UNDETECTED PLAN TO RECALL ENTIRE DELEGATION UNDER FALSE PRETENSES AND DEPART. IF ESCAPE DETECTED

FORESEE MAJOR PROBLEM IF DELEGATION STILL ABOARD. REQUEST ADVISE.

PLAN NO ACTION PENDING FURTHER DEVELOPMENTS.

Pakos then summoned Commander Eustis back to the *Vigilant.* When told of the developing situation, Eustis said he feared that the defection might be phony, a provocation staged by the Soviets to cause an international incident. He warned Pakos not to encourage the man in any way. Before returning to the *Sovetskaya Litva,* Eustis climbed up to the bridge and stepped outside. The would-be defector was still there, his eyes exploring his own ship, the American ship, and the water in between.

It was obvious what he was doing. He was choosing a spot for his jump.

When Captain Fletcher W. Brown, Jr., returned to his Boston office after lunch, his secretary told him of the *Vigilant's* urgent message. He hurried down the hall to Rescue Control Center to read it. Normally the fifty-year-old Brown, who had spent most of his thirty-two-year service career piloting rescue planes, was the district's chief of staff, the number two man. But his superior, Rear Admiral William B. Ellis, fifty-six, was on leave, recuperating at home from hernia surgery. That left Brown as acting district commander, the man in charge.

As soon as he read the message, he recognized its potential significance and ordered a copy sent to the Washington office of Coast Guard Commandant Chester R. Bender. The message from the *Vigilant* asked for advice, and Brown had absolutely no idea what advice to give. He asked his secretary to have Commander John F. Curry, the district's chief of intelligence and law enforcement, come to his office. Without waiting for Curry to arrive, he placed a call to Coast Guard headquarters in Washington and reached Rear Admiral Robert Hammond, the Guard's national chief of operations.

"Bob," Brown said after explaining the situation, "we are going to need some help."

"I'll be back in touch with you," Hammond replied.

But Captain Brown needed guidance immediately. What if the

Soviet seaman jumped now? Brown had been in many tight spots in his Coast Guard career, and he had saved many lives, but he was no diplomat. What if the man jumped while Americans were still on board the Soviet ship? What if the Soviets held them hostage?

Still holding the telephone, he shoved the *Vigilant*'s message across his desk to Commander Curry, who had just entered the room. Without saying a word to Curry, he dialed the district commander, Admiral Ellis, at home. In the weeks that Ellis had been out sick, Brown had called him regularly to update him on developments in the district. He considered Ellis a man of integrity, a source of excellent guidance. He needed some of that guidance right now.

When Ellis got on the phone, Brown explained his predicament. The admiral was firm and sure of himself as always, as befitted a man who had been giving orders for half his life. His career had been a success, he knew, because he had always welcomed responsibility. Whenever clear, firm orders were needed, he had given them. And he gave them now.

"First, don't take any action that would indicate the *Vigilant* condones defection. Do nothing to indicate to the man that refuge will be granted. Second, if the man jumps into the water, we should give the Russians the opportunity to pick him up. We should not let the man drown. Third, if we pick the man up, he should be returned to the Russian ship. Fourth, get Eustis back aboard the *Vigilant*."

Brown thanked Ellis for his help, inquired about the admiral's health, and hung up. Ellis, while on convalescent leave, had absolutely no authority in the Coast Guard chain of command. But Brown felt he had just received his orders. His job, as he saw it, was to run the district the way the admiral wanted it run.

"We're going to return the man," Brown told Curry.

"Why?"

"The decision has been made."

9

Two

As Captain Brown was talking to Commander Curry, Simas Kudirka was sitting on his bunk in the bowels of the *Sovetskaya Litva,* flipping through the Lithuanian–English dictionary he kept hidden among his belongings. He thought the American sailors understood his plan, but to be certain, he would write them a note in their own language. Carefully he composed it, then signed it, rolled it up, put it in his pocket, and headed for the deck. He would throw it across to the *Vigilant.* Then he stopped. What if the wind caught the message and blew it down into the sea or, worse, back onto his own ship? He had to find something to make it heavier. He stole a pack of cigarettes from a friend and stuck the note inside the cellophane wrapper.

When he got back up to the third deck, he saw one of the Americans standing outside the pilothouse. He got the American's attention, pulled the cigarette pack out of his pocket, pointed to it, and threw it across toward the *Vigilant.*

Lunging over the railing, Lieutenant Lundberg caught the cigarette pack. He waved his thanks, pulled out a cigarette, and took several leisurely puffs.

"Good," he said and strolled back into the pilothouse. The instant he was sure he was out of view of the Soviets, he tore open the pack and found the tiny handwritten note.

"My dear Comrade," it read, "I will up down of Russian ship

and go with you together. If is possible please give me signal. I keep a sharp lookout.'' It was signed "Simas.'' He turned it over. There was more. "I up down in the time when the conference is End, and you delegats go into you ships a Board!''

Lundberg showed it to Lieutenant Commander Pakos, who summoned the skipper, Commander Eustis, back from the Soviet ship once more. Obviously, this man Simas was going to jump. Eustis said he would try to close out the fishing conference as soon as possible, to give the man a chance to defect before dark.

In Washington, ever since Captain Brown had called from Boston, members of the Coast Guard bureaucracy had been trying to get him some advice on how to handle a defection. It had not been easy.

Rear Admiral Hammond, who knew nothing about defections, had referred the matter to Captain Wallace Dahlgren, chief of intelligence, who knew nothing about defections either. Dahlgren did know that he should contact the State Department—but who in the State Department? As a start, he called David Webb, a Coast Guard captain assigned to State whom the Guard considered its State Department liaison officer. Unfortunately, Webb did not consider himself a liaison officer; as far as he was concerned he was a marine officer in State's Office of Space, Atmospheric, and Marine Affairs and nothing more. He knew little about how State worked, and, like all the others, he knew absolutely nothing about defections. Webb could only tell Dahlgren that he would try to determine the identity of State's man in charge of defections, if there was such a man.

Webb began his search by asking his immediate superior for advice and was told to call the deputy assistant secretary for security affairs. He called, but the deputy assistant secretary was out of his office. The secretary to the deputy assistant secretary, who was in, suggested that Webb contact one of two lower echelon officials in security affairs. At 2:40 P.M., nearly an hour and a half after Washington first got word of the possibility of a defection, Webb called Dahlgren back with the names of the officials and the telephone number they shared.

11

Dahlgren called that number, hoping to get prompt guidance. What he got was word that he was calling the wrong office. The matter, he was told, should properly be referred to Adolph Dubbs, chief of the Soviet desk. Time was slipping away, and Dahlgren was getting nowhere. He dialed Dubbs's phone number and found that Dubbs was out of his office. Dubbs's secretary referred the call to one of Dubbs's assistants, an experienced career diplomat named Edward Killham. Killham said that yes, he was the right man to be consulted. Relieved, Dahlgren started to explain the situation, but Killham stopped him; he said he wanted to read the *Vigilant*'s message first.

A half hour later, Killham called Dahlgren back. He had read the telegram and was ready to talk. Dahlgren said he needed to know what the Guard should do if the would-be defector jumped into the water. Neither he nor anyone else in Boston or Washington knew how close together the two ships really were.

"What degree or nature of force is the Coast Guard authorized to use in order to retrieve him?" Dahlgren asked.

"This is a very sticky question," Killham replied cautiously. "I don't think I can answer that question myself and, what's more, I don't think I can get you a definitive answer that would do you any good." He said the Guard should simply follow its tradition of rescuing people in distress. As Dahlgren probed for more specific advice, Killham was struck by the absurdity of the conversation. Here was the Coast Guard, whose main business was sea rescue, asking the Soviet Affairs desk of the State Department how to conduct a sea rescue.

Killham said that the Guard should inform State if and when the defector came aboard. He did not say what he was thinking—that the man would probably be brought to shore for interviews to determine whether he was a bona fide defector, not a madman or a spy. He did not say, "Don't return him." He could not imagine that the Guard could even be toying with the idea of handing the man back to the Soviets.

By 3:45, two and a half hours after he had called Admiral Hammond, Captain Brown was staring at his desk, wondering whether

Washington would ever call back and what he would do if that call did not come through in time. Although he found it distasteful, almost unthinkable, to question Admiral Ellis's judgment, he had begun to have serious doubts about whether the Guard had any right to return a defector to the Soviets, just like that. His three top advisers were all against returning the man. Commander Jerome Flanagan, the district's legal officer, had told him that a defection was a delicate diplomatic affair, rightfully handled by the State Department or the White House. The Coast Guard should not be in the business of creating foreign policy, he said. Flanagan had suggested readying a helicopter to pluck the man off the *Vigilant* and bring him to Boston, where he would be turned over to civilian authorities.

Troubled, Brown had called Admiral Ellis again, and Ellis had tersely repeated his earlier advice—the defector was to be returned. But Flanagan's advice still made a lot of sense, even though it conflicted with the admiral's. Fletcher Brown was more confused than ever.

The telephone rang. At long last, Washington was calling back.

"What the fellow at the State Department told me," Captain Dahlgren said, "is that if the fellow goes into the water, exercise your statutory duties of search and rescue and get the man out of the water. Don't let him drown. And call us when the man is on board the *Vigilant*."

"Oh, for crap's sake, Wally," Brown replied. He was angry and disappointed. He had been hoping for something much more specific. "What do you think we are up here—a bunch of dopes or something? That's our business."

"Yes, I know," Dahlgren said, adding that he had been unable to learn what official policy was for handling defections.

Brown thanked Dahlgren for his efforts, hung up the phone, sat back, and waited. Still there was no word from the *Vigilant*. He looked outside and saw a city enveloped in low gray clouds, a sky that was prematurely dark. He doubted anyone would try to jump from a ship if he could not see where he was going. Brown was becoming convinced that there would be no defection attempt after all. He called Admiral Hammond in Washington. The two of them

13

discussed the events of the afternoon and bemoaned the lack of help from the State Department.

"If you get him aboard," Hammond said, "let us know immediately."

Brown said he would. He did not tell Hammond that he had already been told by Ellis to return the defector. He did mention that it was 4:15 P.M.

"Do you think I should remain in the office pending some kind of development or should I go ahead and get my normal commuter service?" he asked.

"I see no reason why you shouldn't shove off," Hammond replied. "Keep us up to date."

On the *Sovetskaya Litva,* Simas was getting ready to jump. He was sitting in the ship's tiny radio room, where he had reported for duty at mid-afternoon. All the Americans had returned to the *Vigilant.* Soon the moment for the jump would be upon him and there would be no time for second thoughts. He would just have to do it or the chance would disappear. He would be ready. He had spent the afternoon sorting through his belongings, knowing that he would have to travel light. He would leave behind everything except a packet of newspaper clippings, radiograms, and letters from home which he had stuck in the breast pocket of his blue flannel shirt.

And he had picked out the spot for his jump. He planned to leap directly from the main deck of the *Sovetskaya Litva* to the flight deck of the *Vigilant,* eight feet across and three feet below. If all went well, he would not even get wet. At the spot where he hoped to land, the *Vigilant*'s flight deck had a railing made of three horizontal cables about a foot apart. As he hit the rail, he would grab for the top cable with both hands. If he missed, he would grab for the second or the third. If he missed all three, he could snag the edge of the flight deck or the deck below.

He stared at his watch and waited for the voice of the ship's captain, Vladimir Popov, to crackle over the public address system, ordering all hands to prepare to shove off. The minutes passed. No order. What could be going wrong? He threw his headset down on the table. He had to see what was happening outside. He headed toward the staircase that led down to the main deck, but before he got to the top of the stairs, he saw Captain Popov approaching down the hall.

"Simas," Popov said. "What are you doing out here?"

"I was just looking for someone who would know whether we're going to be leaving soon."

"We are. I was just on my way to the bridge to give the order."

Simas followed Popov to the bridge and saw him pick up the microphone. The moment for the jump had arrived.

He hurried down the first flight of stairs and stopped on the landing for an instant. He heard nothing, saw no one. Convinced he was not being followed, he ran down the second flight and the third, turned right, and went out the door. He was outside, on the main deck, facing the *Vigilant*.

He walked down the deck, heading for his spot. It was 4:25 P.M., dusk, and there was a stiff, chilling breeze in the air. But he was not going to be in the air long enough for the wind to make any difference.

"Hi, Simas," a passing crew member said. Simas was too nervous to reply. He kept on walking. In a few seconds, he was standing at the spot. He had played the scene out in his head all afternoon. He clasped his hands in front of him in an instant of prayer. Then he lifted one leg over the rail and then the other. He was standing on the ship's giant rubber bumper. Freedom was eight feet away. He looked to either side. No one was watching.

He bent his knees and dove across the abyss, his body parallel to the water, his arms extended, reaching desperately for the railing up ahead. For an instant, he was sailing in between, free of the Soviet ship and not yet touching the American. Then he felt the palms of his hands slam into the top wire cable. Instinctively, he closed his fingers around it and held on tight as both feet landed hard on the edge of the deck. It took a second or two for him to realize that he had a sure grip on the *Vigilant*. He had arrived.

Pushing off with his feet, he vaulted over the railing and tumbled onto the flight deck of the American cutter, landing on his right shoulder. He crouched down to avoid hitting his head against a hanging lifeboat, rolled under it, hopped up, and ran to an open doorway four steps away.

He ducked through the doorway and started up a steep, narrow staircase on his right. Then he stopped. He saw a pair of shoes descending the steps, and the shoes became a man—stocky build, thick face, brown hair. He immediately recognized Ivan Burkal, the acting commander of the Soviet fishing fleet and the host for the meeting with the American fishermen. Unknown to Simas, Burkal had insisted on a brief tour of the *Vigilant* when the fishing meeting broke up. His tour was just ending.

Simas clung to the left rail and burst up the stairs.

"Kudirka! What are you doing here?" Burkal yelled.

"Excuse me," he said as he bolted past. "I don't have time."

Simas got to the top of the steps, whirled to his left, and kept running. He ran past four closed doors, turned left again, and bounded up another flight of stairs, which brought him inside the pilothouse. For an instant, he stood silently at the top of the steps, his chest heaving, his presence unnoticed by the half-dozen Guardsmen who filled the small room. He saw the officer who had caught his cigarette pack.

"Good evening," Simas said in English.

The officers turned from their work and stared at him. For a few seconds, there was silence.

"Good evening," Lundberg said, and the silence erupted into a hubbub of handshaking and hugging and voices all talking at once.

"Comrades!" Simas yelled, hysterical with happiness. "Thank you!"

Simas tried to tell them that Burkal knew he was on the *Vigilant*. But he could not make himself understood.

"Did you jump?" Lundberg asked.

Simas did not understand.

Lundberg crouched, extended his arms in front of him, and pretended to grab a railing. "Jump? Jump?"

"Yes," Simas laughed, mimicking Lundberg's crouch. "Jump!"

He tried to explain who he was. "I sailor in Russian fleet. I Lithuanian, not Russian. I try long time to get sailor's passport and nothing, nothing, nothing. . . . I not alone. I have family—two childs, girl, Lolita, boy, Evaldas.''

After a few minutes, he was led to the rear of the pilothouse, through a metal door, and into a storage closet called the ''stick.'' He was instructed to stand inside the closet behind a padded yellow stretcher. And there he waited for the *Vigilant* to start its engines and take him to American soil.

The moment Simas was stashed inside the stick, Lieutenant Commander Pakos dashed down the stairs from the pilothouse to the captain's sitting room two flights below.

''He's here!'' Pakos shouted.

''Who's here?'' Eustis asked.

''The defector!''

''Where is he?''

''In the stick.''

''Did anybody see him jump?''

''I don't know, Captain.''

''Well, you better put him out of sight,'' Eustis said. ''Put him in the watchstander's head and don't let anybody near him.''

''Yes, sir.''

''And put in a call to Captain Brown.''

Simas watched anxiously as the door to the stick opened. Standing in front of him was the tall redhead, the first American he had talked to.

''We have to move you,'' Seaman Fowlie said.

''Good.''

Fowlie led him down the steps to the watchstander's head. The room was simple and gray, four feet deep, five feet wide, and eight feet high. It had a toilet and a sink, a power hand-drier on the right wall, and a mirror on the left.

''O.K.,'' Fowlie said. ''Listen. Lock the door. Lock the door. Do not open the door for anyone, absolutely no one except me.''

''Yes.'' Simas nodded. ''Understand.''

Fowlie left, closing the door behind him. Simas looked at the doorknob and tried to figure out how to lock it. The knob was

17

round with a metal button in the center. He pushed the button in and it stayed in. He turned the inside knob, expecting it to be locked, frozen. But the knob moved and the door opened. He tried the process again and got the same result. (He did not know that the button locked the door on the *outside*.) He cursed his own ignorance. Fearing that Burkal or some other Russian might break in the head and drag him back to the *Sovetskaya Litva,* he leaned his right shoulder against the door, planted his right foot on the ground, and braced his left foot against the back wall, his body forming a giant, slightly bent capital T. Once the *Vigilant* got moving, he figured, he would be safe and able to relax.

Pakos called Boston and asked for Captain Brown.

"Captain Brown is not here," the duty officer said. "He's on his way home."

"What about Commander Curry?" Pakos asked.

"On his way home."

"Admiral Ellis?"

"He's available." He was available because he was home on sick leave and out of the chain of command. But under the pressure of the moment both Pakos and Eustis forgot that fact. "I'll get him for you," the duty officer said.

Pakos sent for Eustis to take the call. Despite all the official discussions about the would-be defection in Boston and Washington during the afternoon, only one message from the Coast Guard hierarchy had reached the *Vigilant.* That message, from Brown in Boston, had instructed the cutter to allow the Soviets to recover the defector if he jumped into the water. It said absolutely nothing about what to do if the man jumped directly onto the *Vigilant.* Still, Commander Ralph Eustis, the thirty-seven-year-old skipper of the cutter, felt certain that the defector would be granted asylum, assuming the man could satisfy American officials that he was not a Soviet spy. Eustis's reaction was based on instinct, not knowledge. His fields of expertise were navigation and economics, not foreign policy. The defector named Simas had been on board for about forty-five minutes when Eustis spoke to Admiral Ellis.

"Admiral," he began, "we are still waiting alongside the Soviet vessel. We have a man aboard who has defected from the Soviet Union. Believe that they know that he has defected. . . . We are all ready to get away. The man has expressed opinions to my flight operations officer [Lundberg] and my executive officer [Pakos] previously this afternoon about what his desires are. . . ."

"Does the [Soviet] ship know that he has come aboard your ship?" the admiral asked. "If not, I think they should know that. Over."

"Roger," Eustis replied. "Understand they suspect that man has defected and is aboard *Vigilant*. However, they expressed no concrete desire to recover man from ship. Over."

Ellis had been reluctant to talk to Eustis, knowing that Brown, as acting district commander, should be issuing the orders. But now his tone was anything but reluctant.

"In view of the nature of present arrangements with them and in the interest of not fouling up any of our arrangements as far as the fishing situation is concerned, I think they should know this and if they choose to do nothing, keep him on board," he said. "Otherwise, put him back."

Eustis was stunned. The admiral was telling him to return the defector. The admiral seemed so worried about not "fouling up" the fishing situation. If only he knew. The fishing meeting had been a farce. Eustis wondered whether the admiral really understood the implications of his own words. But Eustis was not about to question the wisdom of a respected superior officer—at least not openly.

"If they [the Soviets] have no indication that he is aboard or no desire to recover him," Eustis replied, "will intend to get under way at this time with man on board. If they desire to recover him, will have them return man to mother ship. If he desires to jump from mother ship to *Vigilant* as we depart, will make attempt to pick him up as he leaves mother ship and recover the man and stand by for further instructions. Over."

"If the man jumps into the water," Ellis said with a touch of impatience at Eustis's apparent inability to understand, "give the Russian ship the first opportunity to pick up. . . . Well, make sure you don't preempt them in taking that action."

"Roger on that," Eustis said in a flat voice that hid his depression. The admiral spoke only of returning the man in the watchstander's head, never of keeping him. "Will be under way shortly and will keep you advised of the situation as it progresses."

"O.K., this is Boston. Roger," Ellis said. "Good luck. Out."

A few minutes later, Eustis knew he would need more than good luck to handle the situation. He discovered that Burkal and his two fellow Soviet officers had never left the *Vigilant*. Now they were standing, in stern silence, against the wall of his sitting room. Burkal had opened his mouth once to say, through an interpreter, "One of our sailors is drunk and aboard your ship. He is probably talking with some Americans. Please conduct a search and see that he is returned."

At 5:30, an hour after his landing on the *Vigilant*, Simas heard a knock on the head's door. Remembering his instruction not to open it for anyone, he leaned his shoulder into the door a little harder.

"It's me," a voice said. It sounded like the red-headed seaman. Simas opened the door a crack, then let him in. Seaman Fowlie was carrying two bulky life jackets, both orange, one inflatable, the other not. Lieutenant Commander Pakos had ordered Fowlie to give one to the defector. Simas chose the noninflatable one and Fowlie helped him strap it on.

"You may have to jump in the water," Fowlie said, speaking very deliberately. Fowlie showed him the flashlight strapped into the jacket. "Turn it on when you get in the water," he said. "Don't forget or we will not be able to see you."

Simas wondered why the Americans would want him to jump into the sea. It sounded crazy, but he knew the language barrier would prevent him from truly understanding why it might be necessary.

"Anybody speaking Russian, German?" he asked tentatively.

Fowlie thought for a moment. "Polish, yes. Russian, no. German, no. Japanese, yes. How about Japanese?"

Simas smiled and shook his head.

"I have to go now," Fowlie said. "Remember—don't open the door to anyone."

A few minutes later there was another knock on the door.

"This is the commander," a voice said in English.

Simas opened the door and saw a pale, big-eyed man with reddish hair, wearing a white dress shirt and a thin blue tie. Simas had seen him during the day but had never suspected that he could be the American commanding officer. His face was too boyish, his manner too relaxed. He did not exude the superiority of rank the way a Soviet officer did. The man entered the lavatory and closed the door behind him.

"I am Ralph Eustis," the man said.

"I am Lithuanian, Simas Kudirka, radio operator of *Sovetskaya Litva*. You give me shelter in your great country?"

The captain did not answer. Instead, he asked Simas some questions about his life, his career, and his family, probing as deeply into the man's psyche as the language barrier would allow. He was trying to figure out whether this Simas was what he claimed to be—a Soviet sailor trying to flee the tyranny of his homeland, even at the price of leaving a wife and two children behind. The minutes passed, and Eustis's doubts dissolved. This man was no spy. He was an ordinary man who, in a moment of extraordinary courage or maybe even stupidity, had decided to risk everything in a jump for something he called freedom.

Speaking slowly and simply, Eustis tried to explain the situation that confronted him. But Simas understood little. He caught the phrase "Russians protesting" and sensed Eustis's dilemma, more from his tone and his gestures than his words.

"My orders are to return you," the commander said sadly. "But that might go the other way."

"I cannot leave here!" Simas pleaded. "No give me back! Siberia! Siberia! Killing!"

Eustis had thought of one scenario that might lead to a grant of asylum for Simas. In the light of Ellis's order and the presence of Soviet officers on the *Vigilant,* Eustis knew he could not keep Simas on board once the Soviets insisted on his return. The only way to circumvent these obstacles was to get Simas onto another American ship. Eustis would summon a forty-four-foot Coast Guard vessel, stationed on nearby Martha's Vineyard, to the scene. Then Simas would jump into the water and the forty-four-footer would fish him out. How could the officers of the forty-four-footer possibly be criticized for rescuing a man overboard? Now Simas would be on one boat, and the Soviet officers on another. Simas would then be taken to shore for "medical treatment," since he surely would be suffering from his jump into the chill November waters. Then, with Simas on American soil, the State Department would take over the case and, in all likelihood, grant asylum.

"I will jump?" Simas asked tentatively, after Eustis had explained the option. Eustis nodded. "I will jump! You saving me, yes?" Eustis nodded again. Simas took the packet of papers out of his shirt pocket and gave them to the American. "For you," he said. "When I come to shore, you give to me, yes?"

Eustis said he would. Then, abruptly, he left the room, walked down the hall, and radioed the Coast Guard base on Martha's Vineyard, asking that a forty-four-foot boat rendezvous with the *Vigilant* for reasons of "utmost political importance."

As I stood in the lavatory, my shoulder once again propped against the door, I felt a numb streak from my head to my heel. How had everything become so difficult? The captain kept talking about the Russians protesting, the Russians protesting. I knew Burkal might still be on the ship. Yes, that did complicate matters. But weren't we on an American ship? Weren't the Americans masters of their own vessel?

Commander Eustis seemed sympathetic but a little aloof, as if he wanted to keep me but not if things got too tough. I knew right away that he was a kind man. I just wasn't sure he was a strong man. And maybe he didn't believe I was sincere. I thought that perhaps I had violated the rules—the protocol of defection—in some way in which I, a seaman and not a diplomat, couldn't possibly understand. Maybe the way to correct that breach of protocol was to jump into the water and let the Americans pick me up. I had no way of knowing. But I was not so sure the Americans would be able to pick me up. I knew the Soviets had rescue drills twice a month. I knew how fast they were. The Soviets would get me—unless the Americans were ready and unless I knew precisely where the Americans wanted me to swim. The language barrier was insurmountable. I would be able to understand the details of this rescue plan if it were explained in German or Russian or Lithuanian, but not in English. I was not going to dive into that cold, dark water unless I understood every detail of the plan.

I wondered why this man Eustis had ended our conversation so abruptly. What was happening out there, beyond the door of this toilet, where men I could not see were debating my fate in a language I could not understand? Whatever it was, it had to be bad. I had been on board the *Vigilant* for an hour and a half. If the Americans were going to keep me, the *Vigilant* would already be steaming for shore.

I kept listening for the engines to start. And I heard nothing.

Three

At 6:00 P.M. Fletcher Brown opened the door of his home in Gloucester, about forty miles northeast of Boston. The long train ride home had been a relief after an afternoon full of constantly impending crisis. On the train, at least, he had been where the news—good or otherwise—could not find him. Now he thought how nice it would be if there were no telephone messages waiting for him. That would mean the "defection" had been a false alarm, and Brown could look forward to a relaxing night. But before he could take off his coat, his wife told him that Rescue Control Center in Boston had called while he was on the train. With a gesture of resignation, he quickly telephoned Boston and talked to Lieutenant Kenneth Ryan, the night duty officer. Ryan told him the two central facts: the defector had been on the *Vigilant* for ninety minutes, and Admiral Ellis had already told Commander Eustis to give the man back to the Soviets on request.

"Did you notify Flag Plot [Coast Guard national communications center in Washington]?" Brown asked Ryan, remembering Admiral Hammond's orders that Washington be informed immediately.

"No, sir."

"O.K., notify Flag Plot that the *Vigilant* has the Russian*
aboard."

"Should I call the *Vigilant* first and see if the guy is still on
board?"

"Yes."

Ryan called the cutter. *"Vigilant,* this is Boston radio. Over."

"Boston radio, this is *Vigilant,"* Commander Eustis replied.
Then Ryan hooked the captain's home telephone in Gloucester into
the conversation.

"Ralph, this is Captain Brown."

"Captain," Eustis began, "the present situation is that I have
presently on board one Russian defector, the communications
officer on board, plus three of his superiors that are down in the
cabin. Defector indicates that his intentions are, regardless of what
we do, tonight he's going over the side if he has the chance, if we
depart here. I have talked considerably with the individual within
the last half hour. I believe he is sincere in his intentions to defect
to this country. . . . ."

At that point, the ship-to-shore conversation broke into static,
and Eustis had to start over.

"Roger on that," Brown said after hearing it all a second time.
"Now, are the [Soviet] officers that are aboard—are they aboard by
your invitation?" Eustis said they were. "I understand that, Ralph.
Are these officers attempting to convince the defector that he
should go back aboard the Russian ship—are they trying to convince him to go back aboard the Russian ship?"

"The Russian officers have had no communications with the
defector since he has arrived aboard the *Vigilant.* Defector is presently in watchstander's head at this time. Only person that has had
direct communications with potential defector is myself. Over."

"Roger that," Brown said. "I understand and I also understand
that you are still alongside of the *Sovetskaya Litva,* is that correct?
Are you still alongside the *Sovetskaya Litva?"*

Eustis said he was.

---

*The Guardsmen frequently referred to Simas as a Russian, which was incorrect.
He is a Lithuanian. The term "Russian" properly refers to only one of the Soviet
Union's numerous ethnic groups.

"Are the Soviet officers aware of the defector aboard the *Vigilant?* Over."

"Roger on that," Eustis replied. "Soviet officers have indicated informally via an interpreter aboard that they believe that a member of their vessel is seeking asylum. . . ."

"O.K., *Vigilant,* this is Boston. Have they made any formal request for the return of the individual? Over."

"They have not requested his return by name or position," Eustis said. "It appears to me that the political situation is such that we should return all Soviet officers to their vessel and apprise them that we will stand by with possible political refugee until further advised. Over."

"Roger on that," Brown said. From the vantage point of his living room, the captain was becoming increasingly concerned about an international incident should the Americans try to force the Soviet officers off the cutter. "Do you think they would leave the *Vigilant* [voluntarily] and still leave the defector aboard? Over," Brown asked.

"I believe that they probably would depart *Vigilant* at this time if directed to do so, but would be very unhappy about it. They are presently within U.S. territorial waters and we have full jurisdiction of the situation. Over."

"This is a situation which is going to have to be resolved by State Department," Brown said, overwhelmed by its complexity. "I would suggest that you ask the officers to return to their own ship, ask the officers to return to their own ship and stay in present position. Over."

"Roger," Eustis replied. He felt the tension drain from his body. He was not going to have to give Simas back after all or force him to jump into the water. The *Vigilant* would bring Simas to shore, and there the civilian diplomats would make the decision in a far more relaxed atmosphere. Eustis hung up.

Lieutenant Ryan, who had been monitoring the call in Boston, asked Captain Brown if he should call the Guard's communications center in Washington and ask the duty officer there to contact the State Department. It was a reasonable request. After all, Brown had just told Eustis that the situation would be resolved by the State Department.

"No," Brown said. "Hold on a minute. I'll get back to you shortly."

Brown had, at that moment, realized that he was caught between two contradictory sets of orders. One, from Admiral Ellis, told him to have the defector returned now. The other, from Admiral Hammond in the commandant's office, told him to notify the communications center and have the defector kept on board pending further orders from Washington. He was going to have to disobey one or the other. He hesitated, then dialed Admiral Ellis's home. He admired his boss and he had to work with him every day. He would call Flag Plot only if Ellis approved. He apologized for interrupting the admiral's dinner.

"My God!" Ellis yelled. "Is Eustis still alongside? When I talked to him at five fifteen [ninety minutes earlier] I thought he was getting ready to get under way."

"Yes, sir, he's alongside," Brown said passively. He was acting as number two man now, providing information to his superior so that his superior could make the decision. "He still has the Russian officers in his cabin."

"Go back to Eustis," Ellis said impatiently, "and tell him if they don't know the man is aboard, make sure that they do know he is aboard. Tell them that if they want the man returned they are going to have to make a formal request, that we are not going to give him up without one. If they don't want him, then Eustis can take him to shore."

"Admiral, I have told Eustis to keep the defector in seclusion and to get the Russian officers back aboard their ship and to give us the time to call the commandant's office for further instructions."

"Did you get anything from the commandant?"

"No, sir."

The reason Brown had received no hard advice from the commandant's office or the State Department was, of course, that he had not yet told Washington that there had been a defection. But Brown did not mention that fact to Ellis.

27

"If you haven't gotten anything out of Washington by now, you're never going to get anything out of Washington," Ellis said.

Brown did not contest the remarkable illogic of that statement.

"If the Soviets want the man back," Ellis said firmly, "he will be returned."

Brown felt there was no need to consult the commandant's office, the State Department, or anyone else. He had his orders and he would follow them.

On the *Vigilant,* Commander Eustis hurried down the central staircase to the room where Burkal and his two colleagues were waiting impatiently for something to happen. Eustis walked over to the Soviet fleet commander and told him that no decision had yet been made on what to do with Simas. Eustis was buying time, waiting for the orders he now expected from the State Department.

Suddenly, Lieutenant Commander Pakos burst into the room. Captain Brown was on the radio again, Pakos reported, and now he was talking about returning the defector.

"Why should we have to return him, Paul?" Eustis asked. "He [Brown] just said the State Department was going to decide that."

"That's what he passed on to me, Captain. If they make a request, we have to give him back."

Eustis hurried to the radio room, knowing that he had to try to make Brown understand the stakes.

"Did you get my last message that I passed to Lieutenant Commander Pakos?" Brown asked.

"Captain, roger on that," Eustis replied. "The Soviet officers have still not formally requested that we return subject to the Soviet vessel. The situation appears to be at the state now that we have individual rights at stake possibly. If we direct Soviet officers to return aboard their vessel, I believe they will do so at this time, leaving further situation with Soviet defector aboard. Believe if we direct them to return aboard vessel with subject in company, I believe his life is probably in jeopardy."

"I roger that," Brown said. "You are directed to get a positive answer from the master of the Soviet vessel as to whether he wants individual returned aboard. . . . If his reply is in the affirmative, the individual will be returned to the vessel. Over.''

Eustis wondered what had happened in the past ten minutes to make Brown change his mind so completely. Brown did not seem to care about what might happen to Simas once he was back in Soviet hands. Maybe one of the civilians on the *Vigilant* for the fishing conference—all of whom knew there was a defector on board and favored granting him asylum—could get through to Brown.

"We have a State Department and fisheries officer from Washington, an interpreter named Alex Obolensky, standing by at this time," Eustis said. "I will put him on the phone here to give his informed opinion to you at this time, Captain."

"The fisheries agent has no responsibility in this matter whatsoever. Over," Brown said brusquely.

So much for that idea. "Anticipate this individual will make attempt [during his return] to jump from the Soviet vessel," Eustis continued, "and be picked up by the *Vigilant* or forty-four-footer [the smaller boat] standing by. . . ."

"Roger, and I understand what you are saying," Brown answered. "And you are ordered to take all necessary precautions to preclude any type of incident from occurring from your vessel. Over."

"Will take all precautions necessary to preclude incidents from occurring from *Vigilant*," Eustis said, still trying to slither out of the straitjacket Brown was strapping him into. "However, anticipate that if the man goes into the water, we should make attempts to pick him up from the water and that we may be logical agency to stand by and pick man up from water. Over."

"I think you misinterpret what your last order was. You are to take all precautions to prevent the incident from' occurring. Do you understand? . . . You will assure that no incident occurs during the transfer of the individual from your vessel to the Russian vessel. Do you understand?"

Eustis hung up. He understood.

Sitting on his living room couch in Gloucester, Captain Brown knew that he had given Eustis orders that might ultimately cause

29

death or lengthy imprisonment for the defector. But he was only following orders, and he felt his place in the chain of command demanded that he not reveal his reservations about those orders to the man who would have to carry them out.

"What a lousy job," he muttered into the phone. Lieutenant Ryan, who was in Rescue Control Center, Boston, monitoring the ship-to-shore conversation, was still on the line.

"And he's [Eustis] caught in the middle of it," Ryan commented.

"No, he isn't."

"Well, you are, maybe. I don't know."

"You bet your lovin' bippy."

"Yeah."

"Hey, uh, do you know how to knit?" Brown asked.

"Knit?"

"Yes."

"No, sir."

"K-n-i-t."

"No, sir."

"Maybe I oughta take that up."

"What I meant . . ."

"I got my thirty in anyway," Brown said. He had put in enough years with the Guard to qualify for retirement. He was beginning to think that this evening's events might one day force him to retire. Again, as he had when the defection had been merely a possibility, he found himself thinking that Admiral Ellis might be wrong. "Well, it's a lousy position to be in," he said of his own predicament. "I would have done it differently than Ellis, I think."

But it wasn't too late to prevent disaster, he thought. The defector was still on the *Vigilant*. No one had suggested to Ellis that the defector feared for his life. Maybe that would change his mind. Brown dialed Ellis's home once more.

The admiral was unmoved. To him that Soviet sailor was no dissident seeking political asylum; he was a deserter, a coward. If a seaman fled from a Coast Guard cutter to a Soviet fishing ship, Ellis would expect the Soviet commander to return the louse. The

Americans could do no less. Ellis was not worried about the man's fears of death.

"I don't think we have any reason to believe that this would happen," he said curtly. "They are not barbarians."

Dejected, Ralph Eustis walked past the watchstander's head, where Simas remained a virtual prisoner. He started to go in, then stopped. What could he say? He walked past the head, down the stairs, and into the sitting room. The Massachusetts fishermen waiting there saw his pale, drawn face and they knew—the defector had to be returned. They were furious. Had the State Department been contacted? Eustis confessed he did not know.

"Captain, you cannot do this!" yelled Robert Brieze, president of the New Bedford Seafood Producers Association. Brieze was a Latvian who had himself defected to the United States in 1944. He could not believe that the United States would reject a defector now. "I know how they [the Soviets] treat defectors. You cannot do this!"

"Bob, I'm sorry," Eustis said. "I can't help you. I have my orders."

Eustis walked to the rear of the room, where Fleet Commander Burkal was pacing furiously.

"Would you go back to your vessel without the defector while we attempt to convince him to return on his own?" Eustis asked through a translator.

"*Nyet!*" Burkal replied. That needed no translation.

A few minutes later Burkal delivered a note to Eustis:

During our meeting of November 23, 1970, the radio operator Kudirka penetrated into my stateroom, forced the safe, took money from the safe in the amount of 3,000 rubles, jumped over the fender, and hid on your vessel. I lodge a maritime protest on this matter.
[Signed] Popov, captain of mother ship *Sovetskaya Litva*.

Eustis felt the situation beginning to slip out of his control. He went back up to the radio room, called Brown, and told him of the

31

note. Eustis was sure that Simas was no thief, but the note certainly was a formal request for his return.

"My intentions," he told Brown, "are to return defector to custody of Soviet vessel, *Vigilant* to depart side of Soviet vessel and escort Soviet vessel from territorial seas. If defector—potential defector—departs Soviet vessel, *Vigilant* will stand clear and make no attempt to pick up defector until life in jeopardy. Over."

"Roger on your transmission," Brown said, "and proceed in accordance with your total message. Over."

"Am getting under way at this time. Over."

"Advise when vessel is outside the territorial and fisheries waters. Over."

Now came the tough part. Ralph Eustis had to convince the desperate man in the watchstander's head to give himself up.

As I pressed my body against the door of the watchstander's head, I wondered what would happen next. I had been on the American ship for four hours. With each passing minute, I knew that my chances for receiving asylum were growing smaller and smaller. It had been two hours since anyone had come to visit me. I was becoming frantic. If Commander Eustis wanted me to jump into the water so he could save me, I would do it—no matter how crazy it seemed. So, despite my orders to stay inside the toilet, I opened the door, peered out to make sure there were no Russians around, and walked down the hallway. I wanted to see if the forty-four-foot boat Eustis had promised me was in the water yet. I had to know where it was so that I could swim right to it. Every wasted stroke would give the Russians more time to capture me.

I found a window and looked out. All I saw was blackness. No forty-four-foot boat. No boat anywhere.

My heart sank. Maybe I could swim for shore. It wasn't that far and the water wasn't that cold. But I could not swim as fast as a motorboat. The Russians would catch me before I hit the beach.

Who was I kidding anyway? I had failed. The Americans were going to give me back—I could feel it. I had tried to escape the Soviet Union and somehow, some way, something had gone horribly wrong. I didn't know what the problem could be. But whatever the reason, I was going to have to go back. If I had been away only for an hour or so, I could go back voluntarily and make up some excuse about having become so carried away with talking to the Americans that I had lost all track of time. I probably would have gotten away with a reasonably mild punishment. It was too late for that now, though—much too late.

My world was collapsing all around me, and I was going to be crushed under the rubble. I walked back into the head. There was no point in propping myself against the door anymore. I sat in the corner of the tiny room, pulled my knees up toward my chest, and lowered my head between them. And for a minute, I dreamed I had turned into a bird and could fly away without anyone noticing that I was gone.

While Simas waited and dreamed, Coast Guard Lieutenant Junior Grade Wayne Tritbough was sitting in Washington in a tiny office cramped with filing cabinets, maps, telephones, and tape recorders. The room, on the seventh floor of the Nassif Building, was the Guard's national communications center, Flag Plot. As Flag Plot duty officer for the night, Lieutenant Tritbough's job was to monitor the activities of Coast Guard units all over the country and, when necessary, report those activities to his superiors so that decisions could be made. He was the Guard's night watchman.

When he had come on duty late in the afternoon, he had been told of a potential defection developing on the cutter *Vigilant* off the coast of Martha's Vineyard. He had been told that he would be notified by Boston if and when a defection occurred. On receiving the news, he was to call Rear Admiral Hammond and the State Department immediately. But as the hours passed, he had all but forgotten about the situation. He assumed no defection had taken place.

At 8:25, a phone rang on the counter in front of him. It was Lieutenant Ryan, the duty officer in Boston, reporting that a defection had indeed occurred on board the *Vigilant*. Tritbough, though quite surprised, automatically started taking notes.

"O.K., this—the man came over to the *Vigilant*," Ryan said, "but now because the skipper of the [Soviet] vessel requested in

33

writing the man be returned, he was returned, he is being returned, and shortly the *Vigilant* will get under way. . . ."

"O.K., stand by a minute here, please," said Tritbough, who had fallen a little behind in his notes. "He requested that the man be returned, correct? And they are returning him."

"Right, right."

"What's the man's feeling in this regard?"

"He previously said he did not want to return and he stated that he would probably go overboard if he had the chance. . . ."

"Their [*Vigilant*'s] plans are to detach themselves from the Russian vessel immediately after this?" Tritbough asked.

"Right, and proceed with escorting the vessel outside of the contiguous zone. . . . Chief of staff here [Captain Brown] says he will send SITREP [situation report] in the morning. O.K.—if nothing else comes up, this is it."

Then Ryan thought of one other matter he wanted to discuss. He had received a telephone call from a New Bedford, Massachusetts, radio station asking whether there had been a defection.

"We denied all knowledge," Ryan reported. "Now do you want to handle press at your end, or do you want it handled at this end?"

"Well, I have to check with people on this, of course."

"If I do get calls I'm going to say, 'No comment' or 'I am unable to make any statement at this time' or something like that, O.K.?"

"O.K.," Tritbough agreed. "Unless I advise you otherwise, go ahead with that plan."

"O.K. Good-bye."

Lieutenant Tritbough then did exactly as he had been told. He called Admiral Hammond, and he called the State Department. And from Tritbough's account of his conversation with Lieutenant Ryan in Boston, official Washington assumed that a Soviet sailor had boarded the *Vigilant,* asked for asylum, changed his mind, and willingly gone back to his own ship.

During the afternoon, officials at State had insisted that the Guard keep them informed of the incident as it developed. But now, at night, no one on duty at State demanded to know why those instructions had been ignored. No one—not the watch officer, the Soviet desk officer or the European desk officer—did more than ask Lieutenant Tritbough a question or two. No one tried to find out exactly what had happened and on whose authority.

"He was returned, he is being returned," Lieutenant Ryan had said. As far as Washington was concerned, the case was closed.

Ralph Eustis forced himself to knock on the door of the watch-stander's head. "This is the commander," he said as he opened it. His face was ashen, and his forehead was dotted with beads of perspiration. "A Russian delegation would like to speak with you."

"No!" Simas shouted. "Twenty years of speaking with Russians and nothing. Enough! Enough!"

"The Russians say that you have stolen some money, stolen some money."

Simas frantically ran his hands through his pockets, across his chest, and down his legs, denying the charge by frisking himself.

"Nothing, nothing!" He pointed to the papers he had given Eustis earlier. "Nothing, nothing!"

Eustis nodded, then pulled a handkerchief from his pants pocket to mop the perspiration off his forehead.

"Dear Captain, please not giving me again, again," Simas pleaded, his hands clasped in front of him. "For me is Siberia. Siberia is death."

Eustis turned, walked out, and closed the door behind him. He couldn't bear to tell Simas that his request for asylum had been refused. He staggered down the stairs and informed Fleet Commander Burkal that Simas would be given back.

Burkal offered no words of thanks. "I request that you take measures to return the sailor to our ship," he said through his translator.

Somehow, all evening Eustis had managed to avoid thinking about the mechanics of the return. Now that he did think about it, he had visions of a terrible brawl—of American sailors chasing Simas, beating him into submission, and then carrying his bruised body to the Soviets. He could not let that happen. But Eustis knew that he could not convince Simas to go back on his own, and so now he asked Alex Obolensky, the Russian-speaking translator who had accompanied the Massachusetts fishermen, to try. He escorted Obolensky to the head and introduced him to Simas.

"The captain is requesting that I translate the following to you," Obolensky began in an emotionless tone of Russian. "Asylum has been refused to you and the captain has orders from his superiors to return you to your ship. He has no right to detain you further. You have to make a choice of how you wish to leave the ship."

Simas's spirits wilted. He had expected the bad news. Still, it hurt to hear it, especially from a man whom he had never seen before.

"I will not return! I will not return!" Simas yelled. "I will jump in the water first. If I jump, what are my chances of being rescued by the Americans?"

"The captain will make every effort."

"Do the Russians have the right to pick me up?"

"Yes."

"In that case, I will not jump."

Obolensky did not react. Simas was infuriated by his indifference.

"I cannot return!" he yelled. "Do you understand? You obviously understand the language, but do you understand what I am saying?" Perhaps this new man did not comprehend how serious he was about defecting. "The Soviets asked me years ago to inform against my cousin, who was a hero in resisting the Russian takeover of Lithuania. But I refused. And even though that happened twenty-two years ago, I have suffered ever since. Every other member of the ship's crew has a seaman's passport. Not me. They won't let me leave the ship in a foreign port. Ever! Do you understand what that does to a man? I will not return. Siberia waits for me if I do."

"Yes," Obolensky said, nodding his head. "I see. Still, the captain has no right to keep you on this ship any longer. You must decide how you wish to leave."

"No! I will not return!"

Obolensky left. Simas burst out of the head and paced the length of the hall outside, panting, quivering, and clutching his stomach.

Seaman Fowlie, who had been posted in the hall as a guard, watched in helpless bewilderment.

"Do you have knife?" he asked Fowlie excitedly, pronouncing the word kah-nee-fay. "I making hara-kiri." He pretended to stab himself in the gut to make sure he was understood.

"No, I don't have a knife," Fowlie lied.

"Revolver—you have pistol? I must die."

"No."

Simas heard footsteps and voices on the stairway. He raced back into the head and slammed the door.

The door opened. Eustis was there. He was not alone.

"I believe you know this man," Eustis said to Simas, gesturing toward Fleet Commander Burkal, a short, pot-bellied man with dark, wavy hair.

Burkal stepped up into the doorway. "Now, Simas," he said in a patronizing tone of Russian, "can you look me straight in the eye and tell me you know what you're doing?"

"Yes, I can," said Simas, his voice cracking just a little.

"I advise you, reconsider—come back on your own before it is too late."

"Let's not waste time."

"Simas, how can you shame us so much? Do you know what this means?"

"Yes, I know. And I am not coming back."

"Why did you do this thing?"

"Because I am sick and tired of your eternal lies, sick and tired of your meaningless political instruction classes, sick and tired of your Leninisms. You have lied and lied and lied and today I am putting an end to the lies—for myself!" He pounded his right fist into his left palm. His face reddened. His voice quickened. "You have inflicted incurable wounds, and I am leaving in hopes of healing some of them. Your system is not worth the shit on a dog's tail. All you have done is trample on everything good and decent. Today I have chosen to say good-bye to all that. You can go on and build your empire, but you are going to do it without me!"

"I don't understand," Burkal said with a hard edge in his voice.

37

"What were you lacking? You had a job, a family, an apartment. That society you attack has educated you, clothed you. . . ."

Simas began to fumble with his life jacket. "I defecate on your society!" he shouted. He leaped out of the life jacket and hung it on the wall behind him. Then he tore off his shirt and threw it at Burkal's feet.

"Here!" he shouted. "I'm giving you back everything the Soviet Union has given me." He began to unbuckle his pants.

Burkal backed away from the head entrance and up stepped Gruzauskas, the political officer whose remark about the sailors picking up magazines had put the idea of defecting into Simas's head. He spoke in Lithuanian. "Have you given any thought to the position you put the captain and me in?" he asked.

"You put yourselves in that position."

Someone accidentally turned on the hand-drier, forcing everyone to shout to be heard.

"What about the position in which you put your wife, your children, your mother?" Gruzauskas asked.

"Listen. Don't bait me with my family. You have sucked the lifeblood out of everyone who is near and dear to me." Simas was trembling. "I worked twenty years and for what? All your damned money buys is tears for the eye and acid for the stomach. I can earn more bread in the United States cleaning out places like this than I did as a sailor for you. We have talked about all this before, but this is the last time we will talk."

"You will be sorry," Gruzauskas said, still calm. "But then it will be too late."

Burkal tapped Grusauskas on the shoulder. "Let's get out of here. You can feel the anti-Soviet atmosphere." They turned and walked down the steps, followed by Eustis.

On the way down the steps, through the translator, Burkal told Eustis: "The only way to bring him back will be by force."

For Commander Ralph Eustis, the conflict between his orders and his conscience had finally come to a head. More than four hours before, Admiral Ellis had ordered him to return the defector. Since then he had stalled, hoping that somehow Ellis and Brown would become convinced that the orders they had given him were wrong, that the defector should be taken to shore and turned over to the State Department. Only then could Simas's case get the consideration it deserved. Simas had jumped at 4:30. Now it was 9:30, and the orders were still the same. No savior had arrived to resolve his dilemma, and none was coming. And now Eustis knew there was an excellent chance that the return of the defector would lead to violence on the *Vigilant*. Yet his orders were to let it happen.

There had to be a way out. He summoned his executive officer and friend, Paul Pakos, to the wardroom. Pakos understood Eustis's dilemma. He knew what Eustis really wanted to do. Through the evening, Pakos had tried to prod his skipper into following his instincts instead of his orders. "If you decide not to carry out this order," he said at one point, "the crew and I will support you one hundred percent." Eustis had thanked him for the offer but had rejected it, feeling certain that Brown and Ellis, who he assumed were acting with guidance from the State Department, had to have good reasons for what they were doing. Perhaps, Pakos had replied. But if there was no good reason, wasn't Eustis, by following orders, acting just like the American soldiers who had committed the My Lai massacre? "If these orders are wrong," Pakos said, "and you disobey them, then you're a hero who had the guts to disobey his orders. But if you obey, you may be true to the Coast Guard and wrong in the eyes of the public."

Still, Eustis's inclination was to follow his orders, however reluctantly. The main issue now, Eustis said, was the question of force. Obviously, some force would be needed to remove Simas from the *Vigilant,* but Eustis did not want his own men to do the dirty work. Suddenly, Pakos saw an opening, a chance to get new orders, orders that could be obeyed in good conscience. In all the conversations between Eustis and his superiors, there had never been any talk about force, had there? No, Eustis said. Well, then, Pakos said, considering the new problem, perhaps the old orders no longer applied. Pakos suggested sending out a radio message requesting new advice. Eustis told him to go ahead and draft such a message. Pakos sat at the wardroom table and wrote it out on a legal pad.

There was one aspect of the message Pakos had not mentioned—
to whom it should be sent. Pakos wanted to buck the chain of command. He wanted the *Vigilant* to send its request for new orders to
Washington as well as Boston, hoping to get the commandant's office to overrule Brown and Ellis. Pakos finished his work and
handed the legal pad to Eustis.

The message reviewed the events of the evening and stressed the
new problem—"that force will be required to move Simas. Recom-
mend alternate solution by bringing Simas in custody to U.S. while
Soviets attempt to achieve release through diplomatic channels."
Pakos said he was sure Washington would concur.

Eustis refused to send it to Washington or anywhere else. He
would not question the wisdom of his superiors so directly. All he
would do was call Captain Brown once more. As soon as Brown
was on the line, Eustis started to explain the new problem, making
sure to stress the likelihood of violence. But Brown cut him off.

"Commander Eustis!" he said. Brown always called him Ralph,
except when he was angry. "You have your orders. You have no
discretion. Use whatever force is necessary!"

It was 10:15. The time had come to stop avoiding orders and
start carrying them out. Eustis trudged back down to his quarters
and told Burkal that he could use Soviet force to return the defector
to the *Sovetskaya Litva*. Eustis would not make his own men be hit
men for the Soviets. Burkal asked permission to have six more Soviet crewmen hoisted aboard the *Vigilant* to do the job. Eustis
refused. They argued and compromised on three. Burkal smiled,
shook Eustis's hand, turned to his aides and ordered, quietly and in
Russian, that six crewmen be lifted onto the *Vigilant* immediately.

Eustis left the room and walked back up the steps to say good-
bye to Simas. He entered the head and closed the door. His voice
was shaking as he explained that if it were his decision to make, he
would have granted asylum. Simas did not understand the words,
but he heard the sorrow and regret in the American's voice and saw
the tears in his eyes.

"If you jump into the water," Eustis said one last time, "we
will save you."

"No, no," Simas sobbed. "Russians! Killing!" He hit himself hard on the back of the head. "Siberia!"

There was nothing more to say. Eustis grabbed Simas and hugged him tight. Both men cried. Then Eustis pushed himself away, stared at Simas, turned, and walked down the steps. At the bottom of the steps, he found Burkal.

"He's all yours," Eustis said.

Four

Wearing only his undershirt, pants, and shoes, Simas waited on his knees for the men of the *Sovetskaya Litva* to come and get him. The door of the watchstander's head was wide open. A few minutes passed and he heard faint voices speaking Russian. He walked forward into the hallway and looked down the stairs. At the bottom stood three hefty Soviet sailors, all with reputations as brawlers, taking their positions for the assault. One of them carried a blanket, the second had a rope, and the third had a white piece of cloth in his right hand. They looked up the stairs and they saw him.

"Bastard!" one of them hissed through bared teeth. "You didn't really run very far, did ya, ya bastard?"

Simas took the offensive. He grabbed the steel railings on either side of the stairs, and, in a flash, slid down the stairs on his hands, slamming feet first into his three attackers. They fell, recovered quickly, and began pummeling him. One bit him on the left shoulder. The second pounded his side with punches and karate chops. The third grabbed him around the neck and yanked his head backward so that all Simas could see was the ceiling.

"Help me! Help me!" he yelled in English.

He went limp and dropped to his knees. For an instant, he was loose. Then all three Russians fell on top of him, knocking him flat.

"Tie him, tie him, tie the bastard!" they shouted.

Fighting them off with his right hand, he used his left to grab a railing on the lower part of the wall and pull himself down the corridor. Suddenly, he smelled something peculiar. It was coming from behind him, getting stronger and stronger. He jerked his head around and saw a handkerchief, soaked in ether, closing in on his mouth. In desperation, he let go of the railing, lunged at the cloth, and knocked it flying back toward the stairs. All the Russians turned to follow its flight, and, for a moment, he was free. He jumped to his feet and ran two steps down the hall. He was at the door of the sitting room. Inside sat Eustis and the Massachusetts fishermen.

"Help me! Oh, God! Help me!" he shouted in English.

The Russians were on him again. He grabbed the door frame with both hands as two of them pulled at his feet, trying to drag him back toward the stairs. Burkal and another Russian kicked furiously at his hands and face, trying to break his grip on the frame.

Inside the sitting room, Eustis sat at his desk and wept. Brieze, the American fisherman of Latvian descent, leaped off the sofa, ran to the door, and started pushing Burkal off Simas.

"No, no, you cannot do this!" he screamed. But another civilian restrained him, reminding him that the Russians were acting with American approval.

Burkal then slammed the door on Simas's hands. He yelped in pain and let go. The two Russians, surprised by the sudden lack of resistance, lost their grip on his feet and fell over backward onto the floor. Simas was loose again. He jumped to his feet, hurdled the prone Russians, and bolted out the door onto the flight deck ducking under the hanging lifeboat. He was standing at the very spot where he had landed on the *Vigilant* more than six hours before.

He looked up and saw the *Sovetskaya Litva,* her dark form speckled with dots of light. Her spotlights were trained on the *Vigilant,* obviously ready to search for her wayward radio operator should he run loose. Her decks were lined with dozens of boisterous seamen, his fellow crew members until this afternoon, all of them hoping to see a fight and hoping it would be bloody.

He grabbed the top wire of the railing with both hands and vaulted over it. He was hanging on to the outside of the ship now. He lowered his hands to the middle wire, the bottom wire, and then to the edge of the deck itself. He swung his legs back out over the water and then forward toward the *Vigilant,* crashing hard, feet first, onto the main deck below. He shook off the pain, picked himself up, and looked around. There were no Russians on this deck, not yet anyway. He turned toward the stern of the ship and started to run, but the sailors on the *Sovetskaya Litva* had seen him. They screamed to their bewildered comrades on the American cutter.

"There he is!" they shouted.

The spotlights of the Soviet ship swung crazily along the *Vigilant* in search of the fugitive.

"Over there!"

The Russians on the *Vigilant* looked back at the *Sovetskaya Litva* for instructions.

"Down below!"

Simas kept running, breathing heavily and moaning from the pain of battle. He was running toward the fantail, an open area at the stern of the cutter. From the fantail, he hoped, he would be able to see the forty-four-foot American boat that was supposed to be there to rescue him. If he saw it, he would jump.

When he got to the fantail, he hopped up onto a small metal stand called a gunmount grid, whirled around once and then again. He saw only darkness. No boat. (The forty-four-footer had not arrived and would never arrive. On orders from Boston, it had ignored Eustis's request and stayed in its berth at Martha's Vineyard.)

To his left, he saw an American sailor, wearing a telephone headset that was connected to the ship's superstructure by a long wire.

"Where is the boat?" he cried in Lithuanian.

The American, Commissaryman Third Class Joseph Jabour, stared back. He did not understand.

Now Simas heard footsteps. The Russians were sprinting down the flight deck. They were coming to get him. He decided to jump into the sea, boat or no boat. It was his last hope. He dashed for the high railing on the side of the *Vigilant* away from the *Sovetskaya Litva,* climbed on top of it, lifted one foot outside, then the other. He felt a hand on his left wrist. He looked up and saw the American, Jabour. He guessed the American was trying to comfort him, to talk him out of it. And he hesitated.

Two Russians reached in, shoved the American away, grabbed Simas in a headlock, and flipped him back onto the deck. He landed hard on his stomach. The Russians grabbed his legs and dragged him, feet first, across the rough metal deck. One of the Russians reached for Jabour's telephone cord and started to wrap it around Simas's neck until Jabour ripped the cord out of the Russian's hand.

They dragged him to the base of a steep metal staircase leading back up to the flight deck and then stopped for a moment, unsure of how to carry their prisoner up the steps. In that moment, Simas clasped both hands around the left railing of the narrow staircase and locked his feet around the right. Two of the burly Russians untangled his feet and started carrying them up the stairs. Two others kicked at his hands. Still, he clung to the rail. One Russian grabbed him by the hair and rhythmically banged his head into the rail. Simas shrieked in pain. He felt his hold on his consciousness fading fast. He let go.

They lifted him up the stairs and started carrying him across the flight deck. He let his body go limp, hoping the Russians would relax. When they did, he kicked free and broke loose again, screaming for help. He ran back down the stairs and onto the fantail, not knowing where he was running or why. He came to the rail of the ship, determined that this time he would make it into the sea. He put one foot on the rail and was hit in the back of the knees with a flying tackle.

This time the Russians hung on. His strength was draining, his resistance only token. The Russians carried him up the stairs and along the flight deck toward a net that dangled over the *Vigilant* from a boom attached to the *Sovetskaya Litva.* The net would be used to lift him back to the Soviet ship. At the side of the net, he was allowed to stand while one of his attackers tied a long rope tight around his neck. The burly Russian picked up the loose end, whirled it high over his head, and pretended to throw it across to the *Sovetskaya Litva,* shouting, "We don't need this goddamned net!" Meanwhile, they kept on punching him in the neck and chopping him in the side until his shrieks of pain had been reduced to dull moans.

A young Coast Guard officer, Ensign John Hughes, raced down from the bridge and told the Russians to stop the beating. In the next instant, the *Vigilant* started its engines.

All day I had been waiting to hear those engines start. I had equated the sound of those engines with salvation. The beatings had left me nearly unconscious, but now I felt an incredible surge of adrenalin—and hope. I looked around and those Russian toughs who had been acting like such big, strong heroes as they beat me up were acting like scared little boys as the *Vigilant* pulled away. They didn't understand what was happening. They were trapped on an American ship that was taking them away from their mother ship. An American officer had just ordered them to stop mugging me. American sailors were chopping at the lines that held their ship to the *Sovetskaya Litva.* Other lines were snapping in half as the *Vigilant* pulled away. My agony was ending. The Americans had decided to keep me.

Simas was wrong. He was not being saved. When he had swung down from the flight deck to the main deck five minutes before, the American officers had assumed he had jumped into the water. And Commander Eustis, seeing that the two ships had been only a few feet apart, had feared that Simas would be crushed. He also feared that the menacing sailors who lined the Soviet deck were about to leap across to the *Vigilant* for an international brawl. And he had ordered the cutter to depart immediately.

So the engines started, and the *Vigilant* moved straight backward. The Soviet boom crashed into the top of the cutter, knocking down its antenna and destroying its signal light. The debris fell on the flight deck, and the Russians who had been holding Simas ran for cover. For a few seconds, he stood alone, the rope still tied around his neck, blood gushing from his nose. His exhausted body was quivering in spasms, and suddenly he felt very cold. In his mind, he was dashing away across the flight deck. But his body was standing still. Finally, he took a few steps. Then the Russians grabbed him and shoved him into a tiny metal shack on the flight deck. Several of them went in after him, pummeling him again and again. This time, the sound of the *Vigilant*'s engines did not scare them, and no American stopped them. They knocked him onto the floor and tied his hands behind his back. They lifted him up, spread a blanket on the deck, and dropped him back onto it, stomach down. They bundled him up and pulled the ropes tight around his neck, chest, waist, thighs, and ankles, pressing their feet against his body so they could jerk the knots tighter. When they had finished wrapping him, they dragged him out of the closet and carried him by the ropes toward the dangling American lifeboat Simas had been ducking all day. He was barely conscious as the ropes burned into his skin. His eyes were swollen shut.

They threw him into the boat and he landed head first, face down, with a resigned grunt. Then the ten Russians—three officers, six sailors, and a translator—climbed in. Four Americans were already on board. There was silence.

At 11:40, more than seven hours after the jump, the lifeboat was lowered into the water for the voyage to the *Sovetskaya Litva,* now a little more than a mile away. The American officer in charge of the expedition, Ensign Hughes, sat at the bow alongside Fleet Commander Burkal. Simas lay where he had landed, near the stern. One Russian sat on the back of his head while another sat on his legs. A third periodically kicked him at the base of the skull, and a fourth seemed determined to shove his foot through the small of the captive's back. After a few minutes Simas passed out.

Twenty minutes later, the lifeboat arrived at the *Sovetskaya Litva*. The Russians picked him up and threw him from the stern of the lifeboat to the bow. The jolt brought him back to semiconsciousness. Several other Russians picked him up and threw him into the net, which the mother ship had lowered for him. Several of the Russians climbed onto his chest and stood on it while the net was lifted to the main deck.

Dozens of Soviet sailors watched as Simas's battered body landed on the deck with a thud.

"Let's finish him off!" they shouted.

"Give him a few in the shoulders!"

"Let the fish feed on him!"

Simas tensed his back in anticipation of a series of punches, bracing himself for more pain.

"Knock it off!" someone in authority yelled.

The shouts faded away. Simas was carried to a storeroom and thrown inside. The door slammed.

Ensign Hughes and his crew returned to the *Vigilant* after midnight, several sailors reporting that Simas was already dead or surely would be in a few hours. The *Vigilant* radioed Boston that, "as directed, transfer of defector was accomplished." Then it escorted the *Sovetskaya Litva* out of American territorial waters, turned, and headed for its home port, New Bedford, arriving at 3:30 the next morning. Before the ship docked, Commander Eustis assembled his passengers and crew and told them that each man, in his own conscience, would have to live with the events that had just transpired. Many of the men who heard the speech thought the commander was asking them not to say a word about what they had witnessed.

Five

When Simas awoke the next day in the storeroom, the left side of his head still ached from being banged into that steel railing. His left eye was just a thin slit deep inside a blur of blue, purple, and yellow bruises. His right eye was swollen shut. His nose, covered with congealed blood and puffed to twice its normal size, hurt too much to touch. Since the cartilage inside it was shattered, he could no longer tell whether it was securely anchored in the center of his face. His lower lip drooped down toward his chin. Dried blood was caked against his teeth and his tongue. His unwashed skin felt like it was beginning to rot. His left knee still throbbed hard with his pulse, and his wrists ached from the handcuffs. His arms and legs burned from the ropes that had been wound around him, tight enough to leave permanent marks and burns that had begun to fester, encrusting his undershirt and his pants with blood and pus. His body was racked with chills; the ropes had been wound so tightly that his blood was not circulating properly.

As he stirred, he had to be careful to avoid sliding off the rough wooden bench that served as his bed. The bench was only four and a half feet long and barely a foot wide, too small even for his five-foot, five-inch frame. His stiffened body was balanced on a thin red mattress that flopped over the edges of the bench; his head rested on a bloodstained pillow. He opened his left eye as far as his lumps would allow and saw that he was not alone. He was being watched. One guard sat on the desk opposite his bench, and another was in a chair by the door. They were playing dominoes, the favorite pastime of the fleet, smoking and chatting and eyeing their prisoner. They would sit there for four hours, then yield to two new men for four hours more.

The changing of the guard would be one of the few events of his day. There was almost nothing for him to do except go to the bathroom and wait for the delivery of meals to the storeroom three times a day. When the food arrived, he would stare at it in disgust, even though the food was the same all the crewmen were getting. Gruzauskas warned him that a hunger strike would accomplish nothing, but his abstinence was based on pain, not principle. His mouth still hurt too much to contemplate using it for eating. He refused water as well. Water would burn the inside of his mouth, loosen the dried blood, and start another round of bleeding. He could walk, as much as the pain and the walls would allow. The room, which had not been built with people in mind, was only six feet wide and nine feet long. He could guess the time of day from the angle of sunlight that pierced through the porthole or from snatches of conversation from sailors passing by. He could try to go back to sleep and make the pain go away. Or he could think about the future. That hurt the most. When he did think about it, one image, rather blurred, persisted inside his aching head. He had fallen down a deep well with steep, slimy walls, and he was not sure how he was going to get out—or whether he was simply going to die at the bottom.

A week after the jump, in the middle of the night, Gruzauskas entered Simas's storeroom along with two men wearing business suits and overcoats. They were agents from the KGB, the Soviet Union's vast and mysterious force of political police. They picked up his belongings, handcuffed him to Gruzauskas, and put him on a lifeboat bound for another factory ship, the *Kapsukas*.

"You are under arrest," the captain of the *Kapsukas* said officiously on taking custody of the prisoner. "We have a radiogram instructing us to deliver you to the first Soviet harbor we dock at.

You should not talk. You should make no fuss. If you cry out, we will use force to make you still.''

Simas's new prison was a padded cell, an isolation chamber intended for a deranged seaman. The porthole was kept shut at all times, making the isolation complete. The walls were dazzlingly white, and the corners of all the furniture were rounded—to prevent the occupant of the cell from trying to do himself in. His belt had been taken away on his arrival for the same reason.

As the *Kapsukas* turned eastward and steamed across the Atlantic, he knew that he was heading toward a confrontation with the KGB. He had to come up with a story that his interrogators would believe, a reasonable explanation of why he had jumped to the *Vigilant*. He knew the charge would be treason. His first instinct was to tell the truth, the whole complex truth. He would tell the KGB how he hated the Russians for occupying Lithuania, how he had hated them since he was a child. But what good would that do? He would simply get the maximum sentence to the labor camps or maybe even be executed. And where would that leave his wife, Gene, his daughter Lolita, ten, and his son Evaldas, only four? No, he could not tell the truth.

There was another option. He could confess to the crime and condemn the Americans for their failure to live up to all their propaganda about being the home of liberty. Surely that answer would please his interrogators. Considering what had happened, it was not an unreasonable accusation to make. He had thrown himself at America's feet, and America had looked the other way. In fact, though, he was not bitter about what had happened; he was sure Eustis had wanted to grant him asylum. The order to return him had to have been a decision based on innocent stupidity, not on malice. Somehow the Americans had been tricked by the crafty Soviets. He would not condemn innocent men.

So if he was not going to tell the truth or blast the Americans, what was he going to say? He had to say something, and he had to memorize his story in every detail; for the interrogators would probe it from every angle. An idea came to him, and it would not go away. He would tell a story that was very nearly the truth. He had been frustrated by all those years at sea, years of being so near foreign countries but lacking the passport that would allow him to explore them. The temptation of an American ship eight feet away had been too strong. So he had jumped. He had not been defecting, not really. He had been playing a trick on those naïve Americans. They would think he was defecting and would take him in, show him their country, treat him like a king. Then, in a few weeks or a few months, having seen enough to satisfy his curiosity, he would have come back to Soviet Lithuania of his own free will.

In those long, lonely hours aboard the *Kapsukas*, he tossed the story around in his head. Maybe the interrogators would see his point and understand that he had deserved a passport all along. They ought to. Then it hit him—there was a gigantic hole in the story. His own apartment in Klaipeda contained evidence that Simas Kudirka—hard-working, blue-collar worker Simas Kudirka—sympathized with the political dissidents. KGB agents would search it and find a tape of a British radio broadcast that he had recorded and smuggled off the ship just six months before. They would find his copy of dissident physicist Andrei Sakharov's appeal to the Kremlin on peaceful coexistence. They would find Alexander Solzhenitsyn's open letter to the writer's union. So the story had a major weakness, but it was all he could think of.

He tried desperately to get a message out to his wife, telling her to destroy the evidence of his treasonous thoughts. He wrote his address on a tube of toothpaste and gave it to the woman who cleaned his bathroom. "Tell her what you see here," he begged. "Tell my wife." Reluctantly, the woman took the tube and squeezed Simas's hand. He made the same request of the man who repaired the heating in his padded cell and the woman who delivered his meals. The man said he would try. The woman ignored him. Time was running out. There had been days in his padded cell when he wished that he could have his confrontation with the KGB immediately, but now, as it grew near, he wished he could grab it in his hand and hurl it far into the future.

On December 14, a KGB agent entered his cell on the *Kapsukas*. The agent unlocked his handcuffs and let him get out of the clothes he had been wearing since the day of the jump. "We are nearing port," the man said.

Would they stick pins and matches under his fingernails? Would they make him walk on hot coals until he told them what they wanted to hear? He had been interrogated by the KGB when he was eighteen years old, and they had beaten him then. But that was twenty-two years before. Maybe times had changed.

Shortly before 9:00 P.M., the van stopped and the prisoner was escorted into headquarters. The agents marched him down a long hallway, made him strip, and gave him another internal search, this one more meticulous than the first. Then they deposited him in a cell on the ground floor.

He lay down on a cold metal bed covered with a mattress that was not thick enough to prevent the metal bed frame from biting into his back. He tried to fall asleep, but the stench from the latrine bucket in the corner of the cell kept him awake; the prisoners, he would learn soon enough, called the bucket "Madame Parasha," the filthy lady. The only way he could deal with the odor was to put a bar of soap directly under his nose and wait until its smell overcame the stink and allowed him to nod off.

Morning came and a guard knocked on the cell door. It was time to tell his story. He was led up to the third floor and into a large room with a high ceiling and bare white walls. Urbonas was there in a gray business suit, but the dominant figure was the prosecutor, a tall, dark-haired man in his mid-thirties. He paced back and forth with his arms crossed in front of him and a look on his face that made it obvious how seriously he took his work.

Simas said good morning. Urbonas returned the greeting and began the formalities—last name, first name, birthplace, age, nationality, occupation, education, party membership.

"Now suppose you try to explain why you tried to leave the Soviet Union," Urbonas suggested.

"I didn't want to go to sea this time," Simas began, the words rushing out loud and fast. "I had waited thirteen years for an apartment, and now that I had one I wanted to stay home with my family. I wanted a job in port. But you pushed me to sea, and still you wouldn't give me a passport. And so the bitterness piled up inside me. When we met with the Americans, I couldn't hold it in anymore. You didn't trust me! You didn't trust me! You didn't trust

55

me! I was determined to prove to you that I was loyal. I decided to go over to the Americans to prove it to you. Not forever, but for a few weeks. I would have come back . . .''

They laughed at him.

''Simas,'' the prosecutor sneered, ''how did you plan to come back?''

''I would get on a foreign ship or I would go to the Soviet embassy and say, 'Here I am, loyal Simas, I want to come back. You didn't trust me, but see, here I am, just like I told you.' ''

Simas finished and there was silence. Urbonas let it linger, taking a long puff on his cigarette.

''And you really would have come back?''

''Yes.''

''I see.''

The prosecutor took up the interrogation, peppering Simas with terse questions, interrupting his lengthy answers as soon as he had heard as much as he wanted to hear.

''This is absurd,'' the prosecutor muttered.

The tenor of the questioning disturbed Simas deeply. He did not know that his case—and his desire to defect—had been front-page news all over the world. All he knew was that Urbonas and the prosecutor already knew far more than he wanted them to know. They were not even considering the possibility that his story was true. What was going wrong? Had they searched the apartment in Klaipeda and found the evidence of his treason? Why wouldn't they believe him?

''We advise you to think things over very carefully,'' the prosecutor told him as the session ended. ''Know this, and remember it well. The more open you are with us, the more objective we will be with you. You will be making the consequences easier for yourself.''

The prosecutor stopped his pacing and stared at Simas. ''We will ask the question again, but you'll have to think of another answer. This one won't do.''

Six

By mid-December, as Simas was undergoing his first hours of interrogation in Lithuania, the Coast Guard officers involved in refusing him asylum—Admiral Ellis, Captain Brown, and Commander Eustis—had already had their days in court and were awaiting a verdict. The Coast Guard had not been eager to investigate what had happened aboard the *Vigilant,* to admit formally the possibility that its men had made a mistake. Public relations officers for both the Guard and the State Department made a conscious effort to discourage coverage of the incident in the press. They failed to provide reporters with any dramatic details of the incident and emphasized whenever possible the complexity of the situation that had confronted the decision-makers that day. By making the story as boring and as complicated as they could, they had tried to assure that the incident would be treated calmly, quietly, and briefly on the inside pages of the nation's newspapers—or not at all.

The strategy worked for a few days, and it might have worked longer but for the efforts of a few hundred Americans of Lithuanian descent. When they heard sketchy reports on the radio and read them in the newspapers, they were angry. When they got the rest of the story on their own from Robert Brieze, the Massachusetts fisherman who had seen Simas beaten, they resolved to see to it that the incident would not be swept under the rug.

57

On the night of November 25, two days after the incident, small groups of Lithuanian-Americans gathered in living rooms in New York, Philadelphia, Chicago, Cleveland, and Brockton, Massachusetts, to discuss what could be done to make the general public aware of what had happened on the *Vigilant*. They would have to do something dramatic. The dozen men who met in Brockton discussed hiring a sixty-foot yacht, arming it with automatic weapons, boarding the *Sovetskaya Litva,* seizing Simas, and bringing him back to the United States. Once they dismissed that idea as a little too dangerous, they considered organizing a flotilla of pleasure boats, sailing out to the Soviet ship (assuming they could find it), and surrounding it, hoping the pressure of publicity would force Simas's release.

In the end, cooler heads and less exotic plans prevailed. On November 27, four days after the incident, demonstrators in Philadelphia picketed a Coast Guard recruiting station. That same day, members of the Lithuanian Student Association of North America, who were holding their annual convention in Cleveland, marched to the federal building there bearing a black coffin marked HUMAN RIGHTS. In the plaza outside the building, they burned the coffin, told the story of the *Vigilant,* and demanded an investigation by the government, punishment of the officers responsible, and a promise to work for Simas's release.

It was an even less exotic move, however, that proved the most productive. The New York group put together a simple press release and delivered it that day to every newspaper, radio station, television station, and wire service in New York. The angrily worded release announced a demonstration to be held in Times Square the next afternoon and recounted, in far more detail than any account yet published, exactly what had happened to the would-be defector on the *Vigilant*.

The next day at noon, two hours before the demonstration, an editor at the *New York Times* handed the release to a reporter, Robert McFadden, and asked him to check it out. As soon as McFadden read it, he knew he had an excellent story on his hands if the information in the release turned out to be true. After little more than an hour on the telephone, he had confirmed the guts of it. He had interviewed Brieze and listened to his eyewitness account; he had talked to State Department and Coast Guard spokesmen who agreed that, yes, a Lithuanian radio operator had tried to defect, and, yes, he had been refused asylum. By mid-afternoon, when he was about to write, he left his office to look in on the demonstration in Times Square. About 200 persons were in the street, wearing black arm bands, chanting slogans, carrying signs and a black coffin of their own. Most of them were Lithuanians, but they were joined by Latvians, Estonians, Ukrainians, Poles, and Hungarians—all of whom considered their homelands "captive nations" under the rule of the Soviet Union.

"What has happened to the national conscience of the United States when a man who saw and exercised his opportunity for freedom by pleading for political asylum on a ship that was carrying the flag of the United States was turned down?" one speaker asked the demonstrators. They answered with shouts of outrage. "What has happened to the principles of basic human rights when a man crying out for freedom is tied up while American Coast Guardsmen watch in silence as Soviet goons not only forcibly take him off that American vessel but, before doing so, beat and kick him senseless?"

McFadden watched and listened for a few minutes, then rushed back to his office to type out his story on deadline.

At 2 P.M. last Monday, as the mother ship of a Soviet fishing fleet and a United States Coast Guard cutter rocked in the swells a mile off Martha's Vineyard, a Lithuanian seaman made a dramatic leap for political asylum.

The seaman, a radio operator known here only as Simas, hurled himself across a 10-foot gap from the Soviet vessel, the *Sovetskaya Litva,* and onto the deck of the *Vigilant.*

About 10 hours later, after a flurry of ship-to-shore radio consultations, the seaman was forcibly returned to the fishing ship by Soviet crewmen who had boarded the American vessel with permission of the Coast Guard. The man, according to eyewitness accounts, was severely beaten by the Russians while the American seamen looked on.

59

*

The story, which went on for nearly 1,500 words, had a few minor inaccuracies, but the errors were inconsequential. What mattered above all was that the story appeared the next day on the front page of the Sunday *New York Times*, and a story that appears there is almost impossible to ignore.

By the next morning, the Kudirka incident was the top story in the country.

"Now we naturally and deeply regret that this incident occurred," State Department spokesman Robert J. McCloskey told reporters on Monday morning. "Let me say on background that if the department had been told that a defection had actually occurred, I am confident things would have been handled—or things would have developed—differently."

At the Transportation Department, Coast Guard Commandant Chester R. Bender was trying to explain the thinking behind the decision to return Simas. "While it is not yet clearly established whether or not he [Admiral Ellis] took the proper action," he suggested, "I believe it to be understood how he would make this decision on the existing circumstances. I do not approve of the use of force on a Coast Guard ship by personnel of another nation, but do recognize that considerable force was required, as the defector was resisting strongly."

At the White House, President Richard Nixon's press secretary, Ronald Ziegler, said the president was concerned about the incident, particularly because he had not learned of it until he read his weekend newspaper summaries. The president, he said, had ordered an "immediate and full report" on precisely what had happened and why. "At best," Ziegler said, "there appears to have been some error in judgment, and after the President reviews the investigation's findings, appropriate action will be taken."

At the United Nations, Sadruddin Aga Khan, the U.N. High Commissioner for Refugees, lodged a formal protest over the American handling of the case. And later in the day, without the fanfare of a press release or news conference, Commandant Bender suspended Ellis, Brown, and Eustis, effective immediately. He ordered all three to report to Cambridge, Massachusetts, the next morning for the start of a formal Coast Guard Board of Inquiry.

Newspapers all over America denounced the government for what it had done to Simas.

The *New York Times* called the incident "surely one of the most disgraceful incidents ever to occur on a ship flying the American flag. . . . The real explanation is surely craven stupidity, possibly accompanied by lethargy." The *Buffalo Evening News* found the incident "incomprehensible" and an "outrage." The *Washington Post* called it "sickening and humiliating. . . . The mind clogs, the heart clogs at contemplation of this fantastic parable of our times." The *Chicago Tribune*: "That Lithuanian crewman is a sadder person than when he jumped aboard the *Vigilant*. So are we."

Columnists were even more vitriolic. Max Lerner, a liberal, called the incident "a shocker. . . . Simple humanity would dictate granting him asylum, and simple humanity would have been enough." John P. Roche called it "an outrage against the conscience of every decent American, liberal or conservative." Conservatives were every bit as indignant. Smith Hempstone, Jr., suggested that "every flag should be flying at half-mast today." William F. Buckley hoped that whoever was found responsible would be threatened with punishment so severe that "he will be moved to jump into the water, hail the nearest Russian fishing boat, and ask for asylum."

Thousands of Americans, angered by the news accounts, wrote to their local newspapers, to the Coast Guard, and to the White House. A New York man suggested renaming the *Vigilant* as *Old Yellowstain*; a California couple preferred the *Disgrace*. A North Carolina couple denounced Ellis as a swine; a Pennsylvania man compared him, unfavorably, to Pontius Pilate. "Force Ellis to eat the Bill of Rights and be stripped of rank in public," a Hawaiian suggested. "Give them to the Soviets," wrote a Delaware man, "or take them to deep water and sink same in the contaminated ship that has red sailors on deck." Mr. "U.S. Taxpayer," writing to Bender from East Hartford, Connecticut, said it best: "My taxes pay your salary. . . . Now look, buster, I fought my way through the biggest war this country has seen, and I fought for certain

61

ideals. So long as it is MY money that's supporting you, you will NOT allow this sort of thing to happen again. Do I make myself clear?''

The people of New Bedford, where the *Vigilant* sat in the harbor under twenty-four-hour guard, were reacting with their own special sense of outrage. In the old port city waitresses refused to serve members of the ship's crew, and merchants would not cash their checks. Passersby jeered at them as they walked through town, and street toughs picked fights with them in portside bars. Many crew members decided to stay on board ship, waiting for the rage to pass.

By Wednesday, December 2, President Nixon himself joined the chorus of criticism. He let it be known that he considered the incident "outrageous." The next day, he issued new guidelines designed to prevent its repetition. The new directive stated that "under no circumstances should the person seeking asylum be arbitrarily or summarily returned to foreign jurisdiction or control" until the case has been fully evaluated by the White House, the State Department, and other agencies. Later in the month, in a nationally televised news conference, he would elaborate on his personal reaction:

"Well, as I have already indicated, I was, as an American, outraged and shocked that this could happen. I regret the procedures, the Coast Guard informing the White House, were not adequate to bring the matter to my attention. I can assure you it will never happen again. The United States of America for a hundred ninety years has had a proud tradition of providing opportunities for refugees and guaranteeing their safety. And we are going to meet that tradition.''

Congress could not resist leaping into the fray either. The House Subcommittee on State Department Organization and Foreign Operations, chaired by the crusty and powerful Wayne Hays of Ohio, opened hearings into the case on December 3, four days after the *Times* story and just ten days after the incident itself. The hearings, which concluded late in the month, produced little new information but did provide the Congressmen with a forum from which they could express their outrage and generate headlines.

"How long do you think it will take them [the Coast Guard and the State Department] to whitewash this matter?" Hays asked William Macomber, the deputy undersecretary of state for administration, early in the hearings.

"Mr. Chairman," Macomber replied, "I don't think anybody is trying to whitewash or find scapegoats. I think they are trying to find the facts."

"I will be surprised if anybody ever gets a reprimand out of this."

But Hays was wrong. The Coast Guard was investigating the matter quickly and thoroughly. The inquiry, run personally by Assistant Commandant Thomas R. Sargent III, opened with four days of hearings in Cambridge, December 1 to December 4, and resumed the next week with three more sessions in Washington. Then Sargent reviewed the 900-page record full of testimony, telegrams, memoranda, and transcripts of conversations between the *Vigilant* and Boston, Boston and Washington, Eustis and Brown, Brown and Ellis, Ellis and Eustis.

As he pondered the case, Sargent became convinced that the bungling of the defection had resulted from both a failure of procedures and a failure of men. The procedural flaw had been that Guard officers had never been briefed on State Department policy or given any idea how to get diplomatic guidance in times of emergency. He urged improved liaison between the two agencies so that the Guard would always be aware of the foreign policy it might have to enforce. But, Sargent concluded, the failures of men had been paramount, and Fletcher Brown was the real villain. Brown had been acting district commander that day, and it had been his duty—his alone—to seek advice from above, make a decision, and pass it along to Commander Eustis on the *Vigilant*. Brown had been ordered to keep Washington informed as the defection unfolded. He had disobeyed that order, and he had committed another sin as well. When a decision had to be made, he had reached out for a crutch; he had abrogated his own responsibility. He had called Ad-

63

miral Ellis on the telephone, even though the admiral, while on convalescent leave, had no place in the line of command. "In referring a matter of important decision to Rear Admiral Ellis," Sargent concluded, "Captain Brown failed to exercise his command powers and accept his command responsibilities. . . ."

Sargent recommended that Brown be given a "court-martial for trial on charges of dereliction of duty."

The assistant commandant concluded that Admiral Ellis was not as much to blame for what had happened as Brown. Ellis had never asked to become involved in the decision-making process; he had given advice only when Eustis and Brown asked for it. Still, Sargent said, Ellis "should have known that Captain Brown was treating his remarks not as advice but as orders." Ellis had "infringed improperly" upon Brown's command, Sargent concluded, and had also erred by offering advice without knowing the policy of his government "on complicated and sensitive issues having obvious national and international import."

Sargent recommended that Ellis be issued a punitive letter of reprimand and be asked to retire within six weeks.

Eustis was the least guilty in Sargent's view. The skipper of the *Vigilant* had, in the end, been following his orders. Sargent recommended that he be issued an administrative letter of reprimand—for allowing foreign nationals to commit acts of violence on an American ship—and be taken off the *Vigilant*.

On Friday, December 18, just twenty-five days after the incident, Sargent submitted his findings to Commandant Bender, who had already come to his own conclusions. Bender agreed with the recommended punishment for Eustis, but he did not agree with his assistant's analysis of the relative guilt of Brown and Ellis. It might make good military sense to single out Brown, but the public would not understand the logic. How could Ellis, who had, in effect, given the orders, be less guilty than Brown, who had carried them out? Brown was wrong to have listened to Ellis, but Ellis was equally wrong to have said anything that sounded like an order to Brown.

The commandant wanted both men out of the Coast Guard as soon as possible. He asked his superior, Transportation Secretary

John Volpe, to order courts-martial for both men, to be held only if they refused to retire. Three days later, Volpe announced that both Brown and Ellis would be issued letters of punitive reprimand and forced into retirement. He said he saw no point in subjecting them to courts-martial; they had suffered enough.

"I regret very deeply," Volpe said, "that a young man had to lose his chance for freedom in order to bring to light the deficiencies in government procedures for welcoming victims of oppression to American soil. Also, I regret that the proud history of the U.S. Coast Guard, which has given shelter to hundreds of political refugees, was not upheld in this tragic incident. But the errors in procedure have been corrected. We now can give assurance to the world that an incident such as that which occurred on November twenty-third can never occur again and that America remains the haven for the oppressed."

Seven

For Simas, awaiting trial in Vilnius KGB prison, each day began precisely at 6:00 A.M. A guard walked down the hallway, which was carpeted for soundproofing, shouted "Wake up!" and banged his gloved fist on the cell door, which was sheathed with tin. Simas rose slowly from his cot and took a deep breath of air smelling of mildew, cheap cigarettes, and human waste. That first breath always seemed to stick in his throat. He put his hands on the damp gray floor halfway between his bed and the wooden table in the middle of the cell. He did fifteen push-ups, then ten handstands. He sat back on the bed and reached for his towel and toothbrush, readying himself for the first of the day's two trips to the bathroom. When the guard opened the door, he picked up the latrine bucket, which was kept next to the door, and lugged it down the empty hall. He walked into the blindingly white bathroom, emptied the bucket into a hole in the floor, and rinsed it out with a chlorine solution that made his eyes tear and his skin burn. That done, he crouched over the hole. If he could force a bowel movement here, he might be able to avoid having to do it in the bucket. And if he could do that, the stench in his cell might not grow any worse.

"Hurry up, hurry up," the guard ordered through the peephole. Every door in the prison had a peephole. "Time's up." There never was enough time. He marched back to his cell, sick to his stomach. When he recovered from his queasiness, he touched his toes, did some kneebends, and waited for breakfast, which always arrived at 6:30. First, a hunk of black bread was shoved through a slot in the door. Then a hand reached through, holding an aluminum scoop. The scoop turned upside down and Simas held out a scrap of newspaper to catch his daily fifteen grams of sugar. A fist pounded on the door, and Simas obediently held his kettle out through the slot. A guard filled it with a hot, urine-colored liquid that was alleged to be tea. Simas poured some of it into his cup, added a dash of the precious sugar. and bit into the coarse, dry bread. The bread stuck in his mouth until the tea washed it down.

The rest of the morning was "free" time. Almost all a prisoner's time was free, which was what made prison life so boring.

At 8:00, the guards changed, and at 8:30 the supervisor of the day shift opened the door of the cell. "Is everything all right in here?" he asked. Then he slammed the door shut before anyone could answer.

Some mornings Simas found himself alone in his cell, but most days he had a roommate or two. On those days, at least, he could make the morning pass in conversation. One roommate, Andrius Sadeikis, nineteen, a quiet, passive youth with a slim build, a long face, and pale, thin lips, said he had been put in prison for running away to escape service in the Red Army. But Simas was suspicious; the youth asked too many questions about Simas's case. Perhaps Sadeikis was an informer, put in the cell to soften Kudirka up for his interrogators or gather information about him that could be gathered no other way. Or maybe he was a KGB trainee, learning about political prisons from the inside. Or maybe Simas was just suffering a mild case of paranoia, an affliction that could be a political prisoner's most pernicious enemy.

Simas preferred talking to another roommate, Zubavicius, a criminal pure and simple. Zubavicius was full of insights into prison life; he had been in and out of prisons and labor camps since he was seven. He was only twenty-two now, but he looked fifty. His gaunt, skeletal body provided a living warning of what Simas might expect in the years ahead. Zubavicius's misshapen arms dangled lifelessly at his side; he had been hung by his hands more than once. His cheeks looked as if a sadistic sculptor had attacked them with a chisel; they were covered with permanent red scars. He had tinted the rest of his body blue with tattoos burned into his skin with rubber melted from the heels of shoes. On his eyelids, in protest against his treatment, he had etched the words "Slave of the USSR."

At 11:00 A.M., the prisoners were taken for "outdoor exercise," which meant standing around in a cell that was open to the sky. Then it was time for lunch. The midday menu provided one of the few elements of mystery in the daily routine. The first course could be borscht or cabbage, barley, or pea soup. The second might be potatoes or porridge or fish. Simas washed it down with the cold leftover tea and took a brief nap.

When he woke up, he tried to read. Afternoons were the best time for reading, for the window, which was recessed deep into the wall behind layers of wire mesh, frosted glass, and steel bars, faced west. If the day was clear, the dim cell would brighten at 3:00 P.M. to the point that Simas could read anywhere in the cell. As the light faded in the afternoon, Simas could keep reading only if he stood on a stool and held his book up to the cell's single light bulb, which was tucked away inside the wall behind a wire grating. He kept reading until his head began to ache and his eyes began to burn.

Eventually, a foul fishy odor overwhelmed the other smells in the cell and Simas knew that supper, usually a ladleful of slime-coated fish soup, was on its way. He knew he could not swallow the stuff so he deposited the stew directly into the toilet bucket. After supper, he often tried to communicate with his unseen neighbors in adjacent cells by talking through his metal cup, which, when pressed against the wall, served as a crudely effective amplifier. Or he pondered the future, which, he knew, held a trial, a sentence, and death, if not immediately, then after long years of suffering in the labor camps. But first there would be days and days of interrogations and the same question over and over. "Why did you jump?" He wasn't sure he could explain it, even to a sympathetic listener, which was a luxury he did not have.

———————————

I knew the source of my desire to see America. That much was easy. When I was small, my grandfather and I used to ride into the Lithuanian woods on spring and summer nights to gather branches that would warm our house during the long winter. As our old horse pulled the cart through our village and out toward the dark woods beyond, grandfather used to talk of America. He had seen it for himself. In his youth, he had left Lithuania to avoid being drafted into the army of the Russian czar. He had fled to England, worked in the mines, and then sailed the world stoking the furnace of a British merchant ship. In 1904, he had gone to America with his Lithuanian wife, found a job in a Brooklyn foundry, and lived there for nine years. During that time all his children, including my own mother, Marija, had been born. Then he had returned to Lithuania for good.

I loved to hear him talk about those years and that strange place called America. Until he opened my eyes, I thought the whole world was just like our village, Griskabudis, that everyone spoke Lithuanian, rode into the forest to gather wood at night, and went to church on Sunday morning. I couldn't imagine this place across the ocean. I couldn't even figure out what an ocean was. The only body of water I knew was the pond in the back yard. Grandfather said there were men in America whose skin was white like mine, and men whose skin was black or yellow or red. How could that be? He said they had come from warm climates, and the sun had tanned their skin very deeply. He told me about factories that were hundreds of times bigger than the mill in our village. He told me about the big cities, places made entirely of stone and concrete and full of people. How could a whole city be built on stone?

And there was this train he talked about all the time. It rumbled through Brooklyn on top of miles and miles of stilts. He would be sitting in his third-floor apartment—I had enough trouble trying to figure out what a three-story building or an apartment was—and this train would rush by his window. Why did they have to put it on stilts? Why not put it on the ground, where it belonged? The ground couldn't really be that crowded. He confounded me further by telling me that the tallest buildings in America had little rooms inside them, suspended by some kind of thick strings. Those rooms moved up and down, taking people from one level to another. Surely, grandfather was joking.

He talked about their apartment in Brooklyn. It must have been a very humble tenement flat, but it sounded like a palace to me. In the kitchen there was this amazing cooking device. You walked up to it, turned a knob, and all of a sudden there was this blue flame on the top. At least, that's what grandfather told me. A blue flame? He said the floors had covers on them made out of fabric. Why do you need a cover on the floor, I wondered, if the floor is clean in the first place? And he just raved about the furniture in America. It was wood, but it didn't sound at all like the wood I knew. It was so shiny that you could see your own reflection in it. I didn't believe it. So I went out and got a board and polished it until my arm was about ready to fall off. But I could never see my face in it, not even the vague outlines.

America fascinated me, even if it sounded a little frightening. I loved to talk about it, read about it, and look at pictures of it whenever I could. And I vowed that someday when I grew up, like my grandfather, I would see that teeming land of multicolored people, blue flames, and trains that ran on stilts for myself.

Every day at first and several times a week thereafter, Simas was led out of his cell in KGB prison, up three flights of stairs, and through a pair of doors wrapped in sound-muffling plastic. The guard sat him down in a chair screwed into the floor near the doors. Then the guard walked across the room to Urbonas, who was seated behind a table cluttered by law books, newspaper articles, and a pitcher of water. He gave Urbonas a piece of paper, which the interrogator signed, thereby taking responsibility for Simas's whereabouts.

Urbonas always greeted Simas politely. Except for that, there was nothing predictable about the interrogation. A session could last ten minutes or ten hours. The questions could be personal or political, the atmosphere hostile or friendly, the questions repetitive and sometimes trivial. One day Urbonas would taunt him into writing a letter of apology to Commander Eustis for having ruined his Coast Guard career. Another day he would suggest that Simas's real motive for jumping was to abandon his family, a suggestion that never failed to ignite Simas's temper. Several times Urbonas just talked politics with him, as if the two of them were old chums sharing a bottle of vodka.

"Why did you jump?" Urbonas often asked to begin a session. The interrogator rested his elbows on the table, pressed his index fingers together just beneath his nose, and waited for an answer.

"I wanted to visit America," Simas insisted. "When my visit was over, I would have come back on my own."

Urbonas stared at Simas through half-closed eyes, as he always did when he did not like the answer he was getting. Then he shook his head wearily. He had been patient with the prisoner, but his patience had gone unrewarded. If the prisoner remained stubborn, the interrogator would have to get tougher.

"Who is your father?" he asked.

"What the . . . ?"

"What is his name?"

Simas did not answer; he was too stunned by the question to speak. He had known since he was nine that he was a bastard, that his mother, Marija, who was rarely around the house, had no husband. His grandparents had raised him.

"Where is he from?" Urbonas demanded.

Simas remained silent, trying to contain his explosive temper.

"How many times did you see him? How well did you know him? Did you love him?"

"Stop it!" Simas screamed, leaping to his feet. "It's none of your business. This has nothing to do with politics, nothing to do with why you bring me to this room every day. I will not answer any questions about it!"

Urbonas, as always, was under control. "Have you forgotten just who the hell you are?"

"I know exactly who I am. But even I have my rights."

"You will answer the question."

Simas was silent. He knew he would have to answer—if not now, then later.

"My father was a farmer," he said in a near whisper. "He sired me and then rejected me. He never married my mother. He made

71

me a bastard. I condemn what he did. He did it only to satisfy his lust, and he shoved two people, my mother and me, into lifelong misfortune. He made rubble of her life and poisoned mine.''

''Where is he now?''

''Dead. From what I know, he was a landowner who was deported to Siberia after the war, when all of us were forced into the collective farms. But I don't know all that much about him. When I grew old enough to understand who he was and what he had done, I never made any attempt to get to know him. But he's dead—I shouldn't really blame him.'' He paused. ''I hope you can understand that this is a very sensitive and painful part of my life.''

''Oh, we understand,'' Urbonas said. ''In this place we see a great deal of emotion. And tears are the most common.''

The shame of being a bastard had not been my only source of tears as a boy. I experienced the pain of having my country occupied by foreign armies. In 1930, when I was born, Lithuania was enjoying a rare interlude of freedom after generations of oppression. In that interlude, which lasted twenty-two years, a fierce sense of national pride developed, and the Catholic Church, to which my family and almost all Lithuanians belonged, flourished throughout the land. But the interlude ended in 1940 when the Russians seized my country as part of their secret nonaggression pact with Hitler's Germany. We hated the Russians, whom we considered utter barbarians; they had occupied our country before, from 1795 to 1918. This time, though, the Russians stayed only a year. On June 22, 1941, the Germans broke the nonaggression pact and invaded the Soviet Union, striking Lithuania first. They seized our country—and our village—and occupied both for the next three years.

Our life returned to something close to normal under the German occupation, except for the fact that all the Jews disappeared. Then, in the summer of 1944, the Russians pushed the beaten German army back through Lithuania and occupied our country once more. Three occupations in four years—Russians, Germans, then Russians again. This last one was the worst. Half-starved Russian soldiers stole our potatoes out of the ground and ran off with our hens. Our wheat fields were full of shrapnel, and our grain was bent to the ground. Our house was intact, except that the soldiers had ripped out the pages of our books, our most prized possessions, and had used them for cigarette papers. Reminders of war were everywhere. One day my friends and I wandered off into the battlefield beyond the village in hopes of finding a good pair of discarded German shoes. Instead we found bodies—standing, sitting, lying, reaching—all frozen in the moment of death. Full skeletons rested on the ground, naked except for gunbelts still full of live ammunition. Bones protruded from the ground at crazy angles, covered with scraps of clothing. Loose ammunition was scattered across the field like seed.

Not all Lithuanians accepted this second and "permanent" Soviet occupation. Thousands of them went into the woods and fought a stubborn guerrilla war of resistance against the occupation forces. They called themselves partisans. They were confident that if they kept fighting long enough, the Western democracies would come to their rescue. And despite the odds against them, they held their own against the Soviet superpower for the first four years of the struggle, from 1944 to 1948. The Soviet authorities, hoping to weaken the partisans' support in our village, began to stack the bodies of dead guerrillas in the marketplace and to ferret out weapons kept by partisan sympathizers—like me.

One cold day in December, 1948, when I was eighteen, I was summoned after school to the office of First Lieutenant Kondratov of the KGB. The imposing lieutenant—over six feet tall and a hard 200 pounds—told me he knew I had a gun. He was right. I had found the weapon, a German semiautomatic machine gun, in an abandoned battlefield. I had been keeping it for the day when I would join the partisans myself. He ordered me to turn it in.

I lied. I told Kondratov that I had once owned a gun but had long since thrown it away in a creek. Kondratov bared his teeth and leaned forward across the desk. "Why are you lying? We gave you your chance, and you chose to reject it. So be it!"

Kondratov's soldiers ransacked my grandparents' house but

could not find the gun. So they brought me back to their head-quarters as their prisoner and kept me until the next day, when they summoned me back to the lieutenant's office.

Kondratov greeted me by smashing me across the face. "Where is your gun?"

"I don't have any . . ."

This time a karate chop crashed into the base of my neck and sent me sprawling to the floor. Kondratov grabbed me by the collar and pulled me to my feet. He asked again. I lied again. And he hit me again—this time in the jaw. As I lay on the floor, I heard another voice telling me to calm down. A second, less intimidating-sounding agent had entered the room. "Everything will be all right," this new agent was saying. "My friend here [Kondratov] just gets a little carried away. Tell him where the gun is, and he'll leave you alone."

I got back up.

"Are you going to talk or not?" Kondratov demanded.

"Look, I have told you everything . . ."

"Enough!" Kondratov took his revolver out of his pocket and slammed it down on the table, pointing it directly at me. He stared at me, slapped me in the face, kicked me in the shins, and chopped me in the neck again.

I screamed.

"Shut up!" he yelled, and pushed the gun barrel against the side of my head.

The second agent intervened. "That's enough, that's enough," he said, lifting the gun away from my head. He patted me on the shoulder. "Settle down, stop screaming. You say you threw the gun into the creek. Well, when the water goes down this spring, you go there, retrieve the weapon, and bring it to us."

I relaxed a little, thinking my ordeal was over. Then Kondratov opened a new line of questioning.

"Do you know Vytas Sulskis?" he asked.

So this is what this encounter is all about, I thought. Of course, I knew Vytas. He was my best friend, a relative through marriage. I knew exactly why the KGB would be interested in Vytas. Vytas was a partisan.

"Why don't we make a deal?" Kondratov suggested firmly. "We won't do anything to you now. But for that you also have to do us a favor. Why don't you help us come into contact with this fellow Sulskis? Tell him we'd like to have a little talk with him."

For the next few months, after the KGB let me go, I felt I was being watched wherever I went. I would hear that a friend had disappeared or been arrested—or that there had been a fierce battle in the woods. And I would shudder, not knowing what the news meant, thinking that maybe the KGB was about to call me in for another interrogation and increase the pressure. Were they going to arrest me and deport me? Or were they going to beat me again? I could bring in the gun, but that would be collaboration with the Russian enemy. Or I could end all the agonizing—take the gun and join up with the partisans.

In the end I did not join the partisans. I did not give the gun to the KGB, nor did I lead the KGB to Vytas. Instead, on Vytas's advice, I left Griskabudis and headed for the port city of Klaipeda to try to become a sailor. I wanted to forget all about the KGB, and I hoped the secret police would be equally pleased to forget about me. A year later, I thought again about joining the partisans, but I was too late. The war was almost over; the partisans had lost. Three hundred fifty thousand Lithuanians—12 percent of our nation's population—had been deported in the years from 1945 to 1950. Another 30,000 had been killed, Vytas Sulskis among them. Our only consolation was that the Russians had expended 80,000 lives of their own to win the fight.

———

On Christmas Day, 1970, Simas was led to the interrogation room as usual.

"What would you say if you got to see your wife?" Urbonas asked.

"That would be great," Simas said, thinking of how much he wanted to see Gene, to explain why he had tried to defect, to assure her that he had not been trying to abandon his responsibilities at home. He wanted, too, to find out whether she had destroyed the books and papers that would provide the KGB with evidence to incriminate him. "But I know it's not possible."

"I repeat, what would you say if you saw your wife?"

"You're just taunting me."

"If that's the way you're going to be," Urbonas said, leaning back in his chair, "there isn't going to be any meeting."

"You mean, my wife is here, in this building, now?"

"That's right. She's downstairs, waiting for you. But first, I must be sure of your behavior. You must agree that you will not make any comments about your case. Don't try to pass anything to her or take anything from her. No hand signals. No winks. No rolling eyes. No signals of any kind. Your entire conversation must not go beyond your family life. If we notice anything else, your meeting will be ended immediately. And that won't make your wife very happy, will it?" So he wouldn't find out about the fate of his forbidden books and pamphlets. "You agree to the terms?"

"I agree."

Urbonas led him down to a tiny room on the second floor where Gene Kudirka was sitting in front of a wooden swinging gate. A KGB colonel sat behind the gate, watching her every move. When Urbonas opened the door, Simas ran to her, sat down beside her, and threw his arms around her. He cried and so did she. Her body seemed shriveled, her eyes and cheeks sunken.

I met her in the fall of 1957, when I was twenty-seven, two years out of the army, and a student in Klaipeda learning to become a radio operator for the fishing fleet. One day I went to the food store around the corner from the radio school to check out the new "gypsy" girl my friends kept talking about—the girl named Gene, the one with the dark brown eyes and chestnut hair. I noticed her the moment I walked in. I waited in line, shifting nervously from one foot to the other.

"So," she said, smiling at me, "what are we having today?"

"Well, I'd like some fruit tea."

"That's very good for you," she said cheerily, getting a box of tea for me.

"Will there be anything else?"

"No," I said, fearing the conversation was about to end but too tongue-tied to think of anything to say.

"You go to school here?" she said.

"Yes," I said, relieved that she had kept the conversation going. I was too nervous to come up with anything else.

"What are you studying?" she asked.

"To be a radio operator." I looked behind me and saw that no one was waiting in line. That was a break.

"This store must be convenient for you."

"Yes, I live right down the street," I said, trying to think of something more to talk about. Several shoppers walked toward the counter. It was now or never.

"Ah, ah, excuse me," I said, knowing it would sound forced, because it was. "Would you be agreeable if sometime, when I'm in the mood for a movie, I would invite you to come with me?"

"Fine," she said, without hesitation.

"I'm glad to hear that," I said, backing away. "Good-bye. Have to go now. Maybe I'll see you tomorrow."

A few days later we made a definite date, and soon we began to see each other regularly. I would walk her home, or take her to the movies, or stroll with her through the woods. I fell in love with her almost immediately, enraptured by her wit, her outgoing warmth, her singing and dancing, and her inability to take herself too seriously—all qualities that I knew I lacked. She didn't seem bothered by the fact that I always wore the same shabby suit and couldn't afford to buy her candy at the movies. She was only eighteen years old, but she seemed so mature, so sure of herself. After three months, I told her I wanted to marry her and waited for her reply. There was none.

There were great differences between us. After we had been to a movie of Victor Hugo's *Les Misérables,* Gene left talking sympathetically about the human suffering she had seen while I was horrified at the kind of government that could allow such conditions to exist. When there was no meat in the stores of Klaipeda, she used her charm and a bribe to get meat for her supper. She coped. I just got angry at the government.

In the spring of 1958, I finished training at radio school and began to go to sea for a month or more at a time. I was terribly afraid that I would come back to find that I had lost her to someone

77

taller, better-looking, and more romantic. But finally, in the fall, she accepted my proposal.

Making our marriage official, though, was almost impossible. The state, in order to discourage frivolous couplings, made a man and a woman apply for a marriage certificate and then take time to think it over—thirty days to be precise. Not twenty-nine or thirty-one, but thirty—no more, no less. If they failed to pick up their certificate on the thirtieth day, they had to start the application process all over again. While this rule was just a bureaucratic annoyance for most couples—the kind that was typical of Soviet life—it was a major obstacle for us. My voyages often lasted longer than thirty days, and my stays in port tended to be shorter.

We applied for a certificate, but on the thirtieth day I was still in the North Sea, pacing the deck, chewing my fingernails, and muttering about the insane system and its idiotic rules. I got home seventeen days too late. The second time, the ship missed by just five days. Gene, who had moved into my barracks room in the meantime, was beginning to doubt me. "You never really wanted to marry me," she said. "You just wanted me to move in. If you really loved me, you'd skip the next voyage so we could be sure of getting married." But I couldn't do it; I might never get another chance to sail.

I sailed out again, and by the twenty-ninth day I was in port in Estonia, about 300 miles away from Klaipeda. I got permission to leave the ship, hopped an all-night train, and arrived in Klaipeda just after dawn. I picked Gene up at her store, and we rushed to the marriage office, stood in line all morning, got all the papers signed, and celebrated with a bottle of champagne that we had kept around for months in anticipation of the big moment.

The weeks passed in Vilnius KGB prison, and still Simas clung doggedly to his alibi. He kept insisting that he had never intended to defect, only to take a short, unauthorized tour of the forbidden West. Then a cellmate informed him that the reason Urbonas would not believe that story was that what had happened on the *Vigilant* had been front-page news all over the world.

A few days later, during an interrogation session, Urbonas

handed Simas an American newspaper clipping recounting the incident. Simas stared at the article, then chuckled.

"You know what," he admitted, "I wanted to leave and never return."

Urbonas sighed. "You should have said that long ago. It would have been much better for you."

"I'm not a thief or a murderer. I have done no harm to anyone. But the truth is that the only way I could imagine myself being returned to the Soviet Union is exactly the way I did come back—in shackles."

"Your confession still leaves us with the unanswered question," the interrogator said. He took a puff of his cigarette and stared down at the table. "Why?" He paused again. "Perhaps you were merely running away from your wife and family."

Simas began to object.

Urbonas raised his hand. "Let me finish. You talk so much about morality. Maybe there was no morality at all to what you did. Maybe you are a totally amoral creature. Now, you have something to say?"

"I wasn't running away from my family," he said uneasily. "I was going to bring them to America to join me. You want to know why I jumped?" He ran down a litany of complaints about the Soviet system's failure to provide its citizens with either consumer goods or basic freedoms.

"Now wait a minute," Urbonas said with obvious impatience. "Tell me—why only you? Why is it only you who cannot tolerate these horrible conditions you speak of? If things are so bad here, why isn't everyone trying to jump?"

Simas hesitated before answering. The question was one that had troubled him often over the years. He knew that many of his friends did not share his anger.

"I don't know," he said.

In 1959, after I had become a ship's radio operator and had married Gene, I tried to learn to be happy in Lithuania. All I wanted was an apartment for my family and a seaman's passport for myself. Was that so much to ask?

At the time of our marriage, we lived in a single room in a drab clapboard barracks in a section of Klaipeda called Fishtown. The neighborhood was a slum, a center for drinking, mugging, and prostitution. A giant fish-processing plant was just a few blocks away, and when the wind came off the Baltic Sea, as it did every afternoon, the stench was unbearable. We did what we could to make this room a real home. But there was nothing we could do about the paper-thin walls that let the chill of the winter wind and the raucous voices of drunken neighbors come right through. We had no running water. There was just a pump outside and a filthy outhouse about seventy-five yards away. To cleanse our bodies, we had to take the crosstown bus to the public bathhouse, a trip which could consume the better part of a day.

We had our first child, Lolita, in 1960. On winter days when I was out to sea, Gene would awaken in the freezing room at 6:00 A.M., hop out of bed, clean the dead ashes out of the stove, load in fresh wood, and start a fire, hoping to warm the room before the baby woke up. Then she would breast-feed Lolita, put together a package of diapers, and, just before 8:00 A.M., drop her with a neighbor before running off to her job at the store. Several times a day she hurried home to nurse the baby. When Gene's workday finally ended at 11:00 P.M., she would drag herself home, pick up Lolita, and leave the crying child bundled up in the carriage while she worked feverishly to get a fire going and warm the room, which had been unheated since morning. Then after undressing the child, feeding her, and putting her to bed, she boiled the next day's diapers, chopped the next day's wood, and went to bed at 2:00 A.M., looking forward to four precious hours of sleep.

The arrangement was becoming unbearable, and the room was just too small. As soon as Gene could stop breast-feeding, we took our daughter to Griskabudis to live with my mother and stepfather. We vowed to bring Lolita home as soon as we got our apartment. But in the Soviet Union, which has a chronic housing shortage, a man and a woman cannot just go out and walk the streets in search of an apartment. They must put their names on a list and wait for their names to get to the top. I would have to wait thirteen long years.

Every time I came back from a voyage, before I went back to the barracks, I checked the all-important list; and every time I found that my name had moved up only a few notches, or not at all. At this rate, I would have a grandchild before I had an apartment. My child would grow up hardly even knowing her mother and father. I wanted to find the people who were responsible for this travesty of a list and knock their teeth down their throats. Who were those bastards, dozens of them, who managed to jump ahead of me on the list? Who were the sons-of-bitches who got apartments without even appearing on the list? What gave the privileged few—government officials and party bigwigs—rights that an ordinary working stiff didn't have? I would swear and curse and yell so loudly that Gene feared the police would come.

Once I went to see the great and exalted housing supervisor to try to get an explanation. I was admitted into his office after a long wait, and I was made to feel as if I had been granted an audience with the king on his throne. This man had a huge apartment of his own, a chauffeur-driven car, a generous salary, and all sorts of other privileges. And when I asked for his help, he said he was sorry, there was nothing he could do. I asked him why. He said that was not for me to know. I felt as if he had stabbed me in the gut and poured boiling vinegar into the wound. What could he know about living in a barracks room? You come back from a month at sea, and you want to make love to your wife. How can you do that and enjoy it when the door has no lock and could fly open any time and the walls are so thin that the neighbors can hear the bed creaking?

At first, we tolerated the situation. We told ourselves we only had to suffer a few years there. But as the years went by, we couldn't fool ourselves anymore. We were probably going to be living in this squalor forever.

On board ship, I took out my mounting frustration by listening to the forbidden Western radio stations—the Voice of America, Radio Liberty, and British Broadcasting. The more I listened, the more my hatred for the Soviet system grew. I heard talk of a Russian writer named Alexander Solzhenitsyn and a physicist named Andrei Sakharov, men who called themselves dissidents. At first, I paid them no mind; they were, after all, ethnic Russians. Besides, what could those Moscow intellectuals know about finding an apartment in a provincial town or getting a passport? Gradually, though, I sensed that we were all complaining about the same conditions— the lack of respect for human rights and human dignity.

As the years passed, my frustration grew into a rage that I had to fight at all times to suppress. Once it totally overwhelmed me. In full view of other sailors, I screamed at my ship's political officer, denouncing him, the fishing fleet, the collective farming system, Lenin, Stalin, and the inability of the system to provide a simple apartment for a hard-working man and his family. After that outburst, I was confined to shore for six months and lost six months' salary, a loss I could ill afford with a second child on the way (our son, Evaldas, born in 1966, joined Lolita in Griskabudis with my mother). I knew I could not risk another day of rage. But by the end of the 1960s, as I entered my second decade of waiting for an apartment, my patience was disappearing. My outbursts were becoming more frequent and harder to control. I saw myself walking down a long gangplank. One day soon I would reach the end of it and fall into the ocean, where the sharks were waiting to rip me to bits.

Then one day in the spring of 1970, just before my fortieth birthday, I received a short telegram at sea from Gene. At long last, we had been assigned an apartment. I felt all the tension disappear in an instant. I got drunk that night, and I celebrated again when I got back to port and saw the apartment for myself. The living room alone was bigger than our old barracks room. It was no palace. It needed work. But that was the kind of work I had been waiting to do all my life, work that would create a real home for my family.

I thought my problems were all behind me. But it was not to be. I asked for a permanent job in port so that I could enjoy my new apartment all the time. My supervisor said no. And if I didn't go back to sea, he said, he would make sure I never got any kind of a job ever again. He even threatened to have the apartment taken away. So nothing had changed, not really. The system would never allow me to be the master of my own destiny. Unless I did exactly as I was told, I would lose everything I had worked so hard to get.

So I did what I was told, hating the system more than ever. I had no choice. On November 5, 1970, against my will, I left Klaipeda as the radio operator of the factory ship *Sovetskaya Litva,* not knowing the ship was bound for the coast of North America.

"Why did you choose a career at sea?" Urbonas asked one day. "I'm serious. Why does a peasant from a little town like Griska- budis want to go to sea? Why was it such an obsession for you? You've told me all about your grandfather and how he made the sea seem so romantic to you. That's all very nice. But there's more to it. There has to be. From everything you've said, I get the distinct impression you chose the sea from all other types of work because you thought it would provide the greatest opportunities to escape from the Soviet Union. True?"

Simas laughed. Urbonas was right, of course, to a degree. When he had first tried to become a sailor, when he was running from Griskabudis and the KGB, he had been looking to escape. At the age of twenty-one, in fact, he had plotted with two other men to smuggle himself on board a Soviet ship, hijack it, and force it to sail to Sweden, where all three would ask for asylum. But nothing had come of it. And when, at age twenty-seven, he had enrolled in radio operators' school, the thought of escaping had still been in the back of his mind. Once he met Gene, though, he had forgotten all about going anywhere.

"Considering my circumstances at the moment," Simas said, "considering what happened on the *Vigilant,* how could I convince you otherwise? Is it worth even trying? No matter what I say, you'll twist it around to prove whatever point you want to prove."

"Try."

"What were my choices? Factory work? Construction? Coming back home to the collective farm? Get serious. Financially, the sea was good for me. When I was on ship all my living expenses were taken care of. I could save money for the apartment Gene and I hoped we would get someday. I went to sea because it was the ful- fillment of a childhood dream to see the world. Of course, your wonderful government wouldn't let me see the world. I couldn't get a passport that would allow me off the ship when it docked. I don't know why I wasn't allowed to have one, though I can guess. No one would tell me. I stayed at sea, though, because it was the only way I knew to get money for my family, the only way to build up some savings. My motive was money, pure and simple.

"You think I wanted to escape all those years. If all I wanted to do was run away, I could have done it twenty times, even without a passport. We were always going to Kiel in West Germany for repairs. It would have been child's play to defect there. Once last year we were in Las Palmas in the Canary Islands for eight hours. We were so close to shore I could have waded in. Why didn't I go then, if all I ever wanted was to escape?

"I told you from the first day I arrived in this God-forsaken prison of yours that the jump we've been talking about day after day was not premeditated. Until the morning of the day it happened, I didn't think of doing it.

"Tell me, why should I want to run away at that particular time, when I finally had an apartment? Why would I want to run away? Who would I be running to? I didn't know a soul in America. So why did I do it? You act like you understand it. So if you're so smart, explain it to me."

Urbonas poured himself a glass of water. "No," he said slowly. "We do not understand you at all."

Eight

After nearly three months, the interrogations ended. At the close, Simas was examined by a prison psychiatrist who had the power, by declaring him insane, to send him without trial to one of the KGB's notorious psychiatric hospitals, special hells reserved for the most prized political prisoners. A few years in such a place would make a man truly insane, no matter what the condition of his mind upon entering it. But the doctor found Simas in good mental health, which meant he would have his day in court.

"Who would you like as a defense lawyer?" Urbonas asked.

"Do I need one?" Simas asked. "You know that I am a decent man who has done no wrong. Why should I pay for an attorney?"

"If the state assigned one for you, you would not have to pay."

"You misunderstand. From what I know of the law, the reality of your legal system, and the cold facts of the case, I have no need of an attorney."

"An attorney is a specialist. He can help you."

"Be serious," Simas said. "There is no physician skilled enough to cure the dead."

Urbonas shook his head. "Why do you say that?" he asked in a tone that suggested he could learn to like his prisoner if the man would only come to his senses. "I have told you before. Everything depends on you."

Urbonas was right of course, in a way. Everything did depend on me. I was going to be found guilty, no matter what. But that did not really matter. What mattered was how I behaved during my trial. Would I be meek and respectful? Would I grovel before the court and ask for forgiveness? Or would I say what was on my mind, knowing full well that the consequences would be death?

I could not be a hypocrite. I was not sorry for jumping. I was only sorry that I had failed so miserably. I began to feel a very direct responsibility to speak the truth, as eloquently as I knew how, which I knew would not be very eloquently at all. I felt a responsibility to the partisans, the men who had died fighting the system I had tried to escape. Other prisoners told me that I only had a responsibility to myself—to survive. They said that to speak out was folly. I was getting the same advice in letters from Gene and my mother. They told me not to do anything crazy at my trial, to remember that I had loved ones who wanted me out of prison as soon as possible. But I didn't see what difference my behavior made in terms of my punishment. I felt I was a dead man and had been since that day on the *Vigilant*.

I had to be faithful to the ideals that had made me jump or my jump would end up meaning nothing at all. If I had succeeded, I would have been in America now, using my forum in the West to denounce the Russians and what they had done to Lithuania. I had to make that same denunciation at my trial. But if I did, if I spoke what was in my heart, I would lose whatever chance I had of ever returning to my loved ones. The thought of that hurt so much. I could feel a pain in my side as if the three of them—Gene, Lolita, and Evaldas—had been attached there and then torn away, leaving me bleeding.

I could be a good, quiet boy at my trial and hope for a light sentence. But if I got out of prison quickly by doing that, would my family really want me? I would be physically deformed from the years in the labor camp; and inside that mangled body there would be no spirit left, only the remnants of a man who did not love justice enough to speak his mind, who had trampled on the graves of the dead just to save his own skin. I would not be that man! It was better to end it here, with my self-respect still intact. I was coming to the realization that there was no choice for me and there never had been. At my trial, I was going to denounce the Soviet system for what it was. The writings of Alexander Herzen helped me make up my mind.

Until I got to prison I had never heard of Herzen. My education, after all, was not the best. Herzen was one of the leading Russian intellectuals of the nineteenth century, and his memoirs were permitted reading in prison only because he, like the Communists of the twentieth century, hated the czars. I guess we were very different men, Herzen and I. He was brilliant and a Russian aristocrat by birth, while I was just an ignorant Lithuanian sailor of peasant stock. But we were kindred spirits. He too was a bastard who had been imprisoned for his political beliefs. He loved the West—and its concern for democracy and human rights—and so did I. He had condemned the Russian government, survived his imprisonment, and continued his war of words. He made it seem a great honor to be in a Russian jail.

Herzen described his own life in prison—the spartan cell, the meager food, the mind-numbing monotony of the routine, and the persistence of his interrogators. I read his words and felt that he would feel right at home here in Vilnius in 1971. Nothing had changed—not really. If he could survive without giving up his beliefs, so could I. I vowed to make my day in court the forum that I had been searching for all these years. I would vent my hatred of the system, and the system's representatives would have to sit there and listen. My crime was a political one. My trial should be political, too.

———————

Simas was wearing a short-sleeved shirt, black pants, and deck shoes when he entered the auditorium where the Lithuanian Supreme Court would sit to judge him. The vast chamber made him feel very small; it had a foreboding, almost lonely feeling to it. As the guards marched him toward his seat in the middle of the front bench, he could hear his footsteps echo off the high ceiling. The long windows were covered with thick curtains; this was a closed trial. Only a dozen persons were scattered on massive oak benches that could have handled hundreds. Urbonas and Gene were among them.

He sat down on the front bench, stared straight ahead, and saw a raised stage where the judges, lawyers, and secretaries would soon take their places. Above the stage was the only decoration in the barren gray room—a giant wooden replica of the seal of Soviet Lithuania. Inside a wreath of painted green leaves, the sun was rising behind staves of golden wheat, and above the sun was a black hammer and sickle, and above that the red Communist star. The words "Workers of the World Unite" were emblazoned across the leaves.

A door opened to the right of the stage.

"All rise," a court officer announced, "the court is entering."

Five men walked in. The youngest of them, a tall blond in a navy blue uniform trimmed with gold, marched to a table on stage left. He was the prosecutor. The next three, all middle-aged and wearing gray business suits, took their places behind a raised bench directly under the seal. They were the judges. And last came a stooped-over old man with a folder of papers jammed under his arm. He fell into his table, at stage right, his papers scattering in all directions. He was the defense attorney, appointed by the court.

"Please be seated," said the pudgy man in the middle of the judges' bench. "This court is now in session to hear Case Number Three-thirteen, the case of the dangerous offender who is seated here. My name is Misiunas. I am the chief judge." He introduced the two associate judges, who were not to say a word during the entire trial. He introduced the prosecutor, Petrauskas, and the defense attorney, Gavronskis.

"Are there any questions?" he said to the other judges and lawyers. There were none. "Will the accused please rise?" Simas stood. "The court has appointed an attorney, Mr. Gavronskis, to represent you. Do you have any objections?"

"I don't want an attorney," he said calmly.

Simas turned toward Gavronskis, who was still trying to get his mess of papers arranged on his table. "I feel badly as far as you are concerned, but my experiences give me no choice but to refuse your services as defense attorney." He faced the judge. "If

Gavronskis is an honest man and defends me according to his conscience, then it can only do him harm. But if he is dishonest and plays the role of a second prosecutor, then I think my case is already complex enough. One prosecutor is enough.''

"Do you have anything to say to that?'' the judge asked Gavronskis. The defense attorney was silent. ''You are dismissed.'' The old man stuffed his papers into the folder, thrust the folder under his arm, and hurried out of the room.

The judge turned now to Simas. ''May I have your name, please, for the record.''

"Simas Kudirka.''

"Citizen Kudirka, I will read the charge against you. 'On the twenty-third day of November, nineteen seventy, the accused citizen, Simas Kudirka, did commit a dangerous transgression against the state by going over to a ship belonging to a foreign government, and, by that act, betraying the motherland. On the basis of the Lithuanian Soviet Socialist Republic's Penal Code, Article Sixty-two, Paragraph One, Citizen Kudirka is being brought to trial here, this day, May seventeenth, nineteen seventy-one.' You may be seated.''

The judge then asked the prosecutor, Petrauskas, to give an opening statement, which he did with gusto, flailing the air with his right hand, whirling to point at Simas, and shouting in short, choppy verbal punches.

"I accuse you of being a traitor!'' he exclaimed.

Simas leapt to his feet. ''I accuse you of having created conditions in Lithuania that force men like me to seek a freer land!''

"Sit down!'' the judge ordered. ''Citizen Kudirka, we will not tolerate these outbursts. This is a court of law.'' Petrauskas finished his opening statement without further interruption. ''Now, Citizen,'' the judge said, ''suppose you explain to the court why you have acted in this manner and what led you to betray your motherland.''

"I did not betray my motherland,'' Simas answered, not shouting this time. ''Lithuania is my motherland, not Russia, and I would never betray Lithuania. If I have betrayed her, then open the doors of your secret trial, and let anyone who wants come in and

89

throw stones at the traitor. Apparently, you are not interested in the truth. This is not a democratic trial. I am not guilty. The only court that would have the right to judge my guilt would be the court of a free and independent Lithuania, which this is not.'' He launched into a harangue of his own on the iniquities of the Soviet system.

"Thank you, Citizen," Judge Misiunas said when Simas was finished. "From everything that the accused has said today, we can see that Citizen Kudirka was reared in a bourgeois atmosphere. He saturated himself with the output of capitalist propaganda sources. He came to incorrect, negative conclusions which brought him to his act of treason against the motherland. The court session for this day is finished."

"All rise," the court secretary said. The judges left, and the guards led Simas back up the steps to the waiting room, down a series of halls of the building, and into the Black Maria for his trip back to Vilnius KGB prison.

The second day of the trial belonged to the prosecution. Twelve prosecution witnesses, all of them men who had sailed with Simas at one time or another, paraded before the judges. The first witness, Vladimir Popov, captain of the *Sovetskaya Litva,* was out at sea, so his sworn statement, prepared in advance, was read aloud by the prosecutor.

"As a person," Popov said, "Kudirka was basically a courteous man, with some exceptions. His work was always done conscientiously. Never was he inebriated aboard ship. . . . As for the incident in question, I can state the following. I was forced as captain to retrieve a member of my ship's crew, and I wrote to the captain of the American ship that Simas Kudirka broke the safe and stole 3,000 rubles, which, in fact, did not happen. I ask the court to turn its attention to this fact. His remaining in the capitalist camp would have brought great harm to the Soviet system. As ship's captain, I could not allow this to happen and therefore felt compelled to write the note. I have no doubt that the Soviet court will find a just conclusion."

Then the judge called Ivan Burkal into the room. The fleet commander, whom Simas had not seen since leaving the *Sovetskaya*

Litva as a prisoner six months earlier, entered from the rear of the auditorium. Looking proud of himself, he marched up the stairs onto the stage, stood in front of the judges' raised bench, and looked up at the three justices.

"Citizen," the judge began, "you are hereby instructed to tell the truth. You will be held responsible for the truth. The crime of false witness is punishable by two years in prison."

"I understand."

"State your name, please."

"Ivan Burkal."

"And what do you do?" the judge asked.

"I am the acting commander of the Soviet Lithuanian fleet."

"How long have you known the accused?"

"We first met eight years ago. I would not say I know him well."

"How was your relationship with him?"

"Good," Burkal said. "I was a commanding officer. He was a radio operator. There were no problems."

"What can you tell us about the accused?"

"His most recent act was totally unexpected," the commander said. "I cannot understand what impulse seized him. He had always demonstrated acceptable behavior, even commendable behavior at times. I was shocked by the anti-Soviet outburst that I heard from him on board the *Vigilant*. A deep hatred against Sovietism was spewing forth from his mouth. We offered him the chance to return voluntarily to the Soviet ship. We tried hard to be gentle, but he rebuffed us. And so he had to be returned forcibly."

"Commander Burkal," the judge said, "the accused has stated that he was harshly beaten in this incident. Is this true?"

"I'm not aware of any beatings," he said. "I certainly didn't see any."

Simas jumped up and screamed, "I protest! That is not true. You are a card-carrying Communist. Which of the ten commandments of Communism gives you the moral right to lie?"

The guards behind Simas reached over and pushed him back down onto the bench.

"I've told you before, Citizen Kudirka," Judge Misiunas said sternly, "the court will not permit such conduct on your part. Strike those remarks from the record. The question is unrelated to the case and is not permitted. You have no right to question witnesses in this way, and, if you persist, your right to question them will be taken away. You, of all people, have no right to discuss morality. Now, Commander Burkal, the question was . . ."

Simas jumped up again. "The question was why did your delegation beat me?"

"Because you wouldn't come back any other way!" Burkal yelled at him.

"Commander," the judge said, scolding Burkal for having answered the question, "that will be all."

Several other members of the posse that had brought Simas back from the *Vigilant* testified during the day. One was Devenas, a short, barrel-chested bully of a man for whom words did not come easily. It was torture for him to have to speak in public. He fidgeted constantly while he stood before the judges' bench.

"Citizen Devenas," the judge asked, "was there any beating, as the accused has claimed?"

"No, none that I know of," he said uneasily.

"No beating!" Simas shouted. He pointed to his own face. "Look at this nose. You broke it. Did you do that with a nasty look, or with your fist?"

"We used force, but no one beat you."

The judge tried to restore order, but Simas kept firing questions and Devenas kept answering in nervous bursts.

"Were you the one who kicked me in the ribs?"

"That did not happen."

"Were you the one who bit me on the shoulder?"

"That did not happen."

"You are trembling, Devenas. Or are you going to deny that, too?"

Before Devenas could answer, Misiunas ordered him to leave the room.

The next witness was Gruzauskas, the political officer of the *Sovetskaya Litva*. He, too, was asked whether force had been used to return Simas to the mother ship.

"If force had been used," he said with half a smile, "there would be nothing left of Kudirka."

The long day in court became a sort of nightmarish class reunion for Simas, as nearly forgotten faces paraded out of his past to chronicle his previous anti-Soviet outbursts and give their opinions about why he had committed this treasonous act.

"He must not have been sane," said one.

"He was unhappy with his family life," said another.

"He did not agree with Soviet political views."

"He was bitter about not getting a seaman's passport."

The testimony lasted late into the afternoon, and when the last witness had been excused, Petrauskas summarized his case:

"Having heard all the witnesses, we come to the conclusion that Citizen Kudirka has committed a grave crime. Based on the Penal Code of the Lithuanian Soviet Socialist Republic, Article Sixty-two, Paragraph One, the punishment can be from ten to fifteen years or the highest punishment—death. As prosecutor in this case, my recommendation is fifteen years."

Simas knew that by the time he was finished presenting his "defense," the prosecutor would be sorry he had not asked for more.

On the third day, Simas stood below the judges' bench and opened his case as attorney for the defense by submitting a list of witnesses to testify in his behalf. All were members of the crew of the *Vigilant,* Americans whom he could identify only by rank or rough description—the captain (Eustis), the little fellow with the mustache (Pakos), the dark-haired man on the bridge (Lundberg). Chief Justice Misiunas stared down at the list, then looked up and smiled.

"I'm sorry, Citizen," he said. "The witnesses are not present in court today, and I will not be able to subpoena them. Proceed with your case."

He would have only one witness then—himself.

"My grandfather was a sailor," he began nervously, the words gushing forth, "and I've been drawn to faraway countries. There was the wish to see the world, and besides, at sea I would forget the tragedy of my people, or so I thought. When I was a teenager, not a week went by when the disfigured bodies of Lithuanian partisans weren't stacked up in the marketplace. I wanted to flee the hunger which reigned in the collective farms at that time, and the total lack of human rights, reminiscent of the serfdom of Lithuania one hundred years ago.''

"Just a minute," the judge interrupted. "Let's get to the issue here. You maintain that you wanted to find freedom in the United States, which, in your opinion, doesn't exist in the Soviet Union. How do you explain that they turned you back?''

"The ordinary Americans on the ship received me well," he said, remembering how the Guardsmen had embraced him in the first few minutes after the jump. "And there were tears in the eyes of the American captain when he told me I could not stay. The real tragedy is that I, as a Lithuanian, was seen by the American government as the legal property of Brezhnev, the heir to Stalin, who had to be returned. But from the standpoint of international law, I am not the property of Brezhnev or Stalin. And even if I were, I would not be a criminal. My decision to go abroad does not even contradict your Soviet constitution, which guarantees the freedom to emigrate, as you seem to have conveniently forgotten. I say *your* constitution. It is not mine. If my country, Lithuania, were sovereign and free, I would not be standing here before you. I am innocent, completely.''

"Citizen Kudirka," the prosecutor sneered. "What do you mean by 'sovereign.' Do you have any idea what the word means?''

"I'm not a learned man," Simas said, his temper rising slightly, "but I know what a sovereign nation is. It is a nation that has self-government, its own language, its own foreign policy, its own army. The guards who are guarding me here are supposed to be Lithuanians. I am speaking what should by all rights be their language, Lithuanian. But they don't understand me. All you have taught them is Russian.''

"We're not here to discuss political philosophy, Kudirka," Petrauskas said, glaring down at Simas from the prosecution table. "We're here to discuss you. And your treason wasn't a matter of philosophy, as you would have us think. It was a matter of living up to your family history. Your whole family was full of traitors!''

"That's a lie!''

"Oh, really. Let's look at the facts.'' The prosecutor paused to sift through the papers on his table. "Aha! Here it is. Your real father, the one who had the good sense to abandon you, was deported for his resistance to the collectivization of the farms. Your cousin by marriage, Vytas Sulskis, was one of those hoodlums who fought in the woods in the late nineteen forties. Your uncle, Jonas Kudirka, was a German collaborator in World War Two. Your . . .''

"That's not true,'' Simas yelled, slamming his right hand into the side of the stage.

"It's not, is it?'' Petrauskas smirked. "Well it's right here in the files.'' He made a grand gesture toward the papers spread before him.

Simas grabbed hold of the edge of the stage, vaulted up onto it, and raced for the prosecution table. "Let me see that!'' He grabbed the piece of paper out of Petrauskas's hand and read it. Petrauskas caught him in a bear hug. The soldiers grabbed him, too, and dragged him back off the stage to his assigned seat on the bench below.

"Just stop and think a minute!'' Petrauskas barked, still panting from the scuffle, after order had been restored. "Aren't you demanding more than a man of your education deserves here?''

"In case you have forgotten, even in your Soviet courts a man is entitled to see the evidence being stacked against him.''

"No, no,'' Petrauskas said. "You misunderstand. I mean, haven't you always demanded more than you deserve? You demand a job, an apartment, a passport, as if they were your divine right. What have you ever done for the Soviet Union? You are a Soviet citizen . . .''

"I never asked to be one. I am a Lithuanian.''

"You are a materialist,'' he said, spitting out the words as if they were the ultimate insult. "In your notebooks, we have found notes about the prices in the West of items like tape recorders and refrigerators. And not only that—we have proof that you are corresponding with a person in the capitalist state of [West] Germany. Tell us the truth now. What made you jump?''

''You say you cannot understand why a man would want to leave this paradise you have created. Well, I'll tell you why. Yes, I have listened to Western radio broadcasts, and, yes, I have made notes. I have talked to and written to Western radio operators. And I have learned that the Western standard of living makes those of us here in paradise look like paupers. I was tired of being shoved from one ship to another. My nerves had been frayed from my ridiculously long quest for an apartment. I had heard from my grandfather about foreign lands. I wanted to see for myself. My breaking point came when Gruzauskas said that two kids on the *Sovetskaya Litva* who picked up some American magazines would never sail again.''

''Didn't you care about leaving your family?'' the prosecutor asked.

''Of course I cared,'' Simas said, trying desperately to make the prosecutor understand. ''But my family would not have died of starvation. No matter what kind of work I got in the United States, I would have had more money to send back to them than I would ever have been able to put aside for them here, even if I had the best job. My family would be better off even if I got a job there cleaning toilets. And I would have tried to get my family to join me over there someday.''

''But here you had a good, clean job, didn't you?''

''You call that a good job!'' he retorted in disbelief. ''I was serving a fleet that was Lithuanian in name only. All my superiors were Russians. And besides, you didn't trust me. You gave me access to the ship's radio, the nerve center of the ship, but you wouldn't give me a passport.''

''That was your fault. You were always making anti-Soviet speeches.'' Petrauskas paused and changed the subject. He was always changing the subject, hoping to fluster the defendant by interrupting his train of thought. ''What about your old mother? Would you abandon her?''

''There was nothing I could do to better her life here,'' Simas said. ''She has to work from dawn to dusk now on your collective farms and gets almost nothing in return. . . . Why are you so interested in my private life all of a sudden? You never cared before. You have looked on me as an old sick nag and have given me nothing but dry straw for nourishment, while you, you government officials, have flocked to the trough to stuff yourselves with only the best food.''

Petrauskas leapt to his feet and faced the judge. "Did you hear that? Can you believe it? Who does he think he is? The state gives him a job, an apartment, a salary, and what does he do? He insults the court. He wants it all on a silver platter. This man is not propelled by some high principle. His driving force is avarice. His motto is 'Give me, give me, give me.' '' He whirled to face Simas. "Let's get this straight, Kudirka. You are on trial. Not us.''

"Is that so, Mr. Prosecutor?'' Simas answered, mocking Petrauskas's condescending tone. "If you hadn't repressed our people and killed so many of our countrymen, you wouldn't have any political problems. If you had let me go to sea freely, I wouldn't be on trial. I would never have jumped.'' He gave the court a history lecture, recalling the days of the partisans and the days that followed, when the government set out to destroy the Catholic Church and the family farm. "Already in nineteen fifty waves of Lithuanians with their young were being carted off to concentration camps. The death of Stalin saved my people from physical extermination. However, the essence of the policy remained the same. Now we are destined to die a much slower death, death by assimilation. But we don't want to die, and we will not die! Read your history and you will see that throughout history Russia has done nothing but inflict misery on humanity. And Soviet Russia has brought nothing but hardships, tears, and suffering to people.''

He ranted on and on, long into the afternoon. He had never given a public speech before and his tongue frequently wandered away from his central theme. He was loud, angry, and highly repetitive, punctuating his points by slamming his right fist hard into the open palm of his left hand. Both judge and prosecutor constantly interrupted him, ordering him to confine his remarks to the facts of the case. Finally, he came to his conclusion: "I ask the government of the Soviet Union to grant independence to my homeland, Lithuania. And I ask that the Supreme Court see to it that there are no more trials like mine.''

Urbonas had been watching the trial for three days, and for three days he had sat there in silence. Now he spoke loud enough for Gene, who was seated nearby, to hear. ''For five months, I've been telling him that if he wanted a light sentence, he would have to be discreet,'' he said. ''Well, now he's going to get it. He's really going to get it.''

Petrauskas lifted himself slowly out of his chair. His face was flushed. ''Are you sure you're finished?'' he asked, facetiously.

''Yes,'' Simas replied.

''That's nice of you,'' he quipped. ''From the statement we have heard from defendant Kudirka today, it is obvious that he does not regret what he has done, that he is in love with the capitalist system. You heard him. He's not guilty; everyone else is! He has no understanding of how much harm he has done to the Soviet system, how much slander the Soviet Union has been subjected to in the Western press.'' For a few seconds, he paced across the stage in dramatic silence, then slammed his right fist through the air. ''I was too generous yesterday! Now that we have heard Kudirka, I know that I should have demanded only one punishment—death!''

And then the court adjourned for the night.

As the trial of Simas Kudirka convened for its fourth and final day, Chief Justice Misiunas asked whether the defendant had anything else to say. Struggling to keep his eyes open, Simas rose and stared at the judge. He had not slept much; the prospect of death had kept him awake.

''The bravest and most resolute patriots of Lithuania were physically annihilated,'' he said somberly. ''But a new, young generation has grown up which intends to go the road of their fathers. When I refused to fulfill the wish of the KGB, they threatened me with the death sentence. And now I believe that promise will be fulfilled. I am a believer, a Catholic. Therefore, if the Supreme Court sentences me to death, I would request it to invite a priest to give me the last rites of the Catholic Church.''

Misiunas paused, glanced at the associate judge on his right, then at the one on his left. He whispered to both of them, then turned to face the prisoner again.

"Does the defendant have anything else to say?"

"Perhaps you did not hear me," Simas said. "I want a Catholic priest."

"Does the defendant have anything else to say?"

Simas was silent.

"Then this court will recess to deliberate on its verdict."

The judges rose from their chairs and walked out a side door. Simas was told to remain on his bench. He knew it would not take long. The judges were back in fifteen minutes. Chief Justice Misiunas stood and asked Simas to stand as well.

"In accordance with the Penal Code of the Lithuanian Soviet Socialist Republic, Simas Kudirka is accused of treason." In his deepest, most formal voice, the judge detailed the charges, explained the law, and announced his findings of fact. "Having analyzed all these factors, we have found the defendant guilty and have arrived at our sentences—ten years in strict regime labor camp with confiscation of personal property. Court costs will be taken from the defendant's earnings in the camps."

Simas was as ecstatic as a man can be who has just been told he will lose the next ten years of his life. It was a stiff penalty, but he had convinced himself that he was going to be sentenced to death. Ten years was a price worth paying for the performance he had just given, or so he told himself.

He whirled to face his wife. "Gene!" he yelled, waving excitedly. "We'll have time for living yet!"

Misiunas called for order, then asked Simas if he had any final request of the court.

"I request that you do not harm my family," he said, gesturing toward Gene and his mother, who was sitting with her. "My fondest wish is to see a free and independent Lithuania in whose courts people like me will not be on trial. Today you have placed me on trial, when humanity, by right, should have placed you on trial. There will be a day when the likes of you will be judged. My conscience is clear."

By nightfall, after a final meeting with Gene and my mother, I was trying to focus my mind on the future, not the past. I tried to put the trial, the jump, and even my family behind me. As I waited in my cell for the long future to begin, I tried to tell myself that I had something to look forward to. My cellmates told me that a labor camp wasn't such a terrible place. All it was, they told me, was a fenced-in compound with a lot of space, trees, and other political prisoners—men who could sympathize with what I had done and why I had done it. Think of all the friends you'll make, they told me. Besides, it was a lot healthier to work than to sit in a clammy, dingy old cell day after day.

But as hard as I tried, I couldn't fool myself. I was leaving my homeland and going to a land where the weather was cold and men went hungry. There was something pleasant and secure—even in my situation—about being on Lithuanian soil. From now on, I would be on Russian soil, foreign soil. Leaving my homeland would sever all ties with the past. By the time I came back, if I did come back, my children would be full-grown. Lolita would be twenty-one and Evaldas nearly fifteen. I would miss out on watching them grow. Mother would probably be dead, and Gene might well be a grandmother. What a terrible ten years to miss! After ten long years, the people I would come back to would not be the same people I was leaving. I would be a stranger to them. My place in their world would be gone.

Nine

There was a knock on the door of Simas's cell late one night ten days after the trial.

"Kudirka," a voice said. "Get your things packed."

Simas gathered his belongings. It did not take long; he did not have much. Six soldiers came to the cell and escorted him into another room, where they made him take off his clothes. While he undressed, they searched his belongings, inspecting every seam of every piece of clothing.

"Bend over."

They probed his mouth, his nose, his ears, and his anus, and found nothing. They told him to get dressed, then loaded him into a black van. The van traveled for thirty minutes, then stopped in a dark, barren field. They pushed him out. The moment his feet touched the ground, a soldier shoved his boot firmly into his back, an unspoken order to march through the darkness.

"Hurry. There isn't much time."

Simas had no idea where he was or where he was going. There were no lights ahead. He could picture what would happen next. The soldier behind him would shoot him in the back, shove him into a trench, and throw some dirt on him. And it would be over. He walked on through a field strewn with garbage and broken bottles, through a thicket of trees, and across a set of railroad tracks. Now he was walking parallel to the tracks. A train, shrouded in its

101

own steam, was sitting on the tracks, standing at a loading platform. It looked like a normal Soviet passenger train with the standard drab green cars and white curtains in the windows.

"Go on. Up the stairs. Into the car."

The first thing that struck him as he entered the train was the overpowering stink, a mixture of makhorka—a foul-smelling cheap tobacco substitute—and human waste. His eyes began to burn from the thick blue smoke. Instinctively, he staggered back but the boot of the soldier pushed him forward.

"Go on. Down the hall."

As he forced himself down the darkened corridor, eyes stared at him from above and below. He could see no bodies, only eyes. The train had the same basic passenger compartments that most European trains have, with two benches, each designed for three riders, facing each other. The prison authorities had taken these compartments and converted them into cages. Instead of sliding glass doors, these compartments were enclosed by locked iron grating, and instead of six passengers to a compartment, there were nineteen. Bodies were stacked everywhere. In each compartment, two prisoners were lying on the floor, jammed underneath the benches. Another ten sat on the benches, five on each side. A few inches above their heads was a wooden platform, with five prisoners lying side by side on top of it. Above them all, on the luggage racks, were the last two.

"In that one, over there."

Simas's first ride on this "death train" lasted nine hours. It was only the beginning of five weeks of death trains, black vans, and transit prisons, a prisoner's tour of the Soviet Union. Accommodations were always spartan, the cuisine was heavy on bread and water, and the plumbing ranged from poor to nonexistent. Travel always began with a full body search in the dead of night. He never knew where he was going or how long it would take to get there. All he knew was that he was heading east into Russia. During those train rides he listened, he watched, and he learned what to expect in the years ahead. He found that when men are put in cages, they act like animals. Obscenity was the language of the cages, and the prisoners, particularly the real criminals, often amused themselves by staging rapes, both heterosexual and homosexual, and comparing the sizes of each other's genitals.

As the days passed, the trains took him from Vilnius north to Pskov, an old Russian city not far from Leningrad, then east past Moscow to Gorki, and finally, in early July, south to the entrance to the prison camp world that Solzhenitsyn called the Gulag Archipelago. Under Stalin the camps had contained millions of men and women, most of them sent there to die for crimes of thought and word. But as the Soviet Union had matured, the number of political prisoners had dwindled to 20,000 or so. They were conscientious objectors who refused to serve in the armed forces; believers, many of them Jews, who insisted on giving their children religious training in a godless society; and nationalists who, like Simas, did not recognize the right of Russia to rule Lithuania, Latvia, Estonia, Armenia, Byelorussia, or the Ukraine. Simas's island in the Gulag was to be a prison complex known as Potma, located in the province of Mordovia, 225 miles southeast of Moscow. Once there had been 125 camps in Mordovia with quarters for well over 100,000 prisoners. Now there were only sixteen camps and 15,000 inmates. Most of the Potma prisoners were patriotic Soviet citizens who happened to have committed violent crimes. Only 2,000 were politicals. They were kept apart from the rest to make sure their heretical beliefs did not rub off on the apolitical criminals.

Simas arrived at Potma Camp Number Three on a cool, foggy morning in early July. The soldiers led him and three other new arrivals inside the main gate, searched their belongings, and then marched them across the central courtyard of the camp's residential zone. As he followed the guards across the yard, he noticed that the vast camp had a dozen long, low barracks, all of them the same chalky gray. There were groves of birch and linden trees, but only in the middle of the yard. The land near the barbed-wire fences on the perimeter was barren, giving the armed guards in the watchtowers a clear shot at anyone foolish enough to try to escape. There were men to be seen, too—old men on crutches with shaved heads and watery eyes. Their drab gray uniforms made them fade into the fog and the barracks walls. Only on second glance did Simas notice that many of them were missing arms and legs.

He thought he heard his name being called out loud. He glanced over his shoulder and saw a short bald man with a dark mustache running up behind him. He was sure he had never seen the man before.

"Kudirka!" the man was shouting. "Which one is Kudirka?"

Simas had to keep walking. The guards would not let him stop. But the man with the mustache caught up. Simas introduced himself, and the man in turn said he was Antonas Jastrauskas, a Lithuanian prisoner.

"Don't worry, pal," Jastrauskas said as he walked at Simas's side. "We can't talk now. You're going to the isolator for six days. Everyone has to go there on arrival. They want to give you a taste of punishment first, so you'll behave when you join the rest of us. Relax. There are a lot of Lithuanians here. We know all about you, and we are proud to have you among us. We have been waiting for you." Simas was approaching a small one-story brick building that was separated from the rest of the camp by a wire fence. The building contained the isolation cells.

"Good luck, my friend," Jastrauskas said. "We will see you soon."

Simas walked through a gate in the wire fence and into the isolation cells. His belongings were taken from him, and he was given new clothes—a pair of coarse, shapeless gray pants, a sleeveless undershirt, two pairs of gray undershorts, a collarless, loose-fitting gray jacket, a pillbox cap, two pieces of white cotton cloth to wrap his feet, and a pair of ankle-high boots. He was allowed a hot shower and was shown to his cell.

For six days, Simas was kept in that isolation cell with nothing to do but empty the toilet bucket, eat his bread and water, pace, and lie on a wooden slab bed, savoring the optimism that Jastrauskas's words allowed him. That optimism, and the summer's warmth, prevented him from noticing that there was no heat in the cell or covers for the bed. Six days passed, and on a sunny afternoon he emerged from the isolator and returned to the residential zone, where he was immediately surrounded by other prisoners, most of them Lithuanian. They shook his hand, slapped him on the back, and said how pleased they were to have a celebrity in their midst. Then they told him to go to Barracks Number Six—the patriarch of the Lithuanian community in camp wanted to meet him.

Dutifully, he walked over to the barracks where a bent old man sat in solemn contemplation on a bench outside, smoking a pipe. The man was bald and his long, sunken face was covered with a salt-and-pepper beard. His body, ravaged by lung cancer and chronic stomach ailments, seemed lost under his prison uniform. He looked like a tribal wise man, weighed down by all he has seen and all he knows must come to pass.

The man rose slowly, with obvious pain, and introduced himself as Mecys Kybartas. Simas was shocked to learn that Mecys, who looked seventy, was only forty-two years old, just a few months older than himself. Mecys had been in Soviet custody since the day in 1950 when he and his band of Lithuanian partisans were captured by the Red Army. Those twenty-one years as a prisoner, his entire adult life, had taken their toll on his spirit as well as his body. He had long since tempered the reckless idealism that had propelled him into the woods so long before. Now he was interested in surviving and helping others survive.

Mecys opened the barracks door and led Simas into a small clean room with four neatly made double-deck beds and a large pot-bellied stove. He pointed to a lower bunk. "You will sleep here."

"This isn't so bad, you know," Simas said.

"Oh, yes, we live very well," Mecys replied in a tone dripping with bitterness. "But do not praise the day before the sun sets." He paused long enough to let his cryptic warning sink in. "Simas, tell me about yourself. I mean, what the hell got into your head to make you take a jump like that?"

"It's such a long story," Simas said as he handed him a copy of his sentencing papers, which included a synopsis of the trial.

Mecys sat on his bunk and read intently, shaking his head and chuckling.

"Mecys," Simas said, sensing that the chuckling indicated disapproval, "I may not be the best son but Mother Russia is not the best mama either. It was not love of Mother Russia that brought you here, was it?"

105

Mecys looked up from his reading. "There was a time called youth in my life, and that time was very different and very long ago. During that time, when I came to the camps, I protested everything—the food, the working conditions, the lack of visits from relatives. And look what it got me. I suppose you will want to protest injustice here too."

"Yes."

"Do you think you have enough energy for that?"

"I have inhaled too much stench out there to stop now."

"Well, we shall see. You will find that in this place your stomach, not your head, often dictates your behavior."

Simas began to ask question after question about camp life. "There will be time to answer every question," Mecys said. His tone was deliberate and serious. "Simas, we know a lot about you. We want to help you survive. Do you want to survive?"

"Yes, of course."

"Fine. We have rules. Our most basic, most sacred rule is this: Do not shoot your mouth off without good reason, and especially not in front of people you have never met before."

"Are you trying to tell me there are informers here?" Simas asked in disbelief. "How can that be? We're all political prisoners in this camp. Doesn't that make us brothers?"

Mecys shook his head in amazement at the naïveté of his recruit. "You will live here, and this way of life will teach you. There are only a few men in our room here. But in every quarter there is a rat—and this room is no exception." He pointed to the lower bunk across the room.

"For you, I will make another sacred rule," Mecys continued. "When you are talking to someone, never say anything more [about politics] than is in your sentencing papers. No one will condemn you for choosing to keep your thoughts private; it is the right of every man. If someone pushes you to say more, spit in his face and walk away. Never speak to him again. Don't be insulted by my didactic tone. Remember, I have sown every one of my teeth in the Gulag. I'm just trying to help. There are a lot of things you don't know and can only learn through experience. Be very careful in choosing your friends. This is a very complicated and dangerous world here. Don't tear your guts out at work. Save your energy in every way. There's a long way to go.''

He put his hand on Simas's shoulder. ''Not everyone is an informer. There are a hell of a lot of good people here. A lot of us have been here a long time, and probably will never see the outside again.'' He paused. ''Did they beat you?''

''No.''

''Maybe you'll be one of the lucky ones.''

In the evening, the prisoners gave a welcoming party for Simas. They sat in a semicircle in the grass outside Barracks Number Six, ate pieces of candy and tiny sandwiches, and passed around a single cup of coffee from which each prisoner took two sips. After an hour of introductions and small talk, Jastrauskas asked for attention. It was time for the evening's featured entertainment, the dramatic reading of the new prisoner's sentencing papers. This practice was a fundamental tradition of camp life and for good reason—the old prisoners had to know who the new prisoner was and whether they could trust him.

Jastrauskas, a natural mimic, played each part in the melodrama, reading the judge's comments from the papers and making up lines for Simas. First he played the defendant, his voice loud and forceful as he attacked the Soviet system before an imaginary tribunal. Next he was the judge, his face serious, his eyes solemn, his voice stern. Then he was the prosecutor, pacing, screaming, and slashing the air with his arms. The trial had not seemed funny to Simas when it happened, but now it was hysterical. The prisoners booed, cheered, and laughed wildly, sometimes snatching the sentencing papers out of Jastrauskas's hands to read for themselves. And when the party was over, Simas felt he was among friends.

There were no more parties for Simas Kudirka—only work, nine hours a day, six days a week. At seven each morning, a guard took a hammer and whacked a short piece of railroad track that dangled from a cable. The clang of the ''clattergong'' reverberated throughout the camp. It was time to get up. A few minutes later, another guard threw the barracks door open and yelled ''Up! Up!'' The first week, Simas jumped to his feet the instant he heard those yells, but as the days passed he learned to linger in his bed until the guards ripped the covers off. He learned to hold on to every moment of rest he could. He rarely slept well. It was hard to sleep when a guard shined a flashlight in his face every two hours and held it there until he opened his eyes. He rolled off the thin mattress, donned his gray uniform, wrapped his feet, stepped into his stiff boots, and trudged out the door.

He made his way across the dirt to the drafty outhouse, then returned to the wash-up area outside the barracks. The mass washbasin consisted of two long troughs, one propped a few feet above the other on wooden supports. Clean water, ice cold even in midsummer, was pumped up into the top trough, which had spigots in its underside. Simas turned one of the spigots and splashed himself with the stinging, cold water as it fell into the trough below.

At 7:30, breakfast time, the prisoners began to stroll over toward the dining hall about fifty yards away. They were stopped outside the entrance by a guard, who reminded them that the entire population of a barracks had to enter as a unit. Unless all prisoners were present, none would eat. "Get your asses over here!" Mecys Kybartas, who served as barracks leader, shouted at the latecomers, particularly on mornings when the early arrivals had to await the stragglers in the rain. In a few minutes, every resident of Barracks Six was present. They all crowded around the door, but the guard still refused to let them in. The prisoners, he noted, were not in formation.

"You're not going anywhere that way," the guard said. "Let's go! Line up!" The prisoners began to form lines of five, but the guard tired of watching. "Go on! Inside! Stuff your ugly faces."

The prisoners pushed inside the dimly lit dining hall, a drab wooden building with two rows of eight rough board tables. The walls were decorated with bright red banners proclaiming "The Communist Party of the Soviet Union is the wisdom, honor, and conscience of our epoch" and "Work is the best medicine for all types of illnesses." The camp had 550 prisoners, and the dining hall had room for only 100 at a time. Since breakfast was served for only an hour, each prisoner had to hurry if everyone was to get his share. Simas pushed his way to the line leading to the soup window. A friend, Julius Dubauskas, stood in the porridge line. When Simas reached the window, the "cook," who was a prisoner, stirred the kettle with his ladle, grabbed a greasy metal bowl from a stack, banged it on the counter, slapped a ladleful of soup into it, and shoved it at Simas. "Another," Simas said, "for Julius." The cook shoved another full bowl at him. Meanwhile, Dubauskas was getting a second bowl of porridge for Simas.

Simas found two empty spots at a table. He left the soup bowls there and hurried to the bread table at the far end of the room. A prisoner was entitled to as much bread as he wanted, but the coarse brown stuff was nearly always inedible. If it was too raw, it stuck in a man's throat. If it was too well done, it broke when bitten into hard brown soot that could chip a tooth. Simas picked out a few relatively appetizing-looking pieces and returned to the table. The soup, as usual, was thin and tasteless, and the porridge was so thick it was almost solid. He never looked at the porridge anymore. The first few mornings, when he had looked, he had seen modest chunks of potato, onion, and fat, and bigger chunks of blue-green mold. He had to keep eating, so he stopped looking. He dumped the soup into the porridge, threw in the fifteen grams of sugar he had brought from the barracks to kill the taste, put a spoonful of it into his mouth, and stuffed a chunk of bread down with it. He ate as quickly as he could. This was not food to savor, and other prisoners were waiting for his seat.

At 7:50, a guard whacked the piece of railroad track once more for lineup. No matter what the weather, the prisoners lined up according to their work brigades in spots throughout the yard. The men who lined up in that yard every morning were a microcosm of the Soviet Union—Lithuanians, Estonians, Latvians, Byelorussians, Ukrainians, Finns, Georgians, Armenians, Jews, ethnic Russians, and even a German or two. They ranged in age from eighteen to seventy, but the true age of a prisoner was measured better by the number of years he had spent in the camps. In time, they all came to look the same—their faces gaunt, their complexions gray, their bodies emaciated. Their heads were constantly

109

shaved, reducing the coarse black curls or long blond locks that were characteristic of their peoples to mildly varying tones of peach fuzz.

Over by his barracks, Simas's work brigade was beginning to form. Prisoners were milling around, telling jokes, shouting greetings to one another, tossing pebbles into each other's boots, and smoking—all of which were against regulations.

"Cut the talk!" the guard at the head of the lineup ordered. "Fall in." The prisoners obeyed. "Stand up straight, you scum." He called out their names, and one by one they walked to the camp gate. When all the names had been called, the group was led off to the work zone. The men marched past a barbed-wire fence, a guard with a German shepherd who looked better fed than any prisoner, another barbed-wire fence, a barren no-man's-land of freshly plowed dirt, several spools of wire, an electrified barbed-wire fence, another no-man's-land, and, finally, a high wooden fence. They were, for a moment, outside the camp perimeter. All that separated them from freedom was a cordon of six armed soldiers, three on the right and three on the left—not counting the soldiers in the watchtowers who would have a clear shot at a man if he made a run for it. Simas never thought about running. He crossed the railroad tracks and marched into the work zone, past more fences and guards and dogs. He entered a two-story factory building, went to his locker, took off his uniform, and put on his work clothes, which were caked with cement dust.

He worked in a plant that manufactured huge rectangular sections of concrete, reinforced with steel. The concrete was mixed on the second floor and then dropped down a chute into a large vat on the first floor. Simas's job was to shovel the concrete from that vat into a rectangular mold, over and over again. If his timing was off, or if Dubauskas, his friend and work brigade leader, decided to play a little joke on him, a load of wet concrete might drop on his head, leaving him with a headache and a film on his skin that would not wash off. On other days, he worked outside the building, shoveling loads of cement, sand, and gravel into the jaws of the mixer. When winter came, the piles were covered with canvas and steam was piped underneath to keep the piles from freezing. The sandy steam filled his lungs and gave him a cough that lasted all winter long.

At noon each day he put down his shovel and made his way to a crowded, muddy dining hall inside the work zone. He stood in line for his food, then stood in line for a place to sit in the smoke-filled room. When a place on the rough wooden benches finally did come open, he sat down to a plate of porridge and a bowl of sour soup—pickle soup, pickled cabbage soup, or pickled black tomato soup. He never knew exactly what would be floating in that soup—a cow's udder, a hog's penis, or a chunk of cow lung, which had the consistency of styrofoam. He swilled the soup in with his porridge and thrust it down his throat as fast as he could. He knew when he had been too slow; his sinuses clogged in defense against the odor.

At 12:30 he returned to his job and shoveled concrete for most of the afternoon. The men in the factory worked hard, for they knew that if their brigade exceeded the camp's demanding group quota, every member would get a little more food in his bowl. Still, several times during the afternoon they took five-minute breaks.

"Smoke time!" Dubauskas would yell and the machinery would go silent.

A few feet from Simas a pale Estonian named Karl Vares collapsed on the floor. "I am so fucking tired," he said to no one in particular. He took a few deep breaths. "Hey, guys, did you hear? There's a commission coming to review cases and commute sentences of guys with good work records who've done two-thirds of their time."

"Yeah, sure," Dubauskas muttered. He took a puff of his cigarette. "That's bullshit."

"No, no," said a Latvian. "I heard it, too."

"Don't hold your breath," a Ukrainian yelled from across the room. "If you're not an informant, you're going to do your full time."

"If it's true, it will be announced to everyone," Dubauskas said with the air of authority that came to a prisoner after serving twenty years of a twenty-five-year sentence. "If we all don't hear it in twenty-four hours, it's bullshit."

"But what if it's not bullshit?" Simas asked. "Wouldn't you qualify, Julius?"

111

"Yeah, sure, kid. I'd qualify, just like I did the last time." Dubauskas spat out the words. "I remember the last farce. It was just like this one. They dangled that fucking carrot in front of me, and I could taste it. I kept getting all these hints that I was going to make it out. 'Keep up the good work, just keep it up,' the camp officials told me. I made one big mistake: I let myself start to believe it. Then they called me in for what was supposedly the final interview. This KGB asshole flips through my file. 'Good,' he says. 'Fine. Everything appears to be in order.' Then he stops and stares at one piece of paper. 'Oh, what have we here?' he says. In nineteen sixty-two, in a prison camp in Omsk, I had consumed one shot of an illegal homemade shellac brew. 'We can't release a drunkard, now can we?' He didn't even look me in the eye. And that was it. So you see, kid, I'll believe it when it happens."

"Shit," the Ukrainian barked. "We're going to be here from bell to bell."

"Wait, wait," Simas said. "Maybe times are changing."

"You got your head up your ass, my friend," Vares said. "Nobody forces the Kremlin to do anything. I've been here twenty-four years. So don't have dreams, kid, don't believe that you'll just walk back to the barracks one day and see a note on the board that every motherfucker is free."

Julius threw his cigarette on the floor. "Enough of this crap! Let's get back to work so we can get our extra few grams in the morning. That's the only amnesty I know of."

Simas trudged back to his post and shoveled more concrete until 5:30. Then he stripped off his work uniform, washed, got dressed, and lined up for the march back to the residential zone for supper. Most evenings the main course, in addition to the ever-present porridge, was a small, usually edible square of boiled white fish. On Mondays and Fridays, though, it was replaced by a fish stew that looked and smelled as if it had been scooped directly from a brackish pond full of long-dead fish.

After supper, after another lineup, Simas was free to do as he wished. He could write a letter home, if the authorities allowed him one that month, or read a little Herzen. He could play chess, flip through the Communist Party newspapers, or, as he did most often, walk five or ten times around the camp perimeter with a fellow prisoner, never straying too close to the fences.

Sunday was different. Even in Potma, Sunday was a day of rest.

For the first few months I thought that life at Potma wasn't so terrible. I was new and it was summer.

Then the irritations began to mount. We got paid a little for our work, and I was busting my gut in that plant. But by the time the authorities deducted the cost of my trial, the cost of my uniform, and the cost of my meals, there was nothing left to send home. And, as the warmer weather disappeared, so did my health. I was always coughing, and I was always hungry. I could feel myself growing weaker, and I could see what was happening to the others. They were wasting away before my eyes. Many of the older prisoners, nearing the end of twenty-five-year sentences, were simply dropping off and dying. The food kept getting worse and worse. Late in the summer they served us meat with live worms in it.

When I lay in my bunk and put it all together, I realized that murder was being perpetrated there in a cynical, drawn-out way. And for what? What crimes had we committed? All my instincts told me to say something, to do something in protest, even if we were behind ten layers of fences 225 miles from nowhere. I had been willing to speak out and take the consequences when I was at sea, when I was on the *Vigilant,* and even when I was on trial. I knew I should be willing to speak out in prison too. Mecys and some of the other old-timers told me and other newcomers who felt as I did that we were crazy. They said protest would accomplish nothing other than get all of us thrown into the isolator. No matter what they said, my guts told me to fight.

I looked at it this way: I was not going to survive ten years—not if I had to do that much work on that little food. Someday I'd be a walking skeleton, just like the others. Now, while I was strong, I'd stand up, knowing that other young and strong prisoners would stand up with me. I knew we would not accomplish much. We were in a labor camp. We knew that we would be punished, and that the punishments would insure that we became walking skeletons a few years before our time.

We were willing to pay that price. What did we expect to gain? Our self-respect, for one thing. That was an extremely valuable commodity in Potma, and one that was easy to lose. Beyond that, the rewards would be much less tangible. We worked on the theory that every time the KGB made our conditions worse we had to resist. If the KGB found they could get away with a first step, they would soon take a second and a third. Prisoners years from now would suffer because we were apathetic, because we did not resist. Every time step one was taken, we had to protest; we had to make them know that they would have to pay the price—in putting down our protests—for every step. And then maybe they would retract step one, or at least forget about step two. In that sense, we weren't trying to win anything. We were trying to minimize our losses.

The other motive for our protests was publicity. My friends in camp told me that the system's strength was based on secrecy. All those guards and barbed wire weren't just there to prevent us from escaping; they were there to hide us from the outside world. Our Soviet masters didn't want other countries to be reminded there were still political prisoners in the Soviet Union, and they didn't want the Soviet people to be reminded either. The more the outside world knew about our conditions, we figured, the better our conditions would have to become. What we were saying to the KGB was this: You can execute us if you want. But we want it done for the whole world to see. One man cannot torture another if the whole world is watching.

As summer became fall, Simas began to associate with a small group of camp "dissidents," each of whom brought his own particular skill to what was soon to become an effective protest movement.

David Chernoglaz, a scholarly-looking Russian Jew, was the prison lawyer. In Leningrad, he had been an agronomist who taught the Hebrew language and Jewish history to other Jews in his spare time. At twenty-nine, he had applied to emigrate from Russia to Israel. His application had been refused, but he and his Jewish friends decided to try to leave anyway. In the summer of 1970 the authorities arrested him and charged him with conspiring to hijack a plane to Sweden. He was tried and sentenced to five years in the camps. At Potma, he developed a reputation for his calm and his expertise on camp rules and regulations. When he was overworked or underfed, he protested in writing, citing specific sections of Soviet law. He knew how to fight the system on its own terms.

Lev Lukjanenko, a Ukrainian, was the authority on international law, the man who could develop the legal and moral arguments needed if the prisoners were to take their appeals beyond the prison walls. At the age of forty-three, he was two-thirds of the way through a fifteen-year sentence for writing a pamphlet demanding Ukrainian independence. He had once been a stocky man, but now his ribs stuck through his chest. His liver had been ruined by years of prison fare. When he did try to eat, he usually spent the rest of the day lying in the fetal position, moaning.

Jonas Silinskas, thirty, a Lithuanian, had the ability to write in microscopic letters, a skill the prison dissidents required if they were to smuggle their written protests out of the camp. He was in Potma because in 1970, on the eve of the old Lithuanian Independence Day, he and four compatriots had stuffed anti-Soviet leaflets into hundreds of mailboxes throughout Klaipeda and had hoisted the old Lithuanian flag up on the highest chimney in town. He was in Potma because one of his co-conspirators had turned out to be an informer.

Nikolai Sharygin-Budalak, the oldest of the group at forty-five, was the linguist and translator. He spoke seven languages. The Ukrainian-born Sharygin had spent most of his life in England. During a business trip to Leningrad in 1968 he had been arrested and charged with espionage. His mannerisms and clipped accent were decidedly British, which made him known throughout camp as the Englishman. He walked to work every morning with chin up, shoulders back, and hands behind his back. He kept a handkerchief, folded just so, in the breast pocket of his jacket. He even insisted on proper table manners. He was, in short, a most proper gentleman.

By the start of October, the dissidents at Potma Camp Number Three were getting ready to launch their protests. But Simas hesitated at joining them. Gene would be coming to camp in a few days for a three-day visit. Before he started his protests, he wanted to tell her that he had chosen a course of action that would virtually insure that he would never escape the Gulag. He wanted to tell her to forget him.

Ten

On October 4, 1971, Gene Kudirka arrived at Potma Camp Number Three. The journey that had taken Simas five weeks had taken her less than two days. She was loaded down with suitcases and satchels stuffed with the socks, gloves, muffler, and underwear she thought her husband needed and the notebooks and pencils he said he wanted. Once inside the gate, she showed the guards the papers authorizing her visit, filled out some forms, and was frisked. Then she was led to a sterile white room furnished with two iron cots, a stool, and a tiny cabinet in the corner. The radiator beneath the window was leaking cold water. Just outside the door was a frugal kitchenette with a cold-water faucet, four heating elements, and an assortment of pots, pans, plates, and cups. She unpacked her belongings and all the food she had brought—including a giant chicken, already baked, and a liter jar full of cherries soaked in brandy.

As she sat on the stool, stared at the walls, and waited for dusk when Simas would arrive, she thought about what needed to be said in the hours they would have together. Real communication might be difficult. There had been times during their twelve years together when it had seemed they had not been speaking the same language. The two of them were so different in such essential ways. She had no inflated expectations of what life ought to be; she just cared about living from day to day. He cared about the possibility of fundamental changes in the system. She had never really understood why politics was so important to her man. She just knew that it was a part of him she could not change.

In the eleven months since Simas had sailed away on the *Sovetskaya Litva,* she had talked with him only twice—once on Christmas Day in Vilnius KGB prison and again after his trial. Neither time had they been alone. Now, she hoped, he would explain why he had jumped and, in the process, abandoned his family. Then, together, they would contemplate the future. At home, she had been receiving almost daily visits and telephone calls from the KGB, urging her to ask her husband to behave in Potma. She would ask, only because she wanted Simas to get out with "time enough for living," as he had promised.

He burst into the room and hugged her tight. He still looked healthy, though a little thinner, and the peach fuzz on his head made him look cute, in a strange way.

"So how are you, Gene?" Simas asked.

"I'm fine," she said, too easily.

"No, really, how are you?"

She paused, wondering how much she should tell him. "It hasn't been easy. The KGB confiscated just about everything in the apartment. The sofa and upholstered chair are gone, and so are the radio, the coffee table, the throw rug, the vacuum cleaner, the mirror, and even our raincoats. The KGB is always around. And there are knocks on the door in the middle of the night and voices in a language I don't understand."

"You don't open the door, do you?"

"No."

"Good," Simas said. They sat on the bed. Simas put his hand on her knee. "What about the children?"

"Lolita is doing well in school, as always."

"Do the other kids make fun of her?"

"No," Gene said softly. "Or at least she hasn't said anything about it."

"Have her teachers said anything?"

"Not that I know of."

Simas paused. The words were hard to say. "What are her feelings about me?"

1. A 1946 Kudirka family portrait shows Simas at 16 (*standing, second from left*); his mother, Marija Sulskis (*standing, second from right*); her husband, Teo Sulskis (*standing, right*); and Simas's grandparents, Jonas and Ona Kudirka (*seated in front*), whose nine-year stay in the United States eventually made Simas an American citizen.

2. The house in Griskabudis, a tiny village in rural Lithuania, where Simas grew up.

3

4

6

7

5

3. Simas in 1959 at age 29, after graduating from radio school and just before marrying Gene.

4. Gene, not yet 19, in 1958, the year before her marriage.

5. Vytas Sulskis, the young man on the right, joined the Lithuanian partisans in their fight against the Russians just after this 1947 picture was taken. Two years later he advised Simas, his cousin, not to join.

6. The young marrieds in 1960 with their infant daughter Lolita, in the cramped single barracks room that would be their home for the next ten years.

7. When Lolita grew out of infancy, her parents sent her to Griskabudis to live in the house where Simas had spent his childhood. She is shown here in a mid-1960s photo with Simas's stepfather, Teo Sulskis.

8. Simas, the radio operator, in the radio room of the *Boevaja Slava*, the Soviet fish-processing factory ship on which he sailed before being assigned to the *Sovetskaya Litva*.

8

14. After his release from Vladimir, Simas and Gene say good-bye to friends in Griskabudis on their last night in Lithuania. Only hours before, they had gone to the village church for a quiet, private reaffirmation of their marriage vows.

15. On November 3, 1974, the Kudirka family and friends stand before the train that would take Simas (*in a beret, rear, fourth from right*), Gene, Evaldas, and Lolita (*front, second, third, and fourth from right*) and Mrs. Sulskis (*fourth from left*) to Moscow for their flight to the United States.

16. About a month after his arrival in the United States, Simas, his wife, and mother were guests of honor at a Congressional reception in Washington. Robert Hanrahan, the Illinois Republican who was the first to champion Simas's cause, is at the right. Others pictured (*from the left*) are Congressmen Joseph Addabbo, Benjamin Rosenthal, and Edward Koch, and Senator James Buckley, all of New York.

17. On November 23, 1974, four years to the day after the jump, Simas was given a hero's welcome aboard the *Vigilant*, which was moored in New Bedford for the occasion. Here he is greeted by the ship's chief officer, Commander William Goetz.

Courtesy U.S. Coast Guard

10

9. After Simas jumped onto the United States cutter *Vigilant* and was refused political asylum, angered Americans, many of them of Lithuanian descent, took to the streets in protest. This demonstration, held in Hartford, Connecticut, in early December 1970, about ten days after the jump, was typical.

10. Mecys Kybartas (*left*), a gaunt former Lithuanian partisan, had spent half his life in Soviet camps when Simas arrived at the labor camp in 1971. Before he died at the Perm camp in 1973, he would teach the naïve Simas the reality of camp life. This picture of Kybartas and an unidentified fellow prisoner was taken at the Omsk labor camp in the mid-1950s, when Kybartas was 29 and when camp regulations had been temporarily relaxed to the point that prisoners could wear wristwatches and have their pictures taken.

11. Lev Lukjanenko was with Simas from his first day in the Potma labor camp until his last at Vladimir prison. Imprisoned for his activities on behalf of Ukrainian nationalism, Lukjanenko was freed when his 15-year sentence expired in 1976.

12. Gene Kudirka, daughter Lolita, 12, and son Evaldas, 6, in 1972, when Simas had served two years in Soviet labor camps as punishment for his jump and expected to serve eight years more.

13. Robert Brieze, a New Bedford, Massachusetts, fishing official of Latvian descent, who himself had fled the Soviet Union in 1944, was on the *Vigilant* the day Simas jumped. His eyewitness account of the incident thwarted early attempts by American officials to downplay the significance of what had happened.

Photo by James L. McG[...]

18. Three of the Kudirkas—Simas, Gene, and Evaldas—at home in New York in 1978. Lolita (*inset*) was away at school.

"We talk about you a lot. She mentions you almost every day. She's taking it hard. She misses you a great deal. There's no thought in her mind that you've done anything bad. She just misses you. I'm afraid the suffering has made her far too serious for an eleven-year-old girl."

"What about my mother?" he asked.

"She's calmed down. She's adjusting to the fact that you aren't going to be around to help her. Her health seemed decent when I was there a few weeks ago. I checked to see if she had enough firewood and potatoes for the winter. She does."

"And Evaldas?" He had been hesitant to ask about his five-year-old son. As the result of his voyages and now his imprisonment, he had spent little time with the boy. He was afraid the boy might forget him. "Does he ask for me?"

"Yes," Gene said slowly. "He'll ask, 'When is Daddy coming back?' Not for a while, I tell him. 'Why is he gone so long?' It just worked out that way, that's all. 'Will he be back in time to help with the cement path?' I don't think so. 'Oh.' "

"I don't think he can understand," Simas said with resignation.

"I talk about you with him. That's all I can do."

Simas put his finger to his mouth.

"Shhh," he whispered. "Let's go over to the kitchen area where we can talk in private. I'm afraid this place is bugged." They went out into the hall, and they talked about the jump.

"Hey," Simas began. "Has anyone from the *Sovetskaya Litva* been taken off the ship as a result of the incident?"

"Everyone was. Nobody who was on that ship with you is there now."

Simas smiled, thinking of all the problems his jump had created for his superiors in the fleet.

"Have you heard any other rumors about what happened on the ship after I left?"

"No. . . . One thing did happen. I heard that some sailors in the commercial port were saying they saw some film about you in Sweden."

"What kind?"

"I'm not really sure," she replied. "I have heard all sorts of broadcasts about your trial on the Western radio stations. I was shocked. They reported what you said there almost word for word. That was a closed trial. How did the news get out? It's amazing. Lolita, for a while, would sit by the radio religiously to hear about you.''

"Really? They knew about my testimony?''

"Word for word.''

"I'm stunned.''

Gene smiled. "I can prove it to you.'' She bent over, reached into her shoe, and pulled out a tiny square of folded paper. It was an article from a Lithuanian-language newspaper from America that quoted extensively from the trial.

He threw his arms around her. "Oh, Gene, I'm so happy. The West knows!''

"Shhh!'' she hissed.

"Sorry,'' he said. "I forgot myself. . . . What about our friends. Does anybody give you a hard time at work?''

"Our friends are still our friends. They do not harass me or condemn what you did.'' She stared at the floor. "There are people who have shunned me since the jump. On the streets, once in a while, I hear the talk: 'What kind of wife must that slut have been to force that poor man to jump? He wasn't trying to get away from the government. He was trying to get away from his wife.' '' She looked up at Simas, asking the question with her eyes.

"You don't believe that for a minute, do you?'' he asked. She shook her head. "Didn't you see me at the trial? Don't you understand why I jumped? Don't you know I was trying to help you?''

She changed the subject. She did not want to ruin what should be the happiness of their first night together. There would be plenty of time for serious talk later.

The next day at noon they heard hooting sounds coming from another barracks.

"What's that?'' Gene asked, thinking she was hearing the howl of a strange species of dog or wolf.

Simas walked out into the hall, looked through a window, and saw some prisoners celebrating the death of a particularly sadistic guard. The animal yells were their way of paying final respects.

"Come here, Gene."

She walked out into the hall and peered out the window. He wrapped his arm around her and explained what was going on. "So you see, Gene, it was silly for you to argue with me all those years about what this country is all about. You see, it is full of concentration camps."

"I guess you're right," she said, beginning to sob.

"Take a good look, Gene. Almost every man you see has a twenty-five-year sentence. Look at the eyes and faces. See how tired they look, how close they seem to death."

"I want you to be careful here," she said through her tears. "I don't want you to cause trouble. I want you back."

"I can't do that, Gene."

"Aren't you sorry for trying to jump? Don't you regret it now?"

"No, not at all."

Gene was stunned. "If we could change the past," she said haltingly, "I would be a happy woman."

"I wouldn't want to change it one bit," he said with that tone of self-righteousness she had never liked. "It's not my jump that separates us now. It's the Soviet barbed wire. You know I wasn't running away from family responsibility. You know that what I did, I did for my family. I could not be two-faced anymore. I had to answer to my conscience, to my grandfather, to the partisans."

Gene shook her head. He wasn't talking to her anymore. He was preaching, trying to impress his dead heroes. Years before, when they had met, she had been put off by that cold streak of self-righteousness that she had seen in him. When he thought a moral issue was involved, he could be inhumanly callous. She had mellowed him over the years, made him take himself a little less seriously. But three months in this labor camp had wiped out all the progress she had made. Where was his concern about the living, about the wife he had left and the children whose futures he had blackened forever? Wasn't it human to worry about them and regret what he had done to them?

121

"I couldn't have been any different, Gene. It's not that bad. I've got friends here, men of courage. I didn't know there were any more people like that around anymore."

She was ready to explode. All he talked about was life in camp with his pals, not hope of life outside the walls with her. He sounded as if he enjoyed being in a labor camp. And in a way, she thought, he probably did. What he had experienced at the camp showed him that he had been right to hate the Soviet system, and there was nothing he liked more than being right. She went to take a walk, so she could cry.

"Don't worry about me anymore," he told her when she returned. "Mr. Brezhnev and the camp administration will worry about me. Gene, we cannot live on illusions anymore. We must be realistic. See that barbed wire outside the window. See the death zone. You must know that you're going to have to care for our children by yourself now. There's nothing we can count on any longer. My path is set, and I will not budge. I will not take the conditions here lying down. I will protest."

She cried again, convinced not only that he would never return to Klaipeda, but that he didn't really care whether he did. During their visit just after the jump, he had asked for her forgiveness. She had withheld it. She had come to Potma prepared to grant it, but now it was obvious that he did not care what she thought. The camp had hardened him into a man she found hard to love.

"We have political indoctrination classes here," he said. "Attendance is mandatory. I have seen too much. I will never go. And the administration here will not forgive me."

"But what can one man do alone?" she asked.

"If a lot of individuals act, then we are not alone," he replied.

She jerked free of his arm and cried hard. "You are impossible. If you insist on making things worse for yourself, then who am I to stand in your way!"

In a few minutes, they were back to small talk. They knew they did not have enough time to spend it all in depression or anger. Late in the afternoon, they invited a Russian prisoner and his elderly mother, and an Armenian prisoner and his brother and sister—all having similar visits—to join them in a celebration.

When the three contingents combined their foodstuffs, they had enough for quite a feast, and they partied long into the night, nearly forgetting the troubles that had brought them together at Potma Camp Number Three.

On the morning of the third day, there was a knock on the door of their room. There, with arms outstretched, was the mother of the Russian prisoner who had joined their party the day before. Her withered face, wrapped in a babushka, was wet with tears.

"Help me, please," she sobbed. "Can it be true? They tell me my son doesn't want to see me."

During the party, her son had mentioned that the guards had threatened to cut short his visit with his mother unless he shaved off his beard. The guards had carried out their threat. Simas comforted the old woman, then whirled to face Gene.

"Gene!" he exclaimed in his most outraged tone. "Remember the look on this woman's face. Study it. Take every detail and store it inside your head and your heart. What kind of society takes a sad old woman and uses her as a pawn? And for what purpose? To satisfy the ego of some subhuman camp official."

He turned back to the old woman. "It's not true. Your son wants to see you. They're lying to you. Calm yourself. You're reacting just the way they want you to react. You're playing right into their hands, and you must stop it. It's one of their tricks. I know your son. The only things that would stop him from being here would be death or physical restraint by the guards."

"I know my Victor," she said. "He's stubborn. I've begun to accept the fact that he will never go along with the guards here."

Simas and Gene gave her tea to calm her, and when her tears stopped, she left, thanking them for their sympathy.

"What do you think happened to her son?" Gene asked him.

"Who knows? Don't you see, Gene? We're at the mercy of madmen. Everything is unpredictable. Something like that could happen to me easily enough. Maybe it will happen before this day is over."

Gene had already noticed the parallel between the old woman's son, who apparently put his right to have a beard above the privilege of a visit with his mother, and her own stubborn husband. For the rest of the day and into the next, Simas and Gene's conversation jerked along, punctuated by long depressing silences and interludes of forced optimism. They found themselves strangely eager for the visit to end. When it was time for him to return to the camp proper, he kissed her and held her close.

He had always had trouble expressing his deepest feelings. He was the kind of man who usually suppressed them as long as he could—until he exploded in anger. What he wanted to say was that there was no longer any place for her in his world and no place for him in hers. He wanted to say that their marriage had been wrenched apart by forces far beyond their control. He wanted to tell her that he still loved her, but that the fact of his love was not as important as one other fact—that he was a prisoner in a Soviet labor camp and would be for nine more years.

He wanted to say all those things. But he didn't. His words came out wooden and cold.

"Remember, whatever happens, you have your own life to live," he said firmly. "You may get unpleasant news from here someday. It may well turn out that I never come back. But you must stay strong. You have your own friends to lean on. Tell them what you saw here—that is vital. You are a young woman, and you must think of yourself and the children. Don't worry about me."

And then they parted.

Eleven

Two days after Gene left, Simas began his war against the Soviet prison system by refusing to attend political indoctrination classes. He knew the consequences of his action. He knew that he and the fifty other prisoners who stayed away from class would lose their right to receive packages from home, to have visits with their wives, and to buy candy, sugar, and tea at the camp canteen. But he and his comrades figured the time was ripe for dissent in the camps. The whole world knew of the dissidents in Soviet society, men like Solzhenitsyn and Sakharov who were telling the world that the Soviet Union had not yet outgrown all the excesses of the Stalinist years. The protesters at Potma believed that if the Western democracies got just a little more information about the camps, they would press the Soviet Union to do away with them. The protesters did not consider the possibility that the Western democracies already knew about their plight and did not care enough to act.

They were particularly certain they could count on the United Nations for support. After all, in 1948 the U.N. had authored the Universal Declaration of Human Rights. The declaration, which even the Soviet Union itself had signed, was heady reading for a prisoner like Simas. It seemed to have been written with his own case in mind. According to the declaration, his human rights had been violated when the Soviet Union deprived him of his Lithuan-

125

ian nationality, denied him the choice of a job, prevented him from leaving the country, blocked him from expressing his opinions, and brought him to trial in secret. The United States had violated his rights, too, by refusing to grant him political asylum.

The protesters at Potma adopted the Declaration of Human Rights as their creed and decided to focus their efforts on December 10, 1971, the twenty-third anniversary of its signing. The planning for the protest moved extremely slowly; it was nearly impossible for the fifty dissidents, all of whom found adherence to political principle literally a matter of life and death, to agree on anything. In the end, they resolved to stage a hunger strike, but some of them, Simas included, felt the need to do something more. A hunger strike was too common a tactic to attract the attention of the West.

One evening in early November, Simas and Sharygin-Budalak, "the Englishman," were walking in the camp yard, discussing what else could be done.

"So many of the men in this camp don't know the significance of Human Rights Day," Sharygin said.

"You're right," Simas replied. "Until the last few weeks, I hardly knew anything about it myself. We should educate them."

"And how, my friend, do we do that here? Do we hold seminars or write pamphlets?"

"I guess not."

They walked in silence for a few minutes, pondering the possibilities.

"What if we raised the United Nations flag somewhere in camp," Sharygin said slowly. "Men would see the flag, wonder what it is, ask questions, and get the answer—that it represents an international declaration, signed by the Soviet Union, that our masters in this camp keep trampling on."

"That's great!" Simas agreed. "But how do we pull it off?"

"That, my friend, is an excellent question. It's too dangerous to plan something this delicate in a group. The informers would know about it in two seconds. So it'll have to be just the two of us." He stopped and thought for a moment. "I'll make the flag. We'll need a big piece of blue cloth, some white paint, and a black ribbon to drape it with. I'm not sure where I'll get the materials, but I'll get them, no problem. You decide where we're going to fly the flag and how we're going to get it up there.''

The more they talked about the idea, the more they liked it, despite the obvious risks. The protest would serve two purposes. If word of the flag did get to the West, it would surely generate the publicity they wanted so desperately. But even if the news never got beyond the camp walls, the flag would help raise the consciousness of the more passive political prisoners.

In the days ahead, Simas spent much of his free time glancing upward at rooftops and poles in search of the perfect site for the flag. The location had to be high, accessible, and visible. His first choice was right above the entrance to the dining hall, but it was, on second thought, too visible from the watchtowers on the camp perimeter. The guards in the watchtowers carried automatic weapons. Another possibility was the chimney of the dining hall, the highest point in the camp. He eliminated it for the same reason, and finally settled on a utility pole near a barracks housing the camp's cripples. The pole was not as high as the chimney nor as centrally located as the dining hall entrance. It had two advantages, though: it was near a loudspeaker around which prisoners gathered every morning to listen to Radio Moscow, and it was partially shielded from the watchtowers by surrounding buildings.

Each evening in late November and early December, he met briefly with Sharygin, who reported his progress. He had found an old pair of blue undershorts that had faded to the appropriate pale shade for the flag. He had trimmed the shorts to a rectangle, two feet by three feet, and was painting the white United Nations globe on it at the machine shop where he worked. Simas had obtained a flag pole—a broomstick—from an Estonian prisoner who ran the camp's carpentry shop. Everything was moving ahead on schedule.

On the night of December 9, the eve of Human Rights Day, Simas and Sharygin met at the corner of a vacant barracks near the utility pole where the flag was to fly. It was a foggy night and snow seemed imminent. Simas had the pole stuffed inside his pants leg and some tacks hidden in a pocket. Sharygin had the flag stuffed under his shirt. The two of them huddled close together, using their bodies to shield their treasures as they took them out of their clothes. They tacked the flag onto the broomstick, rolled it up, and slipped Sharygin's black ribbon over it. Then they turned to stash it under some loose boards in the barracks wall.

At that moment, they heard voices, perhaps twenty yards away. They slipped the flag under the boards and walked away as nonchalantly as they could. They were certain they had been discovered, their plot foiled. They circled the barracks at a distance, expecting a guard to rush up at any minute, pull up the boards off the barracks wall, and seize the flag. After ten minutes of pacing, they came together, conferred for a moment, and left the area to avoid creating suspicion. They met again at the hiding place at 10:30, just before lights out. Fearfully, they raised the loose boards and looked underneath. The flag was still there. On the chance that it had been seen, they moved it to an alternate hiding place. Now it was all up to Simas.

———

I was afraid I would oversleep. But I was much too nervous to sleep more than a few minutes at a time. I lay on my back with my hands clasped behind my head and over and over I mentally rehearsed what I had to do. If any little thing went wrong, all our planning, all our work would be wasted. What if a guard just happened to wander by me when I was on my way to pick up the flag? What if a prisoner, going to the bathroom, saw me as I was standing at the base of the pole with the flag in my hand? What if the fever I was beginning to feel made me too weak to climb? What if the watchtower guards spotted me at the top of the pole and shined their spotlights on me? Should I shout out my message? Or should I retreat back down quietly? Or would they shoot me then and there? What if it snowed and I left footprints leading right to my bed? And what if something happened that I had not anticipated at all? Would I have the presence of mind to improvise?

During the night, I lay there feverish and tense, worried but confident. Several times I got up and looked outside. The fog had not lifted. That was a break. It would be that much harder for the guards in their watchtowers to see me when I was on top of that pole, a sitting duck. If only the snow would hold off until mid-morning, I just might make it work.

———————

The clock on the night table in Barracks Number Six read 6:35—time to get going. It was not yet dawn, and the fog made it even darker than usual. Simas sat up, tossed off the covers, and put his jacket on over his underwear. He donned his prison camp slippers and tiptoed toward the door. He had twenty minutes, twenty-two at the outside, to do his work, and he would have to keep track of time in his head.

Once outside, he turned to the left and hurried through the trees toward the outhouse. The camp was quiet. There were no guards in sight. He stuck his head into the outhouse to see if anyone was there. No one. He ran softly through the trees toward the hiding place, about 100 yards away. He was alone. He pulled up the boards and looked underneath. The flag was right where he and Sharygin had left it. He took it out, tucked it under his jacket, and clutched the broomstick against his leg. Running stiff-leggedly to avoid exposing the stick, he hurried toward the utility pole, keeping in the shadows of the trees as much as possible.

Now the pole was five yards away. The most dangerous five yards. Five yards in the open with no trees to sneak behind, no shadows to shield him. He looked all around him. He saw no one and heard no one. Maybe he was safe, or maybe the guards had been watching his every move since he left the barracks and would nab him the moment he raced into the clearing. Or worse. But this was no time for second thoughts. He darted across the clearing and jumped up onto the first of the metal spokes that stuck out from the utility pole on either side. He scrambled up the pole, pulling himself higher and higher with his cold bare hands. In a few seconds, he was twenty feet above the ground, balancing himself against a chill, gusting wind. With a piece of wire, he carefully strapped the broomstick and the flag to the crossbar of the utility pole. Suddenly, he noticed a shadow moving across the ground below. He froze, holding his breath, waiting for the shadow to take shape. Then he relaxed. It was only an old prisoner, staring at the ground

129

and rubbing the sleep from his eyes on a pre–wake-up-time trip to the outhouse. From his perch, Simas quickly surveyed the rest of the camp. There was no sign of movement anywhere else. Relieved, he returned to the task at hand.

In three minutes he was finished, and he climbed quietly down the pole, spike by spike. He raced through the clearing back into shadows and then stopped to listen. Still no sounds of movement. Exhilarated by his success, he rushed back toward the outhouse and then turned toward Barracks Number Six. Now if anyone stopped him he could say that he was simply returning from the toilet. As he walked back to the barracks, he stole a glance at the utility pole; the little blue flag was flapping in the breeze. He came to the barracks, opened the door, and looked at the clock on the night table. It read 6:55. He got back in bed, closed his eyes, and pretended to sleep.

The wake-up gong clattered at 7:00, as usual. The guards burst into the barracks, threw open the doors, and ripped the covers off the beds. The camp day was off to a perfectly normal start. As Simas walked toward the outhouse, he glanced up at the pole. The flag was still flying.

A crowd began to gather around the radio loudspeaker in the yard, as usual. The prisoners smoked their cigarettes and chatted about the latest camp news. Then one of them caught sight of the blue-and-white cloth flying from the utility pole near the speaker.

"What the hell is that up there?" one of them muttered.

"You know," said Sharygin, who had joined the group in the hope that someone would ask that question. "I'm not sure. But from here, it looks a lot like the flag of the United Nations."

"Like the what?"

Another prisoner, a dissident, joined in. "The United Nations flag. You know, the international organization in America."

"Right, I know," said the first prisoner, "the one that's always talking about being humanitarian and stuff like that. But what's the flag doing there?"

"It's U.N. Human Rights Day," said a third prisoner, also a dissident. Simas and Sharygin had counted on the other dissidents to get the discussions going once the flag was up.

Simas walked toward the pole to join in the discussions, but Sharygin stopped him short. "All's well, my friend," Sharygin said. "But you are not, and it's not such a good idea for you to hang around the flag anyway. Go back to the barracks."

Reluctantly, Simas stumbled back to the barracks and collapsed into bed. Now that he knew the flag was flying, the nervous energy that had kept him going had all but disappeared. His fever overwhelmed him.

The flag flew for two hours before the guards took it down. By nightfall, everyone in the camp had either seen it or heard about it. The gimmick had worked, at least as far as educating the camp population on human rights. Simas had not been caught and never would be. The rest—getting the news to the West and the West's reacting—was out of his control. He felt he had made the loudest possible call for help, and now he had to wait for an answer, or at least an echo.

There would be an echo, a faint one. The incident would be noted, briefly, in the Western press. But it would be years before Simas knew that.

He spent much of the winter of 1971–72 writing letters. He wrote to the men who ran the camp and to their bosses in Moscow; he wrote to Brezhnev and to Nixon. He had some letters smuggled out; others he sent out through the regular mail, to give the camp censors something to do and to allay whatever suspicions they might have about him. Some were printed on large pieces of paper, while others were on cigarette wrappings rolled into "bullets." The tone and the message were always the same: Simas Kudirka, wrongly imprisoned by his Soviet oppressors, seeks simple justice for himself, his family, all political prisoners, and the ethnic minorities of the Soviet Union.

"Dear Mr. President," he wrote to Richard Nixon, care of the White House, in December 1971.

I, Simas Kudirka, presently incarcerated as a political prisoner in the Soviet Union, dare to bother you in the hopes of calling to your attention the tragedy of my situation. I ask your personal intervention on behalf of me and my family. I have been sentenced without due process of law to ten years at hard labor because I wanted to exercise Paragraph Number 13 of the Universal Human Rights Declaration. I attempted to gain asylum aboard an American Coast Guard ship. As you surely recall, my request for asylum in the United States was refused in violation of that declaration. I realize it was a mistake, and I ask you to correct that mistake and allow me to come to America. As I told you before, I am not making this request just for myself. Today, because of my hope and desire to come to your country, not only am I suffering but my totally innocent wife, children, and old mother are suffering, too. I appeal to you in the hopes of consideration.

> Thank you.
> Sincerely, Simas Kudirka.

He gave Nixon until April to answer. Then he wrote him again during a presidential visit to the U.S.S.R., in care of the United States Embassy, Tchaikovsky Street, Moscow. He got no answer to the second letter either.

In addition to writing his own letters, Simas participated in the far more frustrating process of drafting group letters to the outside world. While Simas could sit down and dash off something of his own in an hour, a group letter took months. It was difficult to get more than two political prisoners to agree on the most harmless choice of words. Many of these men were in Potma precisely because of words they had chosen to use. Their natural sensitivity about words was compounded by the fact that the only language they all could work in was Russian, a language some of the ethnics spoke poorly and all of them despised.

When a group letter was being composed, two tiny copies of it would be passed from dissident to dissident, with each copy constantly being revised. Passages were constantly added and weeded out until the group reached a consensus, which was far blander than the original. Even then, at least half of the prisoners who had participated in the drafting would not be satisfied enough with the final product to sign it. Each man knew he could be sent to the isolator for signing such a letter, and he wanted it to be something he was willing to suffer for. The first group letter, signed by eight prisoners including Simas, went to the International Red Cross:

"We are writing of the inhuman conditions in which we, as political prisoners, are forced to live in hopes of calling those conditions to your attention and the attention of the world." They wrote of the lack of medical care, of long camp sentences, unsafe working conditions, and punishments meted out arbitrarily. "The entire system of camp detention is designed to transform human beings gradually into unthinking, frightened, and obedient animals, agreeable to doing everything and anything. . . ." They wrote of crowded, stuffy barracks and food contaminated by worms and mold. "People are for many, many years kept in a semihuman state under the threat of outright starvation. Of the officially sanctioned daily nutrition norm of 2,413 calories, we receive barely half."

Another group letter, a particularly long one, was sent to the Supreme Soviet of the U.S.S.R. by dissident prisoners from Latvia, Lithuania, Estonia, the Ukraine, and the Caucasus. The prisoners wrote that their imprisonment was symptomatic of what was happening throughout the Soviet Union—ethnic minorities were being assimilated, and those who refused to be assimilated were being persecuted. "It is typical that in Soviet places of detention where political opponents are imprisoned one finds few Russian nationals . . . while individuals of many other nationalities, which have organized movements for their separation from Russia, are amply represented there."

They demanded that the national republics within the U.S.S.R. be allowed to retain their cultures and control their own internal affairs. "The Russian language has illegally become the state language, acquiring a privileged status as a result," they wrote. "Through the system of state schools, the young generation is compelled to glorify Russia and all things Russian in all ways . . . [while] any movement promoting self-determination is branded as bourgeois nationalism and cruelly persecuted by the state punitive organs."

The letters did get out. The Red Cross letter was obtained by dissidents in Moscow, shown to Western correspondents, and reported in the *New York Times,* among other places. The letter on ethnic groups was circulated widely by émigré groups in the United States. And conditions in Potma just grew worse.

Spring came early in Potma in 1972. In mid-March the mountains of snow melted at the rate of a foot a day and spread out into a layer of ankle-deep soup that covered everything. For the next two months, until the spring rains stopped, the prisoners walked in damp shoes, covered their bodies with damp coats and pants, and slept in damp beds. Nearly every prisoner was coughing and sneezing. The mud was so deep that normal automobiles were useless in it; they had to be dragged in and out of the camp by tractors. The mud was harshest on the camp's several dozen one-legged prisoners. When they tried to walk, their crutches sank into the mud and stuck there. Prisoners had to spend an hour a day cleaning their filthy foot cloths, which were rotting from the moisture, and trying to figure out some way of keeping them dry.

With the spring and the mud came a change in the way the camp was run. Rules that had gone unenforced since Simas's arrival were now being enforced with a seemingly arbitrary vengeance. Simas himself was sent away for four days of solitary confinement on bread and water for refusing to "volunteer" to work on a Sunday in honor of Lenin's birthday. He was sentenced to ten days for calling a guard a "torturer"; months earlier, he might have gotten off with no more than the loss of a month's canteen privileges.

Late one afternoon, a few days after completing his ten-day sentence, Simas took a walk behind the concrete factory with a Ukrainian prisoner named Peshchany and complained about the sudden increase in punishments. But he got little sympathy from Peshchany, who was in camp because he, like Simas, had failed in a defection attempt. Now, after serving four years of a twelve-year sentence, he tired easily, his face had a yellowish tinge to it, and he had a hacking cough that often brought up blood.

"Listen, kid," Peshchany said with contempt, "life is not as simple as you make it out to be." His years in the prisons had ruined his nerves and left him little patience for men who insisted that protest could improve conditions. "You're limited to what you've seen here. And believe me, it's not true that every camp and every prison are the same. Don't ever compare this kindergarten to Vladimir Prison."

Simas had heard of Vladimir before. It was, the prisoners said, the ultimate punishment, the place a man was sent when he was judged "incorrigible." Potma was a camp with trees and grass. Vladimir was a dungeon.

"They didn't like the way I behaved at my trial," the Ukrainian continued. "I called them motherfuckers, which is what they are. So that got me to Vladimir. When I went in, I was strong, healthy, and fit, like a proud Soviet test pilot should be. First they put me in a cell with five nuts, and they all ganged up on me. I was dumb enough to think that big, strong Peshchany could fight back. They beat the shit out of me, and the authorities punished *me* for starting a fight. They put me in an isolator for six months, and that experience left me with two beautiful little holes in my lungs."

"Didn't they give you medicine?"

Peshchany started to laugh, and his laugh became a harsh, wet cough.

"You said you were in the isolator," Simas persisted. "I just came out of the isolator here. It wasn't all that terrible."

"You really are naïve, Kudirka. You're comparing a wooden box to a stone cave. Everything in Vladimir is stone, damp stone— the floors, the bed, the walls. There's no heat. The food here is like a feast compared to the food there. You can't even fall asleep in a cell like that. You protesters here . . . you can't even imagine. . . . You say, 'What can we lose by protesting? Things can't get any worse.' The hell they can't! When they put you in an isolator in Vladimir, you have no idea how long they'll keep you there. The hours become days, the days become weeks, the weeks become months, and you begin to realize that you're blacking out for long periods, just missing them altogether. One day you wake up and you're lying on the floor. You have no idea how you got there. The pains you had when you came into the cell are gone. You feel nothing. You feel great. You hear someone yelling for you to get

135

up, and you don't give a damn. You don't give a damn about anything. The kindest thing they can do to you is leave you alone. But they're not kind. They drag you out of the cell and plop you back in a normal cell. And your senses begin to thaw, but all you want to do is sleep. The only dread you have is of waking up. You realize you'll do anything for them if they'll just let you sleep. Then, after a few days, they take you back to the isolator for another few months. Then out, then in, out, in. Can you understand the feeling? You have nothing left. You just want the whole fucking thing to be over."

Simas still did not believe conditions could be so rough. "I've been in prison myself [in Vilnius]," he said. "I know what you're talking about."

The Ukrainian laughed again. "Like hell you do," he muttered. "You haven't seen anything, and even I wouldn't swear that I've seen the worst. If someone told me he'd seen worse, I wouldn't argue."

"Why? Why do they do it? Why do they torture a man to death? I can't accept it. Isn't Stalin dead? Didn't that kind of thing die with him?"

"Listen, Kudirka, if in your protest you do stand up and do something really effective against the system, you'll see that nothing has changed. You will get a kick in the ass that you'll never forget."

"I know. They've already kicked me ten years' worth."

"How much have you actually served?"

"Over a year."

"That's your problem. When you've served about three years, even if all of it is here in this resort, you'll understand."

On July 8, 1972, a year and a day after Simas's arrival, all 550 prisoners at Potma Camp Number Three were summoned to the central courtyard and addressed by the commander of the guards.

"Tomorrow half of you will be transferred to another work rehabilitation colony." Under his direction, the guards separated those who would go from those who would stay. Simas would go.

"Where are we going?" a hundred prisoners yelled in the next few seconds. Some feared it would be Vladimir, others guessed Siberia.

The commander waved off the questions with a knowing smile. "You will find out when you get there. That is all. Dismissed!"

Twelve

Early the next afternoon, Simas trudged onto a five-car death train, his mind full of the sights, sounds, and smells of the trains that had brought him to Potma. He was shown to a compartment built for two that had been converted into a cage for seven. The guard unlocked the wire mesh door and shoved him into a thicket of withered naked limbs. After he untangled himself, he pulled himself up onto the luggage rack, not knowing whether the rack would be his home for hours, days, or weeks. As he sat on the rack, his body bent at the waist so his head would not hit the roof, he found it nearly impossible to breathe. The air was thick with smoke and stale with the smell of too many bodies in too little space. By the time he was settled in, he was dripping with perspiration. The temperature outside was over 90 degrees, and the car was sitting out in the open, unprotected from the blazing sun. Its door and windows were locked, its vents sealed tight. He immediately stripped to his underpants and started toweling off until he realized he would never get dry.

He tried to get comfortable for the ride ahead. He lowered his back daintily onto the luggage rack, then sat up with a jerk, slamming his head into the roof. The metal rack was sizzling hot, barbecueing its pattern into his back. He spread his towel over the rack before easing himself back down. The new arrangement was not much better, but it would have to do. He lay on his towel, praying for clouds to block the sun and for the train to get moving. The sooner the train got moving, the sooner this ordeal would be over.

Men began to plead for air and water, cursing the solitary armed guard, who seemed to relish ignoring their pleas. The guard was a husky man with greasy hair and piercing eyes; he paced the corridor, stroking his pistol. He grinned at the prisoners and held his gun in front of his face. His eyes glowed with sensual pleasure as he stroked it.

"Go ahead, yell, you bastards," he said. "I'm just waiting for one of you vermin to give me the pleasure of provoking me and my gun." He stroked the pistol again.

As the hours passed and the train did not move, prisoners began to pass out and throw up. Many lost control and excreted waste all over the train and all over each other. The heat was intensifying, the smoke thickening, and the air tightening around them.

Then Simas heard a peculiar noise. It sounded as if an army of rats was running up and down the outside of the car. Then he noticed something else. A heavy mist was forming inside the car. Prisoners were gasping for air and shouting.

Guards outside were hosing down the hot metal cars with ice water to produce waves of steam inside the prisoners' cages.

"Brothers!" one man cried. "This is it. They're going to end it for all of us right here and now. The fucking bastards aren't even going to bother taking us anywhere."

As the steam condensed, it dropped to the floor of the train like rain. The floor was covered with a pool of water, sweat, urine, and feces several inches thick. The prisoners who had been forced to lie flat on the floor were now bathing in this scum-filled pool. If they passed out with their faces down, they might drown. In the early evening, the pleading and cursing stopped. No one had the willpower to keep yelling to a guard who would not listen.

I felt like an animal being roasted on a grill. The heat was penetrating every pore. I felt that my brain was starting to bake. This was no train. It was a steambath on wheels with madmen at the controls. I wondered how long this torture would go on and how

139

long I would last. We were used to suffering, God knows, but even for me this was a shock.

Strange thoughts were going through my mind. I remembered that in 1963 Nikita Khrushchev had said there would be no more political prisoners in the Soviet Union by 1970. It was 1972. Maybe the idea behind this train was to carry out that promise—and get rid of us. Maybe this was just a little going-away party. Then I dropped off into a stupor, in which dream and reality seemed to merge. I had the same dream I had been having for months:

I am standing with some other men—I can't make out the details of their faces—at the edge of a vast black lake full of bubbling, ink-black water. The sky is gray and low. I have been chased here, and whoever or whatever has been chasing me is still after me. So I run to the edge of the water and jump, even though the water is extremely cold, and I am a poor swimmer. I am sure I will drown. But somehow I never touch the water. I am being whisked across the surface of the lake standing up. I am just walking along and not going under, not feeling cold and not feeling wet. I hear this booming voice from out of nowhere saying, ''Of those of you who try to cross this body of water, thirty percent will die at the water's edge, another thirty percent will die in the crossing, and another thirty percent will die at the end. Only ten percent will survive.''

I look around and, sure enough, a lot of my friends are gone and others are going under. I keep walking across the water, and eventually I get to the other side. There aren't too many of us left. Now I am on the shore. On my left, I see white, frozen emptiness. There's a path leading that way, and it disappears off into the horizon. Most of my friends take that path, but a few of us go to the right. We have to hurry. We're still being chased. I look around and think that maybe we are the 10 percent who will survive.

We run a few hundred yards to the right and we come to a canal. We see a big white yacht, maybe sixty feet long. We scramble onto the yacht to cross the canal, but there is something wrong. We run down into the cabin of the yacht, and we can't get the motor started. They're catching up! We fiddle with the dials on the control panel, but nothing happens. We run back out of the boat and onto the shore. The bank is full of people, though they don't seem to be the ones who were chasing us. We look down the canal and see a forest full of palm trees. It looks so calm and peaceful.

So what do we do now? Do we look for another boat? Do we try to swim across the canal? Do we go down to the forest? We're standing there wondering what to do. . . .

———————

Simas was jolted out of his stupor as the train jerked forward. It stopped and started all night long, and when dawn came the prisoners began to stir. The car was a little cooler now, and many of the men who had passed out were reviving. But some of them were not the same men they had been the day before. They no longer made any sense when they talked.

The guard strutted down the corridor, sloshing through the putrid water, to announce that each prisoner would, at last, be allowed one trip to the toilet in the rear of the car. The toilet turned out to be nothing more than a hole in the floor. There was no seat, not even a railing to hold on to. Many of the old and the weak, hovering precariously over the hole, missed the mark as the train rocked beneath them. Others, who had stripped off their clothes to endure the heat, fell into their friends' droppings and stumbled back to their cages covered with human waste.

Mecys Kybartas passed by Simas's cage on his way to the toilet. He scanned the length of the car.

"Well, child," he said, "do you think you have improved our conditions through your protests?"

Simas did not answer. There was nothing to say.

Later in the morning, after the trips to the "toilet" were over, each man got a cup of warm, stinking water. The cup was not enough to quench a thirst or bring a dehydrated body back to life. It was just enough to make the prisoners feel the need for another trip to the toilet, a trip the guards refused. So the pool on the floor got a little deeper. No new food was provided; each prisoner had been given a hunk of bread and two cans of mushy meat, the consistency of dog food, when he boarded the train. The old-time prisoners, the ones who were always talking about how much tougher the camps were when Stalin was alive, said that this train ride was unlike anything they had ever endured. As the day went on and the car heated

141

up again, more prisoners passed out and became hysterical. And the guard just watched.

"Listen, you animal," one prisoner shouted to him. "You get us some medical care or else."

The guard smiled, amused that a man in a cage could try to threaten him. "I'll see what I can do," the guard said. No help came. It never did.

By now the prisoners were so weak that they feared they would start sliding out of control on the slime-covered seats and racks. If the train went through a stretch of curves, their heads might bang into the train walls with fatal results. They began to formulate a desperate plan. They were going to try to derail the train. They would use their last spasms of energy to tip it off the tracks. Every prisoner would have to jump—or lean, if he was too weak to jump—to the same side of the train at the same time. If everything went just right, if everyone was pushing at the moment the train was going around a sharp curve at high speed, the plan just might succeed. In essence, they were plotting a mass suicide. Many of them would die in the accident. But so would the guards, and perhaps a few prisoners would survive and escape. In any event, death on their own terms was better than life on the terms the KGB was offering.

The prisoners in one cage toward the front of the car started it—leaning, sliding, and jumping to the left. Then the residents of another cage joined in, then another. Simas did his part, too. For a few minutes, it seemed that nothing was happening. The train was just as stable as ever. The prisoners were not working in unison; one group was pushing while another was resting. After fifteen minutes, everyone was pushing together.

Simas could feel the weight of the train shifting. Buoyed by the feeling, he pushed harder. The car was rocking.

The guard ran into the car, shrieking and waving his gun.

"Stop it! Stop it!" he yelled, running up and down the corridor. "Tell me what you are so unhappy about."

The prisoners did not answer. They kept rocking the car.

"What do you want?"

"Officer, come join us in our cages and see if you would be happy," said a voice from a cage down the corridor.

"Officer," said another. "Why don't you stop sitting in your nice, cushy lounge and come back in here with us."

The car kept rocking.

"My fingers are no longer itching," he shouted, stroking his pistol furiously. "They are burning!"

"Oh, listen to the big, brave guard," said a third voice.

"What a big man he is with his gun!" said another.

The car was still rocking.

"Stop it!" the guard barked. "We will try to repair the ventilation system."

"And what about medical help?"

"We'll see," the guard said, running out the door to the next car.

The prisoners kept rocking the car until, a minute or two later, the vents started pumping cool fresh air through the cages. They had won, but their victory demonstrated their weakness as much as their strength. For when the fans were turned off again five minutes later, they accepted it with just a curse or two. They no longer had the strength left to resist.

By the fourth day, they had become so docile that the guards felt confident enough to open the curtains and let the prisoners see outside. The train was passing through vast fields of dry brush. It was 800 miles northeast of Moscow, climbing toward the Ural Mountains, the north-south ridge that separates Europe and Asia—and Siberia beyond. By evening, several prisoners had a new complaint. The car was too cold.

The train came to a stop on the morning of the fifth day, and the guard hurried down the corridor, yelling for the prisoners to get dressed. As the door of his cage swung open, Simas eased himself off the luggage rack and lowered himself carefully to the floor. His legs wobbled painfully. He limped down to the end of the corridor and cautiously stepped outside. It was a cool, bright morning. He took a deep breath, and the brisk air nearly overwhelmed his tired lungs. His eyes blinked furiously. After five days of smoke and

143

haze, they were not accustomed to sunshine. He stumbled across the ground and saw a guard who, before the train left Potma, had assured him that the trip would be conducted under the most sanitary conditions.

"I do not know your name," Simas said, pointing at the guard. "But I don't need to know it to know what you are. You are the most outstanding representative I have ever seen of all this great nation stands for. You are a champion of hypocrisy, a master of shame."

Other guards pushed him along and loaded him into a black van, which took him to his new home—Camp Number Thirty-six, Special Correctional Work Institution, Perm Region.

On first inspection, Perm Camp Thirty-six looked clean and almost inviting. All 275 prisoners would be housed in two huge, freshly painted barracks made of unfinished logs. The gravel road, which ran between the two barracks, was lined with shady trees and wooden benches. Grass grew in scattered spots around the camp, and there were flowers in bloom.

Not all the signs were so good. The camp was labeled "special," which, in the language of the labor camps, meant it was considered tougher than a "strict" camp like Potma; and there appeared to be only one bathroom, and that was in the middle of a swamp nearly 100 yards beyond the sleeping quarters.

The older and weaker prisoners, exhausted from the train ride, dragged themselves into a barracks and went to sleep. The others—pale, unshaven, and haggard—collapsed outside on the soft, moist ground. There were no guards in sight. Simas went exploring, finding, among other things, a letter in which a wife of a political prisoner had described Perm Camp Thirty-six as "the hills of death." His explorations complete, he sat in the grass with Mecys and a half dozen other prisoners to share a cup of tea. The men were talking about the train ride.

"You know a guy died on that train," one of them said. "A Ukrainian. A diabetic. He went into a diabetic fit, and they wouldn't give him a shot of insulin. He was in his death throes for hours and the guard just let him go."

"How can they be such animals?" Simas asked. "What is happening to us?"

"I think it's going to be a little tougher writing to your old buddy Nixon from here," Mecys said sarcastically.

"It won't be that bad," Simas replied, ever the optimist. "And if it is, we'll protest." Mecys laughed, but Simas kept talking. "Are we supposed to keep quiet after that train ride? Why are you so set against telling the rest of the world?"

Mecys pointed to the hills that surrounded the camp on all sides. "O.K., look around you. Let's see you throw a letter over them. It's a lovely little garden here, but we're fenced in a little differently than we were before. I have a feeling this place will make Potma look like a resort."

"I don't believe it," Simas insisted.

"Look," said another prisoner. "Nothing happens by accident. There was a reason why we were in Potma, a reason why we were taken out, and a reason why we've been brought here. I'm afraid I know what the reason is."

An hour later, without fanfare, a group of uniformed KGB agents marched into the camp. Among them was a tall, black-haired man nearing middle age who looked a little too elegant for the dirty job of supervising political prisoners. His uniform was impeccable, and he had a graceful, athletic way of walking. He walked over to a group of prisoners who were sitting on the ground and introduced himself as Major Kotov, the camp commander. He asked them how they were feeling.

They answered by complaining about the train ride.

"I remind you," he replied with quiet concern, "that I am responsible only for what happens here in this camp, not what happened on your trip. But I am most interested in hearing about it. If you can document any cases in which a KGB officer followed his whim instead of the rules, I would be interested in hearing about that, too."

"Where should I send my protests?" one prisoner asked, expecting a laugh or a reprimand but hardly a serious answer.

"I'll post a notice about that on the bulletin board," Kotov said. "Look, I understand your outrage. I understand completely. That's

145

why I want you to take your time in getting adjusted here. I want you to relax for a few days. No work. Get your strength back. One other thing—I hope you find the meals to be satisfactory.''

The major nodded good-bye and moved on to another group of prisoners who had come to Perm from another camp. One of those prisoners was a young Lithuanian Jew named Shimon Grilius. Shimon, whose skin was olive and whose face was framed with curly sideburns, was thinner than most prisoners because even in prison he would eat only the food he considered kosher. He asked Kotov whether he would be allowed to keep his thick chestnut beard and the skull cap he wore on his head. Both were symbols of his faith.

''We have the utmost respect for the statutes and all of your feelings and convictions,'' the major answered reassuringly.

Lunchtime came and the meal, the first for the new arrivals at Perm, turned out to be more than the ''satisfactory'' one Kotov had promised. By any standard, it was hearty fare; by camp standards, it was an absolute feast. The meal began with a rich soup filled with floating chunks of onion and bacon. Then came thick, juicy macaroni, covered with warm cheese and garnished with fresh vegetables. The bread was moist and rich and there was fresh fruit, which many prisoners had rarely seen when they were free. Each man even had his own cube of sugar for tea.

Leaving the dining hall, a prisoner spotted Kotov and thanked him for the meal.

''You are welcome,'' he replied. ''It is just our way of welcoming you to the hills of Soviet hospitality.''

After lunch the prisoners were left by the guards to resume their conversations and rest their astonished stomachs. The meal itself was one of the main topics of conversation. Some prisoners said the meal was a sign that conditions were improving in the labor camps and that the worst was behind them. Others were certain the meal was part of a psychological plot by the KGB, although, they confessed, they would not mind being subjected to such a plot if it included more meals like that. Supper turned out to be every bit as good as lunch, and, during the meal, the prisoners were told they could sleep anywhere they wanted. When they went to the barracks, they found the bunks filled with thick mattresses dressed in crisp white linens. Some prisoners, delirious with pleasure, jumped up and down on the beds as if they were trampolines. And Simas went to bed wondering whether Perm would turn out to be "the hills of Soviet hospitality," as Kotov promised, or "the hills of death."

Thirteen

By the end of the first week, Simas knew the truth about Perm—he and his fellow political prisoners had been brought to a psychological torture chamber, where their spirits were to be broken. One by one, all the signs that had provided so much hope disappeared. As the weeks and months passed, the prisoners would wonder if that first day was just a remarkably realistic hallucination that they all happened to share. The heaping plates of food were replaced by tiny portions of black bread, porridge, and fish. The individual sugar servings were gone. The thick mattresses gave way to hard metal cots. The freedom to sleep wherever one wanted was replaced by a strict bunk-assignment system, apparently designed to pair totally incompatible human beings. Simas, who had a pathological dislike for dirt and sloppiness, was paired with a dirty, sloppy Georgian who was constantly spewing pus all over Simas's clothes and toilet articles.

"It has come to our attention that the sentencees are walking around in a very undisciplined manner," an officer of the camp guards told the prisoners at morning lineup on the second day. "That will not be tolerated here. We don't know or care how it was for you in Potma. These are the rules here: Keep off the grass at all times. None of this sitting down and talking. No cigarette butts anywhere. Anywhere! No visiting prisoners in another barracks

without a permit. No beards." Simas looked toward Shimon Grilius, the bearded Lithuanian Jew. "No yarmulkes. Only fanatics
wear those silly little caps anyway. And remember. Your uniforms
will have name tags on them, so whatever you do we'll know who
you are."

The elegant Major Kotov was nowhere to be seen. In his place
pranced Major Fyodorov, a flabby, disheveled man with a blotchy
red face that twitched with nervous energy. He delighted in dis-
covering that a prisoner had transgressed a rule, any rule. When he
found a man whose hair was too long, he would bare his teeth like
a rabid dog, and a gleam would appear in his eye and a crackling
fury in his voice. And then there was Rak, a fat, ugly little guard
with the face of a bulldog and a terrible inferiority complex about
his height and his rank. He compensated for this complex by being
happily sadistic.

All these sudden changes left the prisoners confused and afraid,
not knowing how much to protest or whether there was any point in
protesting at all. As soon as they started to protest one new rule,
another was imposed that cried out for action. The first big change,
the loss of individual sugar servings, was greeted by almost unani-
mous resistance. More than 200 of the 275 prisoners in camp submitted written protests. But that unity was short-lived. When
putrid, rotting fish—far worse than anything served at Potma—
made its first appearance on camp plates, only eighty were willing
to put their anger on paper.

Then forced shavings began, with Shimon the first victim. The
guards yanked the skull cap off his head and tore it into pieces, beat
him, threw him to the floor, sat on his legs, held his hands behind
his back, and twisted them up toward his neck. Then they attacked
the beard with dulled sheep shears that ripped at his face and neck,
leaving scars. The thirty prisoners who had beards staged a hunger
strike to protest the shavings, but only about twenty unbearded prisoners were willing to join. Simas joined; he had joined every protest so far.

One night during the strike, at suppertime, Simas ran into Jonas
Kadzionis, a tall, balding man with cheeks burned by the wind.
Kadzionis had fought alongside Mecys with the Lithuanian par-

tisans in the late 1940s; he had been in the labor camps ever since. That made him something of an expert on camp life.

Kadzionis asked Simas if he was going to supper. Simas said he was on a hunger strike against the shavings.

"Do you understand what you're doing?" Kadzionis asked.

"I understand enough to know that an unfair demand was made," he said, irritated at Kadzionis's condescending tone. "I understand that it's not all right to just stand by and let it happen. And I understand that I'm protesting!"

"In the hopes of achieving what?"

"Righting a wrong!"

"Oh, of course," Kadzionis said. "How silly of me! I didn't even stop to think how you must have the KGB frightened out of its wits by now, what with this tremendous horde of a handful of political prisoners descending upon them and threatening to do themselves in by starving en masse. Are you mad? Or just blind? The KGB has been doing in and starving political prisoners for years, and in greater numbers than you'd care to know. Could it be you think they've been too harshly overworked, that you feel compelled to at least help them out now—by destroying yourselves?"

Simas was shocked at the old prisoner's anger and sarcasm. "And what about principle? Or doesn't that mean much anymore?"

"What about principle? You're the one who seems confused on that."

"Me?"

"Yes, you, boy wonder. The issue of principle is very clear so far—at least it is to me. It's not beards as such, but being made to go against your beliefs; that's the principle at stake. Shimon is being made to do that, and so it's right for him to protest. A protest like that has a rallying effect among us prisoners. It strengthens camp morale. But what's happening here, right now? Look around, Simas. Are the Jews the only ones with beards in this camp? Hell, no! And what does a beard mean to most of the others? Several of them have beards in memory of Marx, as a reminder of how far the party has deviated from pure Marxism. Others invoke the memory of Trotsky, and, of course, there are a few who have beards simply because they like having beards. So what happens? All those beards get mixed up in the same protest, and the issue is muddled.

"What about the unbearded prisoners, like yourself, who join the protest in a show of solidarity? Solidarity with what? It's hard to say. So does your intent get across? Hell no! But the KGB—ah, the KGB—they score again—not only by flushing out a few more activists, but by managing to sap a little of your physical strength in the process. What a pity! What a shame that your conclusions are so limited, because that's just what the KGB is counting on. You're walking right into their trap, and you won't even listen when someone tries to warn you."

"You really think it's a setup, not just another bastard order to make our lives here as miserable as possible?"

"Every KGB order is a KGB setup! Especially here!"

"And this one?"

"Simas," he said, determined to get through his listener's thick skull. "If this is like anything I've ever seen before, the situation is going to get worse. Just watch and see what happens when they start doling out the punishments. They'll have us at each other's throats and flying off in so many protest directions that we won't know whether we're coming or going. And when the really critical situations occur, we'll be so alienated from each other that nothing will gel, and our leaders will have been drained off into the punitive isolators. And no protest will get the attention or support of other prisoners because by then it'll have the stigma of being just another one of those useless little flurries that in the end turn out not to have been so important after all!" He sighed and started to pace. "Well, Simas, that's what I had in mind when I said 'trap.' "

"I guess you've talked this out with Mecys."

"You bet I have. He seems to feel that you, with your temperament and your tendency to pounce on every opportunity to attack the KGB, the system, and state, are walking a mine field. And he already knows you can't be bothered with trifling details like watching your step."

"Look," Simas said, "I'm committed to my protest right now.

151

But I'll talk it over with other unbearded protesters. Look, Jonas, the most I can promise right now is that I'll think about it. Really, I will.''

"I hope you do!" Kadzionis said angrily. "Because you look like hell already. You know, there's no bravado in making yourself vulnerable for the KGB's twisting you around their finger. And making yourself vulnerable is just what you do when you allow your stamina to be sapped. Or didn't you know that? Maybe you have some schoolboy notion that physical degeneration's only consequence is the 'gaunt, martyred look.' You see, Simas, we must try to survive—not at any price. But we must survive if at all possible, if only to live to bear witness to what has been done to us. There is no shame in survival, my friend.''

"Jonas, I realize what you're saying, but my health isn't as bad as you seem to think. And I'm not about to look for ways to make it worse, just for kicks. But I'm not about to make it my primary consideration, either! Hell, I'm not that old yet, nor that dead inside.''

"Nor that smart in the head, obviously!"

"You don't really mean that," Simas replied, a little hurt.

"No, Simas, you're right. It's just that I don't want to see you grab a machine gun to wipe out an ant, when a fly swatter would do the job just as effectively.''

For a time, Simas ignored Kadzionis's advice. He persisted in protesting every injustice. But by mid-August, he began to see that Kadzionis was right. The KGB was trying to divide the prisoners into hostile factions that would be unable to join together to protest any outrage. Prisoners were already on the verge of fighting one another, and the pressure to condemn fellow prisoners was ever more intense. Each prisoner was required to have an informal meeting with a KGB agent of his own nationality. The idea was to make a Ukrainian prisoner think that the Ukrainian KGB agent was his true friend, not the Lithuanian prisoner in the next bunk who wanted him to risk his neck so some Jew could keep his beard. Once that sort of thinking took hold, the prisoners were beaten. They would be tempted to inform on their fellow prisoners to the authorities and condemn them in public. Those condemnations, broadcast throughout the Soviet Union, would damage the morale of the dissidents outside the camp walls and discourage potential dissidents from raising their voices.

It became obvious to the protesters at Perm that the man the KGB most wanted to break was Simas. He was too attractive a target to pass up. His attempted defection had made him famous; his behavior at his trial had made him a symbol of defiance; his eagerness to protest every injustice in camp and denounce the KGB had made him a hero.

To resist the pressure mounting against them, Simas and the camp's fifty other active dissidents—Lithuanians, Latvians, Estonians, Ukrainians, and Jews—needed frequent contact with each other. They began to meet as often as they could in the furnace room where Simas worked. His job was to take huge tins of sand, load them into electric ovens, and heat them to 680 degrees Fahrenheit for use in the heating elements of clothes irons. The furnace room was unbearably hot, and the silicon dust in the air made it hard to breathe. But the guards rarely came by to see how Simas was doing, which made the room a perfect place for the dissidents' clubhouse.

On meeting nights, Simas pushed buckets, crates, and drums of sand into the corner of the room and draped a copy of *Pravda* over the dusty work bench to make it a conference table. He wiped the dust off the windows so that the dissidents would be able to see a visiting guard a few seconds before his arrival. Often, he took some scraps of bread that had been smuggled out of the kitchen, soaked them in oil and water, and toasted them in the sand oven. The aroma of the bread served notice that the meeting was about to begin. He never knew how many of the "literati"—as they laughingly called themselves—would show up on any given night; but six or seven usually managed to think up some excuse to leave their jobs and come down to the stoves for fifteen or twenty minutes. On the night shift, when the guards were particularly lethargic, each dissident might stay there an hour before he was missed.

The meeting never really started or finished. One man would leave and another would arrive. And those who stayed would move constantly around the room so that if a guard did barge in, he would not see a half-dozen guilty-looking dissidents huddled around a table. Sometimes they met to plan a protest. Usually, though, their meetings served little purpose other than to combat the wearying boredom of camp life. To try to bolster each other's spirits, they shared every bit of information they received from the outside world. Letters from home were read aloud; the most private personal problems were discussed. They talked about newly arrived prisoners and worried about day-to-day problems of camp survival: how to get an old man excused from work, how to blunt efforts by camp authorities to force Sunday work, how to get food packages from home for a man who needed the extra food to survive.

They rarely got the old man excused, the Sunday work stopped, or the packages delivered. But they had to try, if only to maintain their self-respect and, ultimately, their sanity.

More often than not, the meeting turned into a discussion of current events. This rather erudite group, many of whom had genuine intellectual credentials, would discuss such subjects as the long-range implications of détente between the Soviet Union and the United States. At first, Simas kept his opinions to himself in deference to all the lawyers, writers, and professors. He had always been aware of the poverty of his education, and he felt particularly ignorant compared to these men. As the months passed, he participated more and more, occasionally exploding with the fury of old. He would make a fist with his right hand and pound it into his left; his face would redden and his neck would bulge. Here he could vent his anger without fear of punishment. He was among friends.

They were never at a loss for news to discuss, despite their isolation. They read the Soviet newspapers and listened to Radio Moscow assiduously. Like intellectuals throughout Soviet society, they had long since mastered the art of sifting through the propaganda and discerning, with reasonable accuracy, what was going on in the world. Besides, they rarely let a lack of solid information stop them from forming opinions. If *Pravda* praised someone, that someone was a bum. If *Pravda* condemned him, he was a hero. They followed the activities of the Soviet dissidents like Solzhenitsyn and Sakharov and their greatest hero on the international scene, Senator

Henry Jackson of Washington. In their view, he alone among Western leaders understood how important the human rights issues, the rights to dissent and to emigrate, really were in the Soviet Union. They considered him every bit as much the senator from the camp at Perm as the senator from the state of Washington. They were particularly enamored of his nickname and occasionally referred to themselves as "Scoop's Troops."

They judged most other figures on the international scene to be villains of one degree or another. They hated Chilean Communist President Salvador Allende, who was portrayed as the savior of the Western world in *Pravda*. Senator George McGovern, who ran for the American presidency that fall, was dismissed as a naïve simpleton who was far too willing to trust the Soviets. Henry Kissinger, whom the prisoners considered the real American president for foreign policy, was hated as the architect of détente, a policy they considered a slap in the face of all Soviet political prisoners. They condemned his silence on the labor camps and labeled him an "international gravedigger."

The one American who fascinated them above all was Angela Davis, the black Marxist who had been accused (and found innocent) of murder in California for her role in a prison escape that led to the shooting of a judge. In the United States, many liberals and radicals contended that the accusations against her were politically motivated, an attempt by a conservative government to silence an eloquent voice from the far left. *Pravda* portrayed Davis as a saint—a poor black woman who was being persecuted solely because of her Communist beliefs. Since *Pravda* considered her a saint, the "literati" viewed her as the devil.

One night in the furnace room, Lev Lukjanenko, the Ukrainian nationalist who had been with Simas at Potma, was using the case of Davis, who had just completed a triumphant tour of the Soviet Union, to illustrate the differences in the American and Soviet systems of law. He was reviewing her complaints about the conditions she had encountered in her American jail.

"She complained about not having enough light to write her memoirs, the coffee being too weak, the candy bars too hard, the rolls too stale. . . ."

Lukjanenko stopped. Across the room, Shimon Grilius appeared to be crying. He was wiping his jacket sleeve across his eyes and sniffling loudly.

"Shimon?" Simas asked, concerned.

Shimon brushed his sleeve across his eyes once more. He leaned back against the far wall, dropped his head, stared at the floor, and uttered a deep sigh. Then he tossed his head back and closed his eyes in mock despair. His upper lip began to quiver. "Poor, poor Angela!" he sobbed. "Oh! Oh!" His body jerked as if he had just been stabbed in the stomach. "Oh, how she suffered! The poor girl!" The back of his hand flew up to his forehead. "How unfair. Oh, cruel, cruel world!"

Abruptly, he straightened his body and abandoned his role. "Just think what those imperialists put this woman through," he said angrily. "Her delicate digestive tract is almost in ruins. Her liquid eyes have suffered strain. She was besieged by danger at every turn, threatened with harm at every step by the diabolical capitalist conspiracy that camouflages lethal instruments as ordinary objects, just waiting for the unsuspecting girl to use them and unleash their violence on her innocent, gentle frame. One such lethal object they deviously disguised as a chocolate candy bar! Luckily, her finely developed senses immediately detected the unusual hardness of the bar and recoiled, escaping what could have been a critical case of chipped teeth. What blatant infringement of human rights! And to think that such things can still happen in the twentieth century! We, all of us here in this room, are political prisoners. Angela Davis, there in the West, from a prison cell, claimed she, too, was a political prisoner. Yet none of us here in this room seems able to identify with her. Why? Where have we lost our sense of kinship?" he asked facetiously.

"I don't know about the rest of you guys," interjected Jonas Silinskas, an old friend from Potma, "but I must have lost mine somewhere between the lukewarm coffee she got and the rotten fish soup we get."

Everyone laughed.

"Mine got stale along with her day-old bun," shouted Yosif Mendelevich, a Jewish dissident.

"Well, I've got to confess," Simas added, "that weak light bulb of hers is more powerful than I ever thought! While it may have strained her eyes, it's still straining my imagination!"

"This isn't exactly the format I had in mind when I started to point out some of the differences between systems," Lukjanenko allowed, "but I must say it's a lot more entertaining and interesting. And it does point out some very stark realities. And there are so many more! We could go on for hours more talking about how Angela Davis's involvement in an actual crime of violence, if mentioned at all, is passed over lightly, while her perception of herself as a political prisoner receives the greatest, if not exclusive, attention of the press. We can only shake our heads and feel bewildered, as we think of the many times we've known of political dissent here being shrouded with trumped-up allegations of criminalities, and the allegations being given the main attention rather than the real issues of political dissent."

"Or the fact that Angela Davis was allowed more visits with family and friends in a month than all of us put together are allowed in a year," Shimon added.

"Or that she and the lawyers of her choice consulted as frequently as they seemed to find necessary," Silinskas said, "and that no threat hung over these lawyers for acting in her defense."

"Or these interviews with the press," said another. "Can you imagine a sprinkling of Western journalists let loose here in this or any other prison camp?"

"That's just it," Shimon continued. "No Western correspondents in the U.S.S.R. have access to the whole truth. They don't have the freedom to gather facts for their news stories. It's our obligation to at least try and get facts to them. So they will know."

A prisoner named Algis Zypre, who had refrained from the merriment, spoke up for the first time. "But knowledge is not enough. The real question is this: Does the West care?"

"Why do you even question that?" Simas asked.

"Because they do know," Shimon answered.

"Because the voices of men like Sakharov and Solzhenitsyn have been heard," Zypre explained. "But has it even begun to affect the fates of the Simases, the Shimons, the Yosifs, and the Jonases? Hell no!''

Zypre's remarks drained the joy from the session. "Let's start getting back to work," Lukjanenko warned. "It's getting late."

Shimon lingered in the furnace room after the others left.

"Simas, you look so dejected."

"I was just thinking about what you and Zypre said, and I was hoping that you aren't right in what you say. Will we ever be any less forgotten?"

"Who knows."

Such discussions, of course, never resolved anything. But they did give sustenance to Simas, a blue-collar man who had never before counted intellectuals as friends. His self-respect—and his self-control—grew as a result of those sessions and the friendships that were nourished there. Years later, he would consider those hours with the "literati" among the best of his life.

Fourteen

The snow began falling in September. It started sticking in October. In mid-November, it came down for four days straight, and, from then on, the paths through the camp were always swept by drifts. By midwinter, the snow in the yard was four feet deep, making the paths seem like tunnels. Collisions between snow-blind prisoners became unavoidable. In the death zone, the no-man's-land between the camp and the outside world, the snow was eight feet high, and outside the drifts climbed over the fifteen-foot fence. The worst times were on January days when it did not snow. The temperature plummeted, and the bitter cold was joined by a thirty-mile-an-hour wind that burned a man's skin, penetrated his chest, and stung his eyes with a constant barrage of blowing crystals. On those days, the temperatures stayed below zero even during the three or four hours of daylight. At night, it fell to 30 below—and lower.

A resident of a Soviet labor camp quickly learned to fall asleep on an empty stomach. His stomach was always empty. But it was harder to fall asleep while shivering from the cold. On a midwinter night, the thin cotton blanket issued by the camp was not enough to keep a body warm. In violation of camp rules, Simas would wear his shabby cotton ''hundred-thread'' jacket—called that because it seemed to have a hundred vertical seams—over his underwear, under the covers. He would curl up inside the jacket, pulling the

159

collar over his otherwise exposed ears. The real problem was his back. It was separated from the cold metal cot by only a paper-thin mattress. He found that a large piece of cardboard would insulate his back from the metal and that a thin piece of wood did the job even better. Several times during the winter, the guards would inspect the bed, discover the forbidden board, and yank it out from under the mattress. Simas would shiver for the next several nights, until he found another piece of wood.

When wake-up sounded and his bare feet hit the cold concrete floor, he felt a shock that he never got used to. He hurried to wrap his feet in cotton foot cloths and put on his pants and shirt. Both fit too loosely to provide much warmth. The round collar on the shirt was several sizes too big for his neck, providing a perfect entrance for the winter wind. His pants, which fit like a sack, were warm at least; he had slept on them to keep them that way. He put on his gloves and his hat, pulling its flaps down over his ears, then donned his hundred-thread jacket once more. He was ready to face the frozen world outside.

He opened the door and, for an instant, felt caught in a powerful suction as two air masses, one 70 degrees colder than the other, collided and mixed violently. A cloud of steam whooshed out from the barracks, and the suction dissipated. He stared straight ahead and saw white—not snow or sky, just vague, endless white. His eyes were always useless those first few seconds. He stood there patiently, waiting for his eyes to adjust. Soon he could make out the lines where the white sky ended and a white snowdrift began, where a white rooftop left off and a white hill rose above it in the distance.

He took a deep breath through his nose. There was no good way to breathe in this weather, but, after long experience, Simas had settled on the nose method. After a while, his nostrils might freeze shut for a few minutes, but that was preferable to the feeling he got when he let the wind enter his mouth and linger in his chest. He tucked his chin into his chest, hunched his shoulders, and started the 120-yard walk to the bathroom. In the first few seconds, the wind burned his skin. After that, he felt nothing. He walked slowly, his boots crunching against the snow. Halfway to the bathroom, he stopped, bent over, picked up a handful of snow, and rubbed it on his cheeks, a crude but effective protection against frostbite. On the coldest morning of the winter, when it was nearly 70 below, he watched as a bird, foolish enough to try to fly, froze solid in mid-air and dropped out of the sky.

When he got to the bathroom and opened the door, warm, steaming air hit him in the face and seemed to stick there, making him feel as if he had been smeared with excrement. The bathroom was a little wooden cabin with sixteen stalls, eight on either side of a head-high partition. Inside each stall was a hole, nothing more. Six inches of a gleaming white ice coated the ceiling, the walls, and the partitions, giving the place the unreal shine of an ice palace. The warm urine and excrement inside the holes gave off steam, which rose to the ceiling and softened the ice, forming wet icicles that dripped onto his head as he tried to relieve himself.

After crunching through the snow back to the barracks, then over to the dining hall for breakfast and back to the barracks again, Simas had to join the other members of his work brigade in the morning lineup. He stood near the back of the formation, running in place or banging his heels together for warmth. After ten minutes or so in the lineup, the pain started. He felt it first in his heels. Then it crawled down his foot to his big toe and shot up his leg. When, at last, his name was called, he trudged off toward the work zone and the welcome heat of the furnace room.

Several times a week, a guard would pick a prisoner at random just before he left the living zone and tell him to unbutton his clothes down to his underwear. If the prisoner was wearing only the permitted amount of clothing, the guard told him to button up and march on. But if a man were caught wearing an extra shirt or sweater, a scarf, or a layer of thermal underwear, he would be forced to strip and pile his clothes in the snow. He would have to stand nude, at attention, while the guard sifted through the pile in search of more forbidden items to confiscate. Then he was allowed to get dressed again—in clothes now covered with snow.

As the winter dragged on, Simas became increasingly morose, depressed as much by the twenty hours a day of darkness as by the crippling cold. His health was failing from the weather, the work,

161

and the diet. When he had jumped onto the *Vigilant* more than two years before, there had been 160 pounds of muscle on his five-foot, five-inch body. Now he was down below 130 pounds, and his pale skin seemed to be stretched tightly over his skull, giving his face that gaunt, martyred look Kadzionis had warned him about. He felt as tired as he looked.

If he ever developed any truly serious medical trouble, he knew his life would be in immediate jeopardy, for he would have to rely on the camp doctor, a sadist named Petrov. Petrov, an elderly man who needed a crutch to get around on, had established his reputation back in July, just after the death train had arrived at Perm. He had concluded that an obvious heart attack victim had been suffering from nothing more than "normal fatigue." He treated most medical problems by ignoring them, accusing the prisoners of being raving hypochondriacs. "I am first, foremost, always a member of the KGB," he declared once. "Then I am a physician." On evenings and Sundays, Petrov disappeared. Anyone falling ill on a Saturday night would have to hope he could survive on his own until Monday morning and then take his chances with Petrov.

By midwinter, though, Simas had a problem that no physician could soothe. He had received three letters—one from his mother, one from a neighbor, and one from a woman he did not know—all telling him that his wife was living with another man. Her new lover, whose name was Vytas, was actually an old lover, a man she had dated before marrying Simas. But the details did not concern him. All that mattered was that his marriage was ruined.

Throughout his days in the camps, he had always tried to comfort his fellow prisoners when they needed comforting. Now that he needed help, he was reluctant to ask for it. When he could stand the hurt no longer, he asked Shimon Grilius to walk with him in the snow. Simas told him the news.

"Oh, Lord, no!" Shimon shouted.

"Shocked?"

"It's not that at all. It's mainly concern about you."

"What I feel?"

"Yes, but more important even, what you are going to do. You know, Simas, it's not just what one feels that's important. It's also how one acts on those feelings that counts.''

"Shimon," he said desperately, "I don't feel like I'm in any position to let this thing loll around in my brain indefinitely. I've got to fight it fast, before I go crazy. My nerves are drawn so tight that a sneeze from Rak or one of Fyodorov's cracks will send me into a rage.''

"Look, it's happened, it's fact.'' Shimon paused, hoping his silence would have a calming effect. "And you don't fight facts, you deal with them. And you don't deal with them by smearing them up with bitterness and anger until you can't even recognize what the real problems are anymore.''

They came to one end of the residential zone and turned to start back the other way.

"Have you figured out what it is you want?'' Shimon asked.

"What I want?'' It struck Simas as a silly question. "Would it make any difference? All I can realistically want right now is to bury the memories as quickly and as deeply as possible.''

"I don't agree with you.''

"You mean you actually think there's a possibility of salvaging the relationship?'' he asked.

"Of course, it's possible. It's not over yet, nothing ever really is, until death, or until all the parties involved make it so. The only thing is, Simas, are you willing to understand what she has done and why—and forgive her? And if you are, do you feel reasonably certain that you would have enough love left to start reconstructing your lives later?''

Simas was silent for a long minute. "You know, Shimon," he said hesitantly, "thoughts very similar to those did come to me, and I couldn't bear to think them through, because they imply a hope I can't afford to have—that I will get out of here someday. So I convinced myself that it was no more than a figment of my imagination conjured up to ease the pain.''

"So you don't want it to be over, do you?''

"No, but how do you even begin to forgive . . .''

"Have you tried thinking about what it must be like for her?''

Shimon asked. Simas shook his head. "How rough these years have been, how empty and uncertain they must have seemed with nothing from you to fill in the gaps? Her last memories of you are behind barbed wire, and she has had no escape from the thought that ahead lie years and years more to widen the gap between you. Simas, what thoughts did you leave her when you last talked? Was it something that would nurture hopes or renew her faith if, in her loneliest hours, she turned to your words for encouragement or comfort? Think about that, Simas. Remember, too, that to stumble under the weight we're given to bear is no greater a failing than being human. And if after all that, Simas, you still can't feel any compassion for Gene, then at least consider how hard the everyday task of keeping body and soul together is for a woman alone with two small children to care for and raise."

Simas started to cry. "You're right, you know. I shouldn't give up. I should try to understand her. Right now I feel that something I cherish as my own was stolen from me, and I'll fight to get it back."

"Good," Shimon said. He put his arm around Simas's shoulders. "But what if it turns out that the game is lost anyway? Suppose she divorces you. Will you still feel it was worth it just to try?"

"Yes, Shimon, I think I will." He paused to ponder the question. "I think I will."

In the days ahead, Simas could think only of Gene. He tried to understand what she had done. Some days it was easy to forgive her. But there were other days when he felt that her decision to live with another man meant his own life wasn't worth a damn anymore. Knowing that gave him a new, wild courage to confront the KGB even more ferociously than he had done during his first days at Potma. He felt he had nothing left to lose.

At noon on February 23, 1973, a few months after he learned about Gene, he was ordered to bring his belongings to Captain Karpavicius of the KGB for inspection.

"It's not much to see," he said, reluctantly hoisting his suitcase up onto the table in front of the captain. Simas hated Karpavicius because the captain was a Lithuanian who, unlike himself, had chosen to become the oppressor rather than the oppressed. "My things have been looked at so many times—entering Potma, leaving Potma, entering here—and every time something else gets confiscated. There isn't much left."

"Don't be embarrassed," said the captain. "Let's have a look."

Karpavicius opened the suitcase and began leafing through Simas's papers, stacking them into three piles—one for Simas, one for the garbage can, and one for the KGB. Simas could feel the vein on the side of his neck pounding and his self-control ebbing. Then the captain found a particularly cherished letter and put it in the KGB pile.

"Why, may I ask," the prisoner demanded, "are you taking away a letter that has gone through so many inspections in so many places and was never taken before?"

"I can't tell you why it was never taken before," Karpavicius replied. "All I can tell you is that it's being taken now. Now don't get angry, pal," the captain said, half as warning and half as reassurance.

He came to a copy of the poem "If" by Rudyard Kipling, a gift from Sharygin, and put it in the KGB file.

"You are a born pickpocket right out of the Dark Ages!" Simas shouted, pounding the table.

"If you don't stop it, you are going to get it!"

Simas calmed momentarily. Then the captain came to Simas's copy of the United Nations Declaration of Human Rights, and took that too.

"Go ahead, take that. It's about time you read it. I already know what is says. You obviously don't have the slightest idea." Simas began to shout. "Where is your might if you, inside this rats' cage, behind layer after layer of barbed wire, fear the printed word?"

The KGB captain did not look up. He kept flipping through the papers until he found a copy of "A Partisan's Prayer for His Homeland," a gift to Simas from a Lithuanian who had spent nearly twenty-five years in the camps. The captain lifted it with his fingertips, as if it were covered with manure, and dropped it into the wastebasket.

165

"You scum!" Simas shouted. He slammed his fist on the table. "You piece of filth. You are Lithuanian, yet you have called me a traitor." Simas pointed to a Russian KGB agent. "From someone like that fellow I don't expect anything. Russians are slaves the minute they are born. But you have no excuse. You were born in a free, independent nation. You were baptized as a Christian. You had an opportunity to get to know what honor and justice really are. You had a choice to make, and you made it. You decided to be a traitor to your country."

Karpavicius leapt to his feet and pointed at Simas. "I want that man sent to the punitive isolator for fifteen days. Starting now!"

In a few minutes, Simas was in the isolator, a tiny cell with brick walls and a wooden floor. Four slabs of wood, which were folded up into the wall and locked there except at night, served as beds. There were no sheets, no blankets, no pillows, and no company.

His first morning in the cell, he was taken into the hallway and told to strip to his underwear. The guards took away his clothing, including his shoes and socks, and brought him the special isolator uniform.

"This thing is filthy," Simas said. He always kept his own uniform spotless. "I'm not going to wear it." The guards handed it to him, and he stepped away, refusing to take it. They dropped it on the floor in front of him. Simas sidled up to it warily, as if eyeing some kind of vermin. He probed it cautiously with his foot. The coarse, gray cloth was stained with blood, spit, and urine, and encrusted with dried pus, mucus, and feces. He lifted it a few inches off the floor with his foot. It was as stiff as a board. He let it drop and kicked it across the floor at the guards. They kicked it back.

"I'm not going to wear that thing," he told them. "I am not a pig. I am not a scum from the sewers like you animals. I'm from the Baltic States. I have a little class."

"Get your ass back into that cell! And take that uniform with you," one guard ordered.

Simas walked back into his cell but left the uniform on the floor outside. The guard tossed it inside after him and slammed the door. Simas kicked the crusty uniform into a corner; he was not going to put it on. Wearing only his underwear, he started to pace, hoping that exercise would keep him warm. But his bare feet quickly grew numb. In an effort to warm them, he sat on a concrete stool, leaned back against a concrete table, and lifted his feet up toward a heating pipe that was barely within reach. The pipe was not exactly hot, but it was warmer than the floor. In a few minutes, a new problem developed. His back and buttocks were becoming discolored and numb from rubbing against the cold concrete. He had no choice but to put his feet back on the floor and start pacing once more. He spent most of the day alternating between sitting and pacing, his mind full of old conversations, old poems, old songs, and old prayers.

When night came and the guards unlocked the wooden beds from the walls, Simas tried to go to sleep, still wearing only his underwear. There were no sheets or covers to warm him, but still he refused to put on the uniform. The hours passed and sleep did not come. He was too hungry and too cold. He tried every position, curling his arms and his legs in toward his stomach to generate some warmth. No matter how he contorted his nearly naked body, he could not get warm. The later it got, the colder it got. The dampness seemed to invade his body in the small of his back and flow out from there in all directions. A guard opened the hallway door to create a draft, making it colder still. Simas nodded off for a second and then awakened with a fierce shiver. After a few hours, he noticed a thin layer of ice on the inside of the wall. He was shaking uncontrollably, certain that he would not survive the night. His head felt light as he teetered on the edge of unconsciousness. At last morning came. Breakfast (bread and water) eased the gnawing in his stomach and raised his body temperature, if only for a few minutes. And eating gave him something to take his mind off how cold he was.

For the next thirteen days, Simas refused to put on the uniform. He lived in his underwear, pacing, sitting, shivering, and trying to sleep. He had thirteen days alone with his thoughts.

For me those days provided a chance to look into the dark little corners of my mind. There were moments of merriment and moments of deep sadness in that cell. The dead became alive for me, and the living almost dead.

I thought a lot about Gene and what she had done. I began to understand how truly difficult it must have been for her alone. If I had not jumped from the *Sovetskaya Litva,* she would not have jumped from my bed. What right did I have to sit and judge her? But that realization didn't change the fact that she was gone from my life. How could there be a reconciliation even if I did get out alive? Only part of me was still alive. The part that had spent all those years with Gene was dead. The pain was always there. Then a numb spot formed, and it grew and blotted out all the sadness and, at the same time, all the good times Gene and I had shared. I was becoming cold on the inside, too.

There were moments when my self-analysis became so painful that I longed to throw my arms around my grandfather for peace and comfort. He seemed so real, I felt I could talk with him. He and grandmother had suffered so much pain and poverty in their lives. All their heartaches and mine seemed to multiply from generation to generation. Our family seemed to be drifting hopelessly in an endless sea of suffering and agony. I began to remember the rules they had taught me as a child. . . . I knew I had not been perfect. Still, except for the fact of my birth—and the jump—I had never caused anyone any real pain. I was not one of the world's carnivores. I did not thrive on eating others. So why did I have to suffer? When was it going to end? It all could have ended so many times before.

When I was five, my grandmother had left me standing near the pond out behind the house with a bucket in my hand. I toddled over to the pond and dipped the bucket into the water. The bucket was too heavy. It started to drag me down. I didn't know to tip the bucket and let the water out. I refused to let go of that bucket and lose it in the pond. I was being dragged into the water. I grabbed for a tree root to hold on to, but I kept slipping. I was already in the water up to my waist when, somehow, the bucket slipped out of my hand, and I was able to get out.

It could have ended during the war so many times, but it didn't. Once, when I was just a teenager, I was fooling around with a hand grenade and it exploded in my hand. All I got was a scratch. It could have ended on the *Vigilant*. What would have happened that day if I had decided to fight to the death? I could have ended it all then and there and perhaps had the satisfaction of taking a few of those Russian thugs to the grave with me. But, no, I would have been dismissed by the world as a simple hooligan, and no cause would have been served.

If I had taken another road, if I were not here in this cell now fighting for my principles in my own crude way, what would I say to the partisans? How else would I be worthy of them? What they thought of me was very important, for those dead heroes were there in that cold cell with me, just as my grandfather was. They were real companions in my shrinking world.

After two weeks in the isolator, Simas's buttocks were bright blue from the cold. No matter how much he paced or rubbed, he could not feel the slightest bit of warmth. His limbs were constantly falling asleep. Every time he tried to stand up, his knees buckled, sending his body crumpling to the floor in a heap. He spent much of the day trying to fall asleep and rarely succeeding, falling only into a stupor that provided no rest.

On the fourteenth day, he received a visit from Major Fyodorov and a Latvian KGB captain named Martuzans. They told him that if he did not get dressed immediately, he would be punished for "insulting the uniform." He refused and was sentenced to another week in the isolator; still, he would not put on the uniform. When the third week was over, he was moved out; the isolator was much in demand for the likes of Shimon Grilius, Lev Lukjanenko, and Jonas Silinskas, all of whom continued to protest. All the troublemakers had to do their time. But Simas, who was considered too dangerous to let back into the camp proper, was kept in the punitive brig, next to the isolator, for six more months. His new cell was just like the old one, except that the rules were different. He had two roommates now, and he was allowed to read. He was given normal prison food, a blanket for his bed, and his old, clean uniform.

There was another rule. He was expected to work. He refused.

In return, the KGB sent him back to the isolator—whenever it was vacant—for two or three days at a time. Out of the next 180 days, he spent at least sixty in the isolation cell. He was not allowed to write or receive letters, although occasionally he was given a tiny scrap of a letter written to him from Lithuania. The KGB wanted him to know that every piece of mail intended for him was being torn up by the camp censors.

He could feel himself changing inside. He wasn't sure whether his will to resist was weakening or whether he had matured enough to know better than to try to fight the KGB every time he had a chance. In mid-September, he was released from the brig and allowed back into the living zone for the first time in seven months. His skin was translucent now, his teeth and eyesight were failing. He was nearly fifty pounds underweight.

"Simas," Shimon said, horrified by his friend's appearance. "Please! Go to work. Play along with them. Cool it for a while. You've got to stay out of the punitive cells. If you go back, and they put you on bread and water again, you may never come out."

Simas had heard those words of friendly admonition before, and in the past he had ignored them, letting his sense of moral outrage propel him to provoke the KGB again and again. But this time he relented. He went back to work and swore off protest. There was no use provoking the rulers anymore. Another long winter was about to begin.

The winter of 1973–74 passed slowly. Simas did manage to stay out of the isolator. The "literati," or what was left of them, met now and then at Simas's stove, but they were totally on the defensive, worrying more about protecting themselves from informers than planning protests. The camp was quiet. There were a few events to brighten the dark winter days. Through a visitor, Simas received a personal message from Sakharov, who wished Simas continued strength and courage. And more good news came from a most unexpected source—Radio Moscow. The commentators reported (and denounced) efforts being made by Senator Henry Jackson to get the Soviets to agree to allow free emigration from the Soviet Union. Late on a cold winter night, a half-dozen dissidents danced in the yard around the loudspeaker, throwing snow into the air as if it were confetti and singing the praises of the senator from Perm.

When spring finally came in mid-April, it was time for a celebration. Antonas Jastrauskas, the Lithuanian prisoner who had welcomed Simas to camp life that first day in Potma, was being released from Perm. He had done his time, ten years in all, and, as was the custom, he gave his own farewell party. He had saved up his canteen privileges for months so that he could fill a table with candies and cakes and a big pot of coffee. During the party, the prisoners came up to him and wished him well, and he, in turn, gave them most of his personal belongings. Those belongings—a fresh uniform, a copybook, a pencil, a spoon—would mean so much to the men left behind, but so little to Jastrauskas once he became a free man.

Simas walked up to his old friend, said good-bye, and thought of another party nearly three years before. Simas, the newcomer, had been the guest of honor that evening in Potma in the summer of 1971, and he had come away from that night with a feeling that prison life would not be so bad. How naïve he had been.

After the party, I thought of Mecys Kybartas, the man who had guided me through my first months in Potma. He had told me that a political prisoner could ask nothing more than survival, and I had scoffed at his tired old cynicism. Mecys was dead now. He had died of lung cancer one night while I was off doing my time in the isolator, during the summer of 1973. I hadn't even been around to comfort him, or to say good-bye. I looked at myself, and I knew that Mecys, Jonas Kadzionis, and some of the others had been right all along. Protest had accomplished nothing of lasting value. I had been punished for my protests so many times—lost so much in canteen privileges, spent so many nights in the isolator—that I was becoming old and disabled before my time. I had aged so much in three years. I was beginning to visualize my own death. I would die like Mecys, like all prisoners, forgotten. And my death would change nothing. I too would close my eyes forever behind barbed wire. All this suffering, and my only reward would be a coffin.

It was only 1974. My sentence would not expire until the end of

1980. My thoughts rarely ventured outside the barbed wire. My life had become a kind of floating thing, no longer anchored by links to the past or future. That meant I had nothing but my life at Perm, which meant I had nothing. It had all come full circle. In 1971, when I had been new and eager to protest, Mecys had been the voice of caution. Now there were new prisoners arriving, young Lithuanians full of outrage over what they saw in Perm. They were ready to protest, and I had to be the voice of caution. I was telling them that they had a lot to learn, that they had to pick their spots, that they had a sacred duty not to throw themselves on the bull's horn. I had become the tired, cynical voice of experience. I had never thought it could happen to me.

Fifteen

Simas would have been much less depressed had he known that while he wasted away in Perm, a serious campaign was under way in the United States to win his freedom. A few Americans, most of them of Lithuanian extraction, had felt from the beginning that it was not enough for the United States to punish three Coast Guard officers and promise that the outrage would never be repeated. For them, the Kudirka case could never be closed until Simas himself was freed from the labor camps and given the chance he had grasped at so desperately—the chance to live in the United States. In the year after the incident, they had labored mightily to keep the case in the public consciousness. They had campaigned to have the *Vigilant* renamed the *Simas Kudirka,* petitioned President Nixon to trade Angela Davis to the Russians for Simas, deposited wreaths in the sea at the spot of the jump, dropped leaflets welcoming would-be defectors onto Soviet fishing trawlers, and sent their children to the doorstep of the Soviet embassy in Washington with food and clothing for the prisoner.

The most daring stunt was the work of an ex-paratrooper named Leonard "Jock" Milne, a Scotsman living in Canada. Milne, a social planner with a taste for "dabbling my toes in an action situation," flew to Finland with the idea of kidnapping a Soviet official. He would force the official onto an American commercial jet at gunpoint, make the plane take off, and threaten to shoot him over the Atlantic unless Simas was freed from the camps and allowed to emigrate. Milne abandoned his plan on arrival in Helsinki, finding security around the Soviet embassy too tight. Instead he went to a downtown hotel, found the flight crew for the next Pan American flight to New York, unbuttoned his trenchcoat to show them his gun, and asked, politely, if they would allow him to pretend to hijack the plane as a publicity stunt for Simas. The flight crew reported him to the local police, and he was arrested.

But by 1972 even the most committed Lithuanian-Americans were giving up the cause. An organization called Americans for Simas did exist, but it was little more than a letterhead backed by two individuals—Daiva Kezys, a petite, blond Queens housewife who had helped organize the Times Square demonstration the week of the jump; and a middle-aged New Jersey man, a radio operator himself, who had managed to get some letters through to Simas and, more important, to get letters back from Simas. The letters provided evidence that Simas was still alive and his cause still worth pursuing, although some skeptics dismissed the letters, which were written in English, as forgeries.*

"It seem to me that you are well informed about my fate and condition I am in," Simas had written in July 1972. "Though last winter was not very kind to me, but I survived as well as many others and now summer is here! Your heart-warming letters and above all your moral support which give me greater hope than ever."

By 1973, though, even the letters had stopped, and Daiva Kezys was on the verge of giving up hope. It seemed there was nothing more to be done for the man.

The break in the case came in September 1973, about the time Simas was finishing up his seven months in the isolation cell and punitive brig at Perm. One day, Daiva's husband, Romas, who hosted a Sunday-morning Lithuanian-language radio program in New York, received a call from a constant listener, an old Lithuanian émigré named Narbertas Kulikauskas. Kulikauskas, who knew of the Kezys family's interest in the Kudirka case, had startling

* The letters were genuine. Sharygin had translated them into English.

news. He said that Simas's mother had been born in New York.

The information had been discovered quite by chance. A few months earlier, one of Kulikauskas's relatives in the old country, a woman named Ona, had met an old woman selling berries in the marketplace of a small Lithuanian village. The sad old woman turned out to be Simas's mother, Marija Sulskis. (Simas's mother had recently been widowed by the death of her husband of thirty years, Teo Sulskis.) The two women had talked and had discovered that Mrs. Sulskis had been a close childhood friend of Ona's sister, who was now living in Connecticut. At Mrs. Sulskis's request, Ona wrote her sister in Connecticut, whose name was Mary Achenbach, and informed her of the coincidental meeting and the fact that Marija was Simas's mother. And Mary Achenbach was absolutely certain that her old friend from Lithuania, Marija Sulskis, née Kudirka, had been born in New York.

It took the Kezyses just two days to verify Mrs. Achenbach's claim. They called a parish priest in Maspeth, Queens, who told them to check an old Lithuanian parish church in Williamsburg, Brooklyn. There they found it. According to the brittle, yellow baptismal records of St. Mary of the Angels Church, Marija Kudirka had been baptized on September 29, 1906, at the age of one day.

So it was true. Marija Kudirka Sulskis was American born and possibly an American citizen. The question was whether that made Simas an American citizen as well. And what should Daiva and Romas Kezys do with their piece of information and their question? Stage another demonstration? Hold a press conference? Write a letter to President Nixon? Call the State Department? Whatever they were going to do, they were going to have to do it with the help of Roland and Grazina Paegle.

Grazina Paegle, a tall, long-haired woman who was Kulikauskas's daughter, had helped organize the Times Square demonstration three years earlier. Her Latvian-born husband, Roland, a balding pathologist, was a hard-line anti-Communist who had also been active in the Kudirka cause, even before marrying Grazina. He had formed his own tiny organization, the Seaman's Education Federation, and worked to get New England coastal radio stations

175

to broadcast messages to Soviet seamen. Those messages, spoken in Latvian, Lithuanian, and Russian, invited the sailors to defect and assured them of a warm welcome in the United States, despite the Kudirka debacle.

The four of them—Daiva and Romas, Grazina and Roland—met on a fall afternoon at the Paegles' ranch-style home in Locust, New Jersey, and worked out a two-pronged plan. They would go to Washington to claim American citizenship for Simas and his mother. At the same time, they would try to make contact with Mrs. Sulskis in Lithuania, win her trust, and invite her to visit the United States, where she could plead her son's case herself.

On the morning of December 17, 1973, Daiva and Grazina brought their case to Capitol Hill, which was all but abandoned due to a snowstorm. They were accompanied by Algimantas Gureckas, a member of the Executive Committee of the Lithuanian-American Community of the U.S.A. and sometime lobbyist who had set up a series of meetings for them in the capital. They were a bit confused and a bit intimidated; lobbying was not their line of work. Their first stop was the office of a lawyer for the House Judiciary Committee who was supposed to be an expert on citizenship claims. He told them that Mrs. Sulskis, by virtue of her American birth, was almost certainly a citizen, but Simas's own claim was weak because his illegitimate father had not been an American citizen, at least as far as Daiva and Grazina knew. The two women left the lawyer's office and wandered through the hallways of congressional office buildings, toying with the idea of finding an old Lithuanian-American who would be willing to claim to be Simas's long-lost illegitimate father. It was far-fetched, of course, but finding a father, real or otherwise, seemed to be their only chance.

They stopped in at every congressional office where they had reason to expect a sympathetic hearing. But with the storm, few congressmen were in their offices. So the women trekked on through the snow to the office of the Commissioner of Immigration and Naturalization, where an assistant commissioner, David Ilchert, said he could give them a few minutes of his time.

Ilchert listened to their story and told them that Mrs. Sulskis definitely was a citizen. "Now, as for her son," he said, and paused. "When did you say he was born?"

"Nineteen thirty," Daiva answered.

"O.K. You'll have to get a lawyer to check this, but this is what I think. If he had been born legitimately, in wedlock, to an American-born mother and a Lithuanian-born father, that's easy. He wouldn't be a citizen. In those days, American citizenship was determined purely by the father. But the law was changed." He paused again. "Just a minute." He grabbed a thick volume of immigration regulations from the top of his desk and flipped through the pages rapidly.

"Here we go," he said, running down the page with his eyes until he found Section 205 of the Nationality Act of 1940. "This is the situation. In 1940, a law was passed that applied to persons born before 1934. So it applies to your man. It says that a child born out of wedlock to an American mother retains U.S. citizenship from the mother." He read the law to them. "It was changed later, but that doesn't concern you. If you can substantiate everything you've told me, and there's no legitimate father, you can go to the State Department and tell them that your man has a claim to American citizenship. Now, without question, the Russians have a claim on him, too, and they may very well tell our State Department to mind its own business. But you've got a chance."

In the next few weeks, Daiva and Grazina did have a lawyer check out the validity of Ilchert's legal logic, and they filed a citizenship claim for Simas and his mother with the State Department. They enlisted the support of a number of congressmen, most of them from New York and New Jersey, to prod the State Department along. They worked on a daily basis with Robert Hanrahan, a freshman Republican representative, whose office they had visited on their Washington trip. Hanrahan had become interested in the case two years before while campaigning through his heavily Lithuanian congressional district in Chicago and its suburbs. He had promised the voters to work for Simas's release and, on his arrival in Washington, he had set out to fulfill his pledge. He had sent off a constant barrage of letters to Secretary of State Henry Kissinger,

177

Soviet Ambassador Anatoly Dobrynin, and United Nations Secretary General Kurt Waldheim, none of which accomplished much of anything.

Hanrahan was eager to help, but the State Department was less than eager to move. In fact, before the citizenship claim was filed one American diplomat told Hanrahan that Simas's chances of release were about those of a "snowflake in hell." Even after the claim was filed, no one from the department was interested enough to even attempt to determine the authenticity of the baptismal certificate, the main piece of evidence in the case. Every congressman who inquired about progress on the claim got the same cold form letter in reply.

"Information about the nationality of Mr. Kudirka's mother indicates another claim which he has upon the sympathy of the American people," the State Department wrote. "Unfortunately, any right to U.S. citizenship which he may have derived through her could not assist him under present circumstances since he is also certainly a Soviet citizen and the Soviet government does not recognize dual citizenships." The letter infuriated Daiva and Grazina because, according to official American policy, Lithuanians were not Soviet citizens. The U.S. had never recognized the Soviet takeover of Lithuania. "We believe that the most effective assistance to Mr. Kudirka is that of private individuals and groups whose activities remind Soviet authorities of the continuing interest of the American people in Mr. Kudirka's fate."

Hanrahan was losing his patience. It had been one thing for the State Department to dismiss him as a well-meaning pain in the ass when he had nothing more to go on than a campaign promise. But now there was evidence—hard evidence—that Simas might be an American citizen. One afternoon in March 1974, nearly a month after the citizenship claims had been filed, he called Frederick Smith, the Deputy Director of Security and Consular Affairs at State, and demanded that someone be sent to Brooklyn to take a look at the baptismal certificate. Smith promised that the evidence would be examined.

Two days later, Betty Burger, Hanrahan's caseworker on the Kudirka affair, received a call from William J. Dyess, who identified himself as the State Department's chief of U.S.–Soviet Bilateral Relations. Dyess had known of the new "evidence" in the Kudirka case for nearly two months, but he had been skeptical of its authenticity—so skeptical that he had authorized all those discouraging letters the department kept sending out. He was skeptical because, after fifteen years in the department, he had learned to what extremes people would go to try to get loved ones out of a Communist country and into the United States. After all, a baptismal record could be faked. As a consular officer in Yugoslavia in the early 1960s, he had learned the hard way that even a priest could do a very professional job of lying—if he thought he could get one of his flock to the United States. He was skeptical, too, because he knew how many hundreds of man-hours State Department workers had invested in the search for a way to get Kudirka out of the Soviet Union, or at least out of the labor camps. Even though the department considered itself blameless for what had happened to Simas, the case remained a national embarrassment that would be erased only by freeing the man. If Kudirka had a genuine claim to citizenship, he felt certain the department would have uncovered it long ago. And so he had been certain the new information was phony.

Now, as a result of Hanrahan's prodding, the department had checked out the baptismal certificate and found, beyond any doubt, that it was genuine. Dyess was calling Congressman Hanrahan's office to say that the citizenship claims of Simas and his mother would get priority treatment from then on.

"Hello!" Grazina Paegle shouted through the telephone in Lithuanian. "Is this Mrs. Sulskis?"

It was 2:20 on a mid-March morning in the Paegles' New Jersey bedroom, 9:20 in the morning at the other end of the line, the post office in Griskabudis, Lithuania.

"Mrs. Sulskis, yes," Simas's mother replied.

The line was fuzzed with static.

"Hello, this is Grazina."

"Hello, hello, Grazina."

"Did you receive all the documents?" Grazina shouted. In carry-

179

ing out the second part of their strategy—the part about winning Mrs. Sulskis's trust—the Paegles had begun by sending the old woman a Christmas card. Then they had written letters, sent packages of clothing for Simas's children, and, finally, had mailed a formal invitation for her to visit the United States. They had arranged for prepaid airplane tickets to New York to be left for her in Moscow. But they had not heard from her in the past few weeks, and their anxiety had become unbearable. They wanted to be sure she was willing to come to America—and they wanted to hear her voice.

"Yes," the old woman said, "the passport office in our region rejected everything because there is no [U.S.] stamp [on the invitation], and he said that if I can leave, it will only be in three months. . . ."

Grazina asked whether Mrs. Sulskis had received the packages. Then the conversation returned to more substantive matters.

"About my daughter," Mrs. Sulskis said, remembering that the Paegles, in their letters, had told her to refer to Simas as a girl in all communications, to confuse the KGB. "I don't know anything. I don't get any letters from her."

"How is your health?"

"Now, it's fine, thank you. I am leaving on Monday for Klaipeda, and from Klaipeda to Moscow to get the stamp. . . . I'll call you and let you know what I hear in Moscow, yes?"

"Please."

Marija Sulskis arrived in Moscow by train late on the afternoon of March 19, accompanied by Birute Pasilis. Birute, the mother of a Lithuanian political prisoner, was along to protect her and translate for her, since the old woman spoke only Lithuanian. The two of them went straight to the American embassy. While Birute watched from behind a tree, Mrs. Sulskis walked up to the main entrance and told the Soviet policeman guarding it that she had to get inside. He yelled at her and refused to let her in. She retreated in tears.

From the embassy, the two women took a taxi to the apartment of a woman who belonged to one of the Russian dissident groups.

Birute told the woman what had happened. The woman listened, then made a few phone calls. A few hours later, two men arrived at the apartment—one, a heavy-set, balding man with glasses, a biologist named Sergei Kovalev; the other, a thin, dark-eyed physicist named Andrei Tverdokhlebov. Both were dissidents, members of the Moscow Human Rights Committee, founded in 1970 by the famous Andrei Sakharov. The two men sat on a mattress in the middle of the room and leafed through Mrs. Sulskis's documents in silence. As they were certain the apartment was bugged by the KGB, they conversed only by scribbling notes and passing them to one another. Then Kovalev rose from the mattress, went to the phone, made a brief call, then wrote out a note that said it was time to leave.

The four of them—Kovalev, Tverdokhlebov, Birute, and Mrs. Sulskis—piled into a taxi and rode to a small two-room apartment on a wide boulevard that is the perimeter of central Moscow. Sakharov was waiting for them in the front room.

Tall, graying, and slightly stooped, he greeted his visitors, then sent the women into the kitchen to prepare supper. He and the other men ensconced themselves in a corner of the living room next to an overstuffed, glass-front bookcase. There Sakharov sat behind his typewriter, studied Mrs. Sulskis's documents, and quickly typed out a copy of them, just to be safe. He did not say a word. Then he wrote out a letter on her behalf to the American embassy. Later he passed a series of notes around the dining hall describing the plan of action that he had developed. Each time a note went all the way around the table and returned to Sakharov, he lit it with a match and dropped it into an empty bottle, where it burned into ashes. They talked as well, but the conversation was staged solely for the benefit of the KGB microphones which everyone assumed were present.

"There is no need for you to go to the American embassy," Sakharov told Mrs. Sulskis through Birute's translation of the notes. "Kovalev will do it for you. I want you to stay in that apartment all day. Do you understand?" Mrs. Sulskis nodded in agreement. Who was she to question Sakharov?

The next morning, while she sat obediently in the apartment,

181

Kovalev went to the American embassy. A half-dozen dissidents were outside, standing behind poles and waiting in taxis so they could watch. The moment Kovalev got out of the taxi, a black sedan pulled up behind it. Four plainclothes KGB agents got out.

"Give me the documents," their leader told him.

Kovalev pretended not to hear.

"We know who you are and why you are here," the agent said. There was no response. "Where is the old woman?"

"I don't know," Kovalev said. "Visiting relatives, probably."

"Give me the documents."

"You can have all of my documents," Kovalev said with a calm that came from experience in these sorts of situations. "My passport, whatever you like. But you can't have hers."

"Get in the car."

Kovalev obeyed. Tverdokhlebov, who was watching in a taxi, followed the black sedan to KGB headquarters.

Later in the day, Kovalev was released. He went right back to the embassy, where, this time, two American consular officials, Steve Steiner and Robert Ober, were outside the gates waiting for him. They took him inside and stamped Mrs. Sulskis's documents. By nightfall she was on the train back to Lithuania with her documents, knowing that she had cleared one bureaucratic hurdle on the way to America and that the Moscow Human Rights Committee would help her clear the others.

A month later, as the State Department's Dyess had promised, Mrs. Sulskis received a telegram inviting her to the American embassy in Moscow to discuss her citizenship claim. She was told to bring three photographs, her marriage certificate, and her Soviet internal passport. On April 27, the day before she was to leave for Moscow, a KGB agent in a trenchcoat appeared at her door.

"I hear you're going to America," the agent said.

"That's right. You have good ears."

"Why do you want to do that?"

"There's nothing here for me anymore."

"I'm telling you," he said, trying to intimidate her. "You're not going to get there. You won't even get to Moscow."

Mrs. Sulskis did not look intimidated.

"What don't you like about your life here?" he asked.

"Everything."

"Such as . . ."

"Well, there's my measly pension. I know widows who get fifty-six rubles a month. I get twenty-six. Is that fair? What of my grandchildren? No one helps me with food and clothing for them. Nobody asks. Nobody cares." She summoned tears. "While my husband was alive, we wouldn't complain or even think of going to America. But he's dead and I have to eat!" She opened the cabinet in her kitchen. "Look at how much medication I have to take. I'm very high-strung. My heart is bad and my nerves aren't so good. How am I supposed to keep paying for the medication?"

"Hmmm," the agent muttered, collecting his thoughts. "I hear that if you go to America, you figure your son will follow. Don't count on that," he laughed. "It'll never happen."

He offered her a deal. He would see to it that she would have food for her house, wood for the fireplace, and hay for the cow if she would give up the idea of going to America. She ordered him out of the house.

She left the house that night—to avoid the KGB—and set out across the muddy fields, wading through puddles and slipping into drainage ditches in the darkness. She stopped at a friend's house for a few hours' sleep and started out again at sunrise, heading for a bus stop well outside of town. To avoid being followed, she changed buses a half-dozen times and eventually made it to the Vilnius train station. There she waited on the platform for the train to Moscow.

Suddenly, she felt a hand on either arm, dragging her along the platform. She started to scream, then passed out. When she came to, she was in a KGB cubicle inside the station. The KGB agent standing in front of her gave her a glass of water.

"We warned you not to go," he said.

"I know. But the Americans were expecting me."

"I see," the agent said. "You won't be going today. This is the [May Day] holiday season. You can go later in the month, if you still want to."

183

"What's wrong with now!" she cried. "I'm not carrying a bomb. I'm not going to set Moscow on fire. I'm just a little old lady."

"I told you—not today."

"The agents who came to my house told me I couldn't go there at all," she said. "They didn't say anything about it being all right later."

"They were wrong. You can go later. Now get out of here!"

On May 15, Marija Sulskis left Griskabudis again for Moscow. Again the dissidents had mapped out a wildly indirect route to make it harder for the KGB to follow her. She took one bus, then another, then a train, then another bus, then hitchhiked a ride on a truck which left her off in the middle of the woods. Frantically, she flagged down a motorcycle and hopped on. Wearing a crash helmet, clutching her suitcase with one hand and the cyclist with the other, she rode for miles through rain and sleet to a remote railroad station. There she boarded the train for Moscow.

The next day, when the train arrived in Moscow, she walked off into the station and tried to look casual, even though she had no idea where to go or what to do. A woman whom she recognized from her previous trip walked up alongside her, kissed her on the cheek, and said, "Hello, Mother." The woman took her to Kovalev, and Kovalev told her that he would accompany her to the embassy the next day. He had a Lithuanian–Russian translator with him. The Americans would need to get a lot of questions answered, he said, and they might not have anyone at the embassy who understood Lithuanian. So through the translator, Kovalev asked her all the questions he thought the Americans would ask and wrote down the answers in Russian.

At 3:30 the next afternoon, followed by an unmarked KGB sedan, Kovalev took Mrs. Sulskis in a taxi to a tree-filled park about 200 yards from the embassy. The American consular officers, Steiner and Ober, were in the park waiting for them. The Americans escorted them into the embassy and the office of Leonard Willems, a thin, curly-haired consular officer in his mid-thirties. Willems took the internal passport, marriage certificate, and photographs Mrs. Sulskis had brought with her. He looked at the passport, which listed place of birth, and smiled.

"Brooklyn, New York!" he shouted.

Willems asked a series of questions, most of which Kovalev could answer in Russian for her. But soon there were questions Kovalev had not anticipated. Had Mrs. Sulskis ever been a member of the Communist Party or the Communist Youth? Had she ever signed anything to waive her U.S. citizenship? After fifteen futile minutes of hand signals and charades, Willems suggested that Mrs. Sulskis call Grazina Paegle in New Jersey and let her translate the answers over the phone.

"Grazina!" the old woman shouted through the static once the call was put through. "I am here!"

"Oh, thank God! Finally! We were so worried!"

"You know, I no longer resemble a person, all that I have lived through. I only got here through good Russian people," she said, referring to Kovalev and other members of the Human Rights Committee.

"Yes," Grazina replied. "I know about those people. Listen, did the people at the embassy give you an American passport?"

"They are making it up now."

"What will you do now?"

"I don't know—whatever the people here tell me."

"You still don't have your visa from the Russians?" Grazina asked.

"They won't even talk to me there. They won't even look at the documents. I went there three times now. I don't know what to do."

"Today, were there problems?"

"No," Mrs. Sulskis said. "Today there were no problems. . . . The KGB followed me every day. I didn't think I would make it here. . . . Now, how I will return, I don't know. Your government official wants to talk to you."

Mrs. Sulskis handed the phone to Willems.

"Obviously, you speak Lithuanian and English," he said with relief. "We are having a little problem here; in fact, we are having a lot of trouble here because of the language barrier. . . . We are able to communicate with a little bit of Russian and pantomime.'' He asked Grazina the questions he had been unable to ask Mrs. Sulskis, then put Mrs. Sulskis back on the phone. Grazina asked the questions in Lithuanian, got the answers, and translated them back into English for Willems.

"Sir," Grazina asked, "is she getting her passport?"

"Well, we've issued her one, but we are holding it in the embassy. In other words, it's her passport and she can use it anytime she wants. It's just here for safekeeping."

"Do you have any indication as to how soon she'll be allowed out?"

"No," he said, "none at all. . . . She's not the only case like this, you know. We have a list of twelve or fourteen U.S. citizens that the ambassador has raised with the Soviet government on a high level for whom we are trying to get exit permission. And you know, it's a hassle. It goes on and on. Some of these cases go on for years."

"So what happens?"

"I just can't offer you any sort of false optimism, that's all, that her case is going to get resolved quickly."

The next day, after Mrs. Sulskis had reluctantly left the embassy to return to Lithuania, Willems sent a cable to Washington suggesting that Mrs. Sulskis's citizenship surely made Simas a citizen, too. Willems wanted permission to press the case by requesting immediate access to Simas under the Soviet-American consular convention.

Permission was denied. From the beginning, the State Department had moved with caution in pursuing the Kudirka case for fear it might become a "major irritant" in U.S.-Soviet relations and the grand design of détente. On several occasions, the department had warned embassy officials, who were eager to resolve the matter quickly, "not to precipitate premature confrontations with Soviet or Lithuanian officials." Willems's recommendations drew a similar response—orders for a safer, slower course of action.

The return cable from Washington read:

Department wishes to resolve Kudirka citizenship case as expeditiously as possible. However, we will be in stronger position to support a request for consular access to him if we have some documentary evidence to show that he has a potential claim to U.S. citizenship. Accordingly, as first step, embassy should endeavor to obtain Kudirka's birth certificate and other pertinent documents from Mrs. Sulskis which would be helpful in establishing his claim. . . .

If Mrs. Sulskis is unable to locate copy of Kudirka's birth certificate, embassy should request copy through [Soviet] Ministry of Foreign Affairs in accordance with usual procedure. Depending on results of these efforts, we can then consider requesting consular access to Kudirka.

A few days later, toward the end of May, a letter for Simas arrived at Perm from his daughter, Lolita. The letter had come from Griskabudis.

"Mommy and I are here on a visit," Lolita wrote. "We did not find Grandma at home. She's away in Moscow in hopes of making preparations for her trip to her homeland. . . ."

Simas understood. His mother was trying to go to the United States to plead his case to the American government.

Sixteen

Summer was normally the most tolerable time in a labor camp. The sun burned the lingering cold out of a man's bones and dried the mud that covered the camp. But the summer of 1974 at Perm began on a grim note. The camp authorities simply stopped giving medical treatment; the injured and the sick were being allowed to die. One prisoner, with only days left in a twenty-five-year sentence, had a stroke chopping wood and the camp doctor, Petrov, never raised a hand to stop him from dying. Another man, suffering from a painful and undiagnosed ailment that had caused the skin on his shins to crack, could not stand the pain when he was deprived of his medication. He hanged himself, leaving this note: "There is no more strength left to suffer."

Then a young Ukrainian dissident named Sopyliak was beaten by a KGB captain for refusing the captain's order that he stop exercising. Even in a labor camp, guards were not to strike prisoners. Now, for the first time since the death train had rolled into Perm nearly two years before, there was mass support for protest.

Two days after the beating, fifty prisoners refused to go to work. Many of the strikers were newly arrived prisoners, eager to test themselves against the camp administration. Simas was on strike, too. His mother's activities and the prospect of America were hazy and far away. What was happening at Perm had to be dealt with first. His fellow protesters from Potma, men like Jonas Silinskas, Lev Lukjanenko, and David Chernoglaz, joined the strike as well. Others, too ill to risk punishment, submitted written protests in support of the action. The strike continued for a second day, without the expected mass arrests. The administration had decided to wait, then pick out the ringleaders. At least thirty prisoners were still off the job when, on the fourth day, Major Kotov, the camp commander, made an extremely rare appearance before the entire camp population at evening lineup.

"We have a problem," he said, as he paced slowly in front of the prisoners with his hands clasped behind his back. "It is a mutual problem. We cannot meet your demands immediately. We have to coordinate with Moscow, and before we can do that we must have a clear understanding of the grievances. I ask you to understand my position. I understand that your protests may be well founded, but I cannot negotiate with an entire camp population. I am interested in working this out. Send me your leaders, and we will talk."

After the lineup, the strikers met in the yard and agreed not to send their leaders to Kotov. Any "leader" who walked into Kotov's office to chat would probably never return. But the guards already knew who the leaders were, and the next day they were called in one by one.

"Kudirka," Kotov said when Simas arrived. "What I have to say to you won't take long."

"What do you want from me?" Simas snapped.

"I want to know whether you will be going to work someday soon."

"Most definitely not."

"O.K., then, eight days in the isolator for you."

Simas, who had expected worse, blithely entered the cell, finding Chernoglaz and Lukjanenko already there. They stayed in the cell for two days, discussing the strike and plotting the moves they would make once they got back out into the living zone. On the morning of the third day, they were awakened before dawn, taken back to their barracks, and told to pack their belongings.

"Where do you think we're going?" Simas asked Lukjanenko.

189

"Probably down to the next camp. They just want to get us away from here. They must think we're a bad influence. Wonder where they'd get that idea?"

"Think we're going to Vladimir?" Simas asked, recalling the vivid image of that prison Peshchany had painted for him years before at Potma.

"No. They can't commit us to Vladimir without a trial," Lukjanenko said. "And we haven't had a trial."

They rode for three hours in a black van over bumpy, dusty roads. Then the van stopped and the prisoners climbed out, expecting to see their new camp. Instead they saw a dilapidated barn that smelled of cow dung. They were led inside, where there were two rows of benches, a table in front, and three uniformed guards. An overweight man in a worn gray business suit was shuffling papers at a desk off to the side.

"All rise," one of the guards said. A stern-faced, middle-aged woman walked in and sat at the bench in the front. This old barn was the Perm Region's version of a courtroom. In this ludicrous setting, Simas and his friends were about to go on trial.

"The court will come to order," the woman said. She conferred with the man in the gray suit, then looked toward Simas. "You are first. State your name."

"Simas Kudirka."

The judge summoned a KGB captain from Perm to recite the prisoner's alleged sins. "He has demonstrated himself to be an extremely undisciplined incorrigible who has not fulfilled his work quotas, has been totally uncooperative with the camp administration, and has committed numerous transgressions against camp regulations. Because such behavior was a negative influence upon the camp population, we appeal to the people's court to channel Kudirka into a closed prison atmosphere." The man in the gray suit, the prosecutor, added the specifics.

"Will the accused please stand?" the judge asked. He did. "What is your response to this?"

"It is insanity to discuss anything with you and a colossal waste of time," Simas replied. At his last trial, he had spoken his mind.

But there was no point in giving a speech if there was no audience to hear it.

"This court will adjourn to deliberate on its verdict," the judge announced as she left the room. She was back in two minutes.

"On the basis of the evidence presented against this man, the property of Camp Thirty-six, Perm Region, this court finds the complaint justified," she said. "This court exercises its right to isolate Simas Kudirka from the general prison population of the camps and sentences him to three years of isolation and detention in Vladimir Prison. Next case."

The guards took Simas back out to the van. The trial had taken twelve minutes. It took thirty minutes more for Lukjanenko to be sentenced to eighteen months in Vladimir (the balance of his labor camp sentence) and for Chernoglaz to get ten months (his balance) at the same place. The black van took them to the station, where they boarded a death train for Vladimir.

Simas's mother was sitting in the office of the KGB regional commander in a town fifteen miles from Griskabudis. In the six weeks since her return from Moscow, she had found that being declared an American citizen did not guarantee a person a free pass out of the Soviet Union.

"Would you like to visit your son?" the commander asked.

Of course she would. She had traveled all the way to Perm in December 1973, even though she had no formal invitation, only to be turned away at the camp gate.

Without waiting for an answer, he handed her two forms. "Fill these out and have him fill them out when you see him—and he's a free man."

"I don't believe it. What are these papers anyway?"

"He just has to write that he's sorry for what he did to get arrested in the first place. It can be short, nothing elaborate. Something like this: 'I made a big mistake. I admit that I was guilty, and I ask that the state forgive me.' "

"He won't sign it."

"What kind of mother are you if you can't make him sign it?"

"I'm telling you he won't sign it."

"That is the offer. If you'll take the papers to him, you and his children can go visit him with an escort we'll provide. You'll leave on July 15."

"I'm not going," she said, dropping the forms into the trash can on her way out.

She hurried back to Griskabudis and called Grazina Paegle in New Jersey to tell her what had happened.

Grazina immediately called Richard Combs, one of William Dyess's assistants on the Soviet Desk at the State Department. She told Combs of the offer; she did not tell him that Mrs. Sulskis had rejected it. She hoped that the prospect of establishing direct contact with Simas—via his mother—would get the State Department moving.

It did. Combs knew that the American embassy in Moscow and Mrs. Sulskis in Griskabudis had both been rebuffed in attempts to get a copy of Simas's birth certificate. He knew that the embassy had already told Mrs. Sulskis (through the Moscow Human Rights Committee) that an affidavit, signed by friends or relatives, would suffice in the absence of a birth certificate. If Mrs. Sulskis was going to visit Simas, Combs figured, American officials should talk to her first. And that talk would give her the chance to file her affidavit.

Late on the afternoon of July 13, Consular Officer Leonard Willems met Simas's mother in the lobby of a tourist hotel in Vilnius. At the outset, she told Willems that she would not be visiting her son. The American was surprised, but not perturbed. At his request, she filled out an application formally requesting American citizenship for Simas. Then he asked her for the affidavit. She gave him an unnotarized statement, handwritten in Lithuanian and signed by three neighbors, that Simas was indeed Marija Sulskis's boy, born out of wedlock.

"I think Simas now will be an American," Willems said before boarding the train back to Moscow.

Two days later, the embassy in Moscow cabled Washington that it had registered Simas Kudirka as an American citizen. Two days after that, the State Department issued the following statement from Washington:

> After an investigation of all available evidence and on the basis of his mother's application upon his behalf, the U.S. embassy in Moscow has determined that Simas Kudirka derived U.S. citizenship from his mother, and in the absence of evidence to the contrary, has retained U.S. citizenship. With the department's concurrence, the embassy has therefore registered him as a U.S. citizen. We are consulting with the embassy in Moscow on how we can best protect Mr. Kudirka's interest in his present situation.

The next day, an American consular officer went to the Soviet Ministry of Foreign Affairs in Moscow and handed a note to an official there. The note quoted Article Twelve, Paragraph Three of the Soviet–American consular convention and asked that American representatives be allowed to meet with Simas without delay.

The Soviet official said the ministry would examine the request and reply. He did not say how or when.

By the end of July, after three weeks in Vladimir Prison, Simas knew that the citadel deserved its reputation as the hell of the Soviet prison system. He had not suffered much yet, if only because it was still summer. In warm weather, the cement floor, the stone walls, the dampness, the darkness, and lack of heat were only inconveniences, not serious threats to a man's health. To understand what lay ahead, all he need do was look around the narrow room. The cell had six residents: three newcomers—Simas, Chernoglaz, and Lukjanenko—and three veterans of Vladimir. The veterans all looked like skeletons.

Anatoly Afanasyenko, a twenty-six-year-old dissident who slept below Simas, spent all day in bed, too weak to get up. Underneath Chernoglaz was a twenty-four-year-old Ukrainian nationalist named Mikhail Jacysin, a tall, olive-skinned man whose skull seemed to bulge through his skin. And underneath Lukjanenko was Vladimir Bukovsky.

At thirty-two, Bukovsky was already a legend in the Soviet dissident movement. A slight man made even slighter by months of bread and water, he had spent the previous eleven years going in and out of labor camps, prisons, and mental hospitals for owning forbidden books, demonstrating on behalf of nonconformist writers, and supporting other dissidents. What made him special was what he had done in January 1971. He had transmitted to the West solid evidence that Soviet psychiatrists were certifying perfectly sane political dissidents as psychotics so they could be committed to special mental institutions—without trial and without appeal—for as long as the KGB wanted.

"The most important part of it is that you never have, you never know, the end of your being in such a place," he would say of the mental hospitals in an interview in the United States after his own release. "Any prisoner may be in very bad conditions of imprisonment; all the same, he has a light in the end of the tunnel. . . . But when you're in a psychiatric mental hospital, they put you in without any certain term. Your liberation would depend upon the decision of doctors, decision of psychiatrists. They demand of every prisoner in such a place to recant, to condemn, to denounce his own actions, to recognize himself mentally ill. Without such recognition, without such expression, they will never let anybody go. And when you refuse to recant, to change your beliefs and attitudes, they never will say that they will punish you. They say to you only one thing. You are an ill man. You cannot understand how ill, how ill you are."

Simas was in awe of Bukovsky. He was too intimidated by the man's knowledge and reputation to even attempt becoming close to him. When Bukovsky talked, however, Simas listened, and Bukovsky spent many afternoons lecturing to his cellmates on psychiatric repression. He was obsessed with the subject. He wanted his cellmates to be ready when the authorities at Vladimir started playing psychiatric tricks, as he was sure they would. One day early in August, a month after Simas's arrival, the six prisoners were summoned, one at a time, before a doctor who was supposedly going to determine their work potential. The first five prisoners were interviewed for thirty minutes each. The last man—quiet, passive Jacysin—was gone for five hours. When he returned, he stood motionless and glassy-eyed for several minutes.

"Mikhail," Lukjanenko pleaded, "what did they do to you?"

Jacysin broke into uncontrollable sobs and began pounding the door, screaming over and over again, "I am not a swine! You will not turn me into a swine!" He whirled around with his fists clenched and his teeth gritted, his face distorted with tension. He paced the length of the cell for an hour, saying nothing, staring at the floor. Then he sat on the bed, picked up a book, flipped through it for a few seconds, and hurled it on the floor. He picked up a pencil and a piece of paper and started scribbling furiously. Then he was on his feet again, pacing at a furious clip.

"He's been drugged," Bukovsky said. "We're all being programmed for something. I just hope we see it coming before it arrives."

Throughout the next week, Jacysin became ever more frenetic. He never spoke a word, and his writing was incoherent. On the sixth day, he entered a new stage, wedging his body into the eight-inch opening between his bed and the wall and standing there for hours, as if he were hiding. He crossed and recrossed his arms and stared blankly at the wall.

"He's reaching a crisis," Bukovsky said.

For the next three days, Jacysin refused to use the toilet bucket in the corner of the room. He seemed squeamish about pulling down his pants in front of the five other men. He paced long past lights-out, not going to bed at all. After four days and nights without sleeping, he stopped. He stood by his bed, put his hands together in front of his chest, and rocked back and forth on his heels, his stiff body quivering, his eyes unblinking for hours on end. Just before daybreak, there was a loud thump as Jacysin crashed to the floor. Simas jumped out of bed and crouched at Jacysin's side. He heard no breathing. He picked up the man's hand. It was cold.

"Brothers!" he shouted. "Jacysin! He's dead!"

The others awakened quickly and wrapped the body in a blanket, picked it up, and laid it on a bed. They leaned over the body and heard faint breathing. They put more blankets on him, and the breathing picked up. His whole body started trembling.

"Guards!" they shouted, banging on the cell door. "Guards! Help us!" They piled jackets on top of the blankets. The trembling subsided and Jacysin dozed off.

A half hour passed. No guards came. Simas, Bukovsky, and the others sat up watching Jacysin, wondering what he would do next. Jacysin stirred, took off the covers, and stood up. His face was still tense, his features drawn. He turned toward the toilet bucket in the corner. His cellmates turned away and pretended not to watch. He pulled his pants down and sat on the toilet seat. A minute later, he pulled up his pants, turned around, and looked down into the bowl. Then he thrust his head into the bowl and began shoving his own waste into his mouth.

Without a word, the other five grabbed his arms and pulled him away from the bucket. He struggled ferociously to get loose, growling, "Let me go!" Then he relaxed. For a few seconds, he seemed almost normal. He broke free with a sudden burst of energy and lurched into the bucket again, soaking his entire body with water and smearing his face with excrement. He grunted and growled some more.

"Guards!" Bukovsky shouted. "We need help right now! We have a man who's going out of his mind!"

No guards came. Eventually, the prisoners subdued Jacysin, carried him to bed, and sat on top of him until he fell asleep. An hour later, he awoke with a shudder. "Let me go!" he yelled. "I am a swine." He hurled his body onto the concrete floor. His cellmates dove on top of him, then helped him to his feet. He began to bend at the waist, as if trying to touch his toes, and crashed head first into the concrete.

"We cannot let him kill himself!" Bukovsky shouted as they dragged Jacysin back into bed. Finally, Jacysin's body sagged. He was spent.

At 8:30, three and a half hours after the outburst began, a KGB captain and the doctor who had interviewed them all ten days earlier entered the room. The doctor put his hand on Jacysin's shoulder. "What happened here?" he asked, as if talking to a five-year-old. He stared into the prisoner's eyes. "Quietly now, we will go." Like an obedient dog, the prisoner followed him out the door.

Simas and his cellmates never saw Jacysin again nor learned what became of him. They just wondered which of them would be next to lose his mind.

For Daiva Kezys and Grazina Paegle, the summer of 1974 was a time for waiting and worrying. There was almost nothing more they could do, now that Simas had been declared a citizen. It was the Soviet Union's move.

The women had already succeeded in getting their powerful friends on Capitol Hill to pressure the State Department to pressure the Soviets. On July 22, five days after the citizenship declaration, Senators Henry Jackson of Washington and Jacob Javits of New York had brought the case to the personal attention of Secretary of State Kissinger. Jackson was conferring with Kissinger almost daily about the so-called Jackson amendment, which would tie any increase in U.S.-Soviet trade to increased emigration out of the Soviet Union. Over the years, Jackson had received thousands of requests to intervene on behalf of would-be Soviet émigrés, but he had nearly always refused, feeling that his clout was best applied to the overall issue, to the amendment. But this time, he made an exception. Both he and Javits told Kissinger they wanted every effort made to get Simas out of prison and into the United States. Kissinger assured them that he would do what he could.

"As I indicated to you at breakfast this morning," the secretary wrote both senators later that day, "I intend to raise the case with Soviet Chargé Vorontsov [the number two man in the Soviet embassy] to ensure that the Soviet government understands the importance we attach to the matter and that Mr. Kudirka receives the full protection due him as an American citizen."

In fact, Kissinger did not talk to Vorontsov; Deputy Assistant Secretary for European Affairs John A. Armitage talked to him on July 25.

Stressing that he was speaking on direct instructions from and on behalf of Kissinger, Armitage summarized for Vorontsov the procedure by which Simas's American citizenship had been established. Then he reviewed the clause of the consular convention entitling American officials to quick access to American citizens in the Soviet Union. He noted that "more than four days" had passed and said "we expect the Soviet government to meet its obligations under the convention and afford embassy access to Kudirka." He went on to warn Vorontsov what might happen if access were denied.

"In our view," Armitage said, "as the fact of Kudirka's American citizenship registers among the American public, public attention will be increasingly directed and focussed on the issue. The question is most unlikely to go away and could become something of a cause célèbre, constituting persistent and continuing irritant in our relations. This would be in neither of our interest. We recognize the issue is a difficult and sensitive one, but we believe it would be in the overriding interest of both sides if the Soviet government could find a way to arrange that Kudirka and members of his family be allowed to come to the United States. While difficult, such a decision now likely would be easier than later, when prestige considerations might become involved."

Armitage closed with a reminder that "this presentation should be treated as coming directly from the secretary." Vorontsov said he would pass the message along to his government.

The next day, American officials in Moscow increased the pressure by returning to the Ministry of Foreign Affairs and once more demanding access to Simas. They made the visit on these direct orders from Kissinger:

> Embassy should stress that consular convention expressly provides for access "without delay" and that in particular circumstances of Kudirka case, where Kudirka's whereabouts and situation are well known to Soviet side, we cannot understand delay beyond the four days specified in paragraph two of the convention's protocol.
>
> If Soviets seem genuinely perplexed over our finding that Kudirka is U.S. citizen, embassy may, of course, explain relevant

sections of U.S. law. Focus of our representations should not, however, be allowed to shift from Soviet obligation to provide prompt consular access and U.S. sovereign right to determine questions of U.S. citizenship.

The visit was made, but still the Soviets refused to respond to the American request.

Meanwhile, on Capitol Hill demands for Simas's release were mounting, just as Armitage had warned the Soviets they would. Republican Senator Charles Percy of Illinois kept bringing the case to the attention of his own contacts in the Soviet embassy. The House of Representatives, acting on the urging of Congressman Robert Hanrahan, passed a resolution urging Kissinger to devote his full energy to obtaining Simas's release. Congressman Edward Derwinski, a Chicago Republican who had long been a spokesman for Eastern European ethnic causes, was taking up the case with his long-time congressional colleague Vice-President (soon to be President) Gerald R. Ford. And lawmakers in both houses were receiving thousands of letters on Simas's behalf, many of them generated by a campaign organized by the Knights of Lithuania.

Two weeks passed with still no answer from the Soviets. On August 9, another cable went from Kissinger to the embassy in Moscow. It ordered embassy officials to return at once to the Soviet Ministry of Foreign Affairs and reiterate the American demand for access. The State Department was becoming angry.

Embassy officials were ordered to make the following points:

A. Over three weeks have elapsed since the embassy presented the ministry with a note requesting consular access to Simas Kudirka. . . . We have since had no official response from the Soviet government.

B. This matter involves a question of principle which transcends our concern for the individual, important as that is on its own merits. At this stage in our bilateral relations, it is essential that all agreements we have concluded be fully and faithfully adhered to.

C. . . . In our view, the [consular] convention is not consistent with the three-week delay. . . .

D. As the Soviets must know, this case is a matter of personal concern to the Secretary of State as well as to a number of leading senators and congressmen. Further delay on the question of consular access could be acutely embarrassing to both our governments since it could lead our congress and public to question the efficacy of the consular convention.

E. We recognize the Soviet Union's sovereign right under international law to consider Mr. Kudirka a Soviet citizen. We are not questioning his status under Soviet law. By the same token, we trust the Soviet government recognizes our sovereign right to determine matters of U.S. citizenship. . . .

F. In view of the above considerations, we feel compelled to call this matter to the attention of the U.S.A. division [of the ministry] and urge consular access to Mr. Kudirka be arranged without further delay.

The men from the American embassy went to the Soviet ministry and made all those points. The Soviet officials listened. There was no answer, and no indication of when there would be an answer. And in Washington and Moscow, the American diplomats waited some more, knowing at least that no answer was better than a negative answer.

At noon on August 23, almost two weeks after Jacysin's breakdown, a guard came to Simas's cell in Vladimir and told him to pack. Simas was shaken, thinking that perhaps his turn for the psychiatric ward had come. He packed quickly and turned to face Chernoglaz and Lukjanenko. He had shared the last three years of his life with hundreds of men like these two. He had known Chernoglaz and Lukjanenko since the first months in Potma. They were his last links to the men who had become his family: Nikolai Sharygin-Budalak (now in Vladimir), Mecys Kybartas (dead), Jonas Kadzionis (in Perm), Jonas Silinskas (in Perm), and Shimon Grilius (free and on his way to Israel). He hugged them tight and started to cry.

"Now I want both of you bums to stop smoking," said Simas, who did not smoke, hoping that talk would stop his tears. "That stuff is garbage. You have to go easy on your hearts." But it did not work. He could not get his mind off the future. "What do I do if they try to drug me?"

"There are ways that you can make them break off the hypodermic needle in your vein," Lukjanenko said solemnly. "At least that way you kill yourself before they drive you insane."

"But Simas, that won't happen to you," Chernoglaz insisted, crying too. "You haven't done enough to deserve it."

They exchanged small gifts—a cube of sugar, a crust of bread, a piece of candy—and Simas pressed their hands hard and walked into the corridor.

He was led from his cell, which was on the second floor of Cellblock Two, through a tunnel, and down the stairs to the first floor of Cellblock One. His heart felt tight. The guard led him into a large room where there was an officer, a civilian, and a tripod with a camera on top of it.

"Get undressed!" the officer ordered.

Simas began to undress, expecting the familiar KGB internal search, the prelude to a long journey.

"Stop right there!" the officer said when Simas had removed his jacket and his shirt. "Here, take this." He was handed a clean white shirt. He put it on and began to button it up the front. The civilian handed him a tie. All of a sudden, Simas had a vision of his picture in a newspaper. He was wearing a white shirt and tie. The picture purported to show how well political prisoners were treated at Vladimir.

He tore off the shirt and threw it on the floor.

"Why don't you take this shirt and go hang yourselves!" he yelled. "But before you do that, would you mind explaining to me what this little masquerade is all about?"

"We must photograph you," the officer said.

"I have a uniform. I am a prisoner. I will be more than happy to be photographed in my uniform."

"Our orders are to photograph you in civilian clothes."

"Well, look, you're going to photograph me in my uniform or not at all."

"Let's not waste time, prisoner."

"I've got plenty of time to waste," Simas said, smiling. "About

201

six years and three months. . . . Why don't you tell me what this is all about?''

''I have my orders.''

''Why don't you bring the guy who gave you your orders here and let me talk to him.''

The officer stalked out of the room. He was back in a few minutes.

''We don't need the picture,'' he said. ''Get dressed.''

Another guard led him out the door and into the courtyard back past Cellblock Two, then back toward Cellblock One, right, and then left, into one building and back out again. He was totally bewildered. Where was he going, and what did the photographs have to do with anything? He was given lunch and led to a tiny cell.

The guard left him there for a few minutes, then came back and took him for another long walk. This time the path led through a glass door, up a flight of steps, past a secretary, and into an elegant office. A KGB colonel sat behind the main desk. A fat, middle-aged civilian was off to the left. Simas stood with his hands behind his back, wondering what he had done to merit being sent to the warden's office.

''Kudirka here.''

''Sit down,'' the colonel ordered. There were ten seconds of silence. ''Kudirka, tell me, what did you dream last night?''

''What kind of dreams can a man have in a fortress like this?''

''Kudirka, you had to have a pleasant dream last night.''

''My pleasant dreams ended the day your occupation of my homeland began. I have tried not to dream at all.''

''Why don't we get to the point?'' the civilian in the corner suggested impatiently.

''All right,'' the colonel replied. He faced Simas. ''Why do you think you're here?''

''There is bad news from home?'' he said, thinking that his mother might have died.

''Wrong, Kudirka. You should be a very happy man today.'' He lifted a piece of paper in his right hand. ''Do you realize you are free?''

"Ugh," Simas groaned, thinking he was the victim of some particularly cruel joke.

The colonel stood, unfolded the paper, and read it aloud. "The Presidium of the Supreme Soviet, in its mercy and by this decree, has ordered that Simas Kudirka be released from further imprisonment." The colonel looked up. "The order is dated August 20, 1974. What do you have to say now?"

This had to be a trick.

"Tell me," Simas said. "Where the hell was the mercy of the Presidium of the Supreme Soviet when I was arrested and tried?"

The civilian in the corner laughed. "Amazing," he said. "No sign of gratitude. He's not even happy."

"Why should I be grateful? You tell me I have my freedom, now that you've burned out my insides and made me think the only freedom possible was in the grave."

"You're young, Kudirka," the colonel interrupted. "You will go back home to your mother. She's waiting for you. She's making plans to go back to the land of her birth."

The words jolted Simas. He knew from Lolita's letter that his mother was trying to go to the United States. Perhaps this was not a joke.

"If it's true," he said slowly, "and I'm going out of this fortress, then I turn to you as warden and as a man. As my last request, I ask you to go easy on the men in your cells. Show a little humanity, for you may get there yourself someday."

"You talk just like a BBC news commentator," the fat man in the corner noted. "Undoubtedly, once you get to the United States you'll throw all sorts of dirt at us. I advise against it."

"I will only tell the truth about what I have seen."

"Kudirka," the colonel said, "why don't you have a picture taken for us now? It's for the documents you need to leave here."

"Take it in my uniform," he insisted.

The colonel shook his head. "You can go."

———————

I walked out of the warden's office, and a guard took me to a tiny room and locked me inside. As I waited there, I remembered the last time I had felt close to freedom. I had been on the *Vigilant,* inside a gray little room much like this one. On that day, three years and nine months ago, I had been certain that I was a free man. But I had been wrong, terribly wrong. My hopes had risen, only to be crushed. I would not let myself be tricked this time. I would not believe it until it happened.

An hour passed. I told myself that if the person who unlocked that door had my belongings and a train ticket in his hand, I would start to believe it was true.

A guard opened the door. I stared at the man. No belongings. No train ticket. I felt sick. "Out!" he ordered.

I was led down the hall to a room where another camera was set up. They took my picture without making me change clothes and locked me back inside.

An hour later, the door opened again. This time, the guard was carrying my supper—meat, mashed potatoes, and fried onions. The meal was new evidence of my freedom; a prisoner did not eat meat and mashed potatoes. Then I remembered my first day at Perm, when a fine meal turned out to be the prelude to two years of torture.

The door opened again. The guard was carrying my belongings.

"Hurry up," he said. "It's seven thirty-five and you've got an eight o'clock train to catch."

I changed into a clean uniform, and the guard rushed me into the lobby of the prison administration building.

"Sit down," the guard ordered.

Several documents labeled "Release Papers" were pushed across a table to me. I stared at them.

"Sign them, quickly." In exchange for my signature, I was given fifty rubles.

"This way." Following the guard, I ran through a set of double doors, and suddenly I realized I was outside the prison. Outside the prison!

"Hurry! Hurry!" I ran after the guard, feeling that my suitcase was dragging me. My stomach was gurgling from the rich meal, my legs felt rubbery, and my whole body was soaked in sweat. I was still convinced there had to be a catch.

"Couldn't we go a little slower?" I gasped.

"Not if you're going to make that train."

When we arrived at the station, the train was already in. The guard took my fifty rubles, bought me a ticket to Moscow, and gave me the change. He led me onto the train, found me a seat, and left. I looked around me. This was no death train. It was a normal, everyday Moscow local full of men, women, and children. There were no guards, no German shepherds, no guns. The train jolted forward. I started to cry.

Seventeen

For the first few hours on the train, he would not allow himself to believe it was happening. Everything he had experienced since his jump—in Vilnius, Potma, Perm, and Vladimir—had taught him to assume the worst. What if a bunch of drunks boarded the train and decided to pick a fight with the newly released prisoner, the little man with the shaved head? What if some KGB agents had arranged for him to "fall" out of the train before it got to Moscow? Gradually, his pessimism weakened. The time had come to stop worrying about the KGB and start thinking about his own future, for the days ahead held a series of difficult choices, the first of which was coming up in a matter of minutes.

Where was he going once the train arrived in Moscow: toward Griskabudis and his mother, who had helped win his freedom, or toward Klaipeda and his wife, who had been living with another man while he had been in prison? When the train arrived in Moscow, he had still not decided where he was going. He just knew he wanted to get out of Russia as fast as possible. He took a taxi across town to the station from which trains to Lithuania left and checked the schedule. The first train to Lithuania would take him to Klaipeda—and Gene. He took it.

As the train headed west toward home, he became increasingly angry with Gene for having dared to live with another man. It had been so much easier to think of forgiving her when he had been in prison, when a thousand miles and another seven years of hard labor separated them. He had not expected he would ever see her again. Now, as he was speeding toward the rendezvous, the pain was as sharp as it had been the day he learned about the other man. He could not bear the thought of seeing her. He certainly couldn't go to the apartment. What if that man were there with her? What if Simas lost his temper and started a fight? What if the police arrested him? Wouldn't the KGB love an excuse to ship him back to the camps?

When he arrived in Klaipeda, he went to his uncle's house and found, to his relief, that Gene was out of town. She had gone to Griskabudis to pick up Lolita, who had spent the summer with his mother. Simas spent a day with his aunt, uncle, and cousins, catching up on family news. The next night, accompanied by his cousin Maryte, he boarded the overnight bus for Griskabudis.

It was nine o'clock on the morning of August 26 when Simas and Maryte arrived in the village and started walking up the dirt road toward the farmhouse where he had grown up. Maryte saw Mrs. Sulskis in the distance and ran ahead to tell the old woman the news. Mrs. Sulskis shoved the girl aside and stared down the road as her son's figure became larger and larger. He ran the last few yards into her arms.

"Hello, Mother," he whispered. "Even the condemned come back."

She tried to say something, but all she could do was sob.

In minutes, the news that Simas had returned was all over the village. Dozens of well-wishers ran out from the square and crowded around Simas and his mother as they stood in the road. One of the later arrivals reported that four black sedans had arrived in town, carrying KGB agents.

His mother looked shaken.

"Don't worry about that, Mama," Simas said, holding her close. "It's to be expected. If they let me out of Vladimir, they're not going to arrest me now. . . . Where's Gene?"

"God! You just missed her. She left with Lolita a few hours ago. They were going back to Klaipeda."

Simas and his mother walked to the house, and Evaldas, who

was eight years old, ran out to greet his grandmother. He stopped short when he saw the man with her.

"My child," she said, "do you know who this is?"

The boy held his hands behind his back and stared at the ground.

"Son, do you recognize me?"

The boy remained silent. Simas ran up to him, and bent down and hugged him; but the boy was stiff in his arms. Simas let him go, hoping that in time he would remember.

Later in the day, Simas and his mother sat at the kitchen table and talked about Gene.

"What are you going to do about her?" Mrs. Sulskis asked.

"I'm going to try to make it work."

"You are?"

"I can't say for sure right now, Mother. Maybe she doesn't want me back."

"Well, if you want to start trying now, she has a telephone."

He couldn't bring himself to call her. Now that he was in Griska-budis and she was in Klaipeda, he wanted her to make the first step. No one had forced her to start living with another man. She would have to come to him.

She came the next morning. She walked into the kitchen while he was eating breakfast.

He looked at her and his whole body stiffened. He stood up, but he could not move toward her. He just stared. In prison, he had envisioned her sometimes as a grief-stricken prisoner's wife, torn by her pain, who had little choice but to find another man. The real Gene did not look like she had suffered much. She had gained at least twenty pounds. For a second, he hated her more than ever.

She put down her packages—she had brought him some clothes—walked over to him, hugged him, and tried to kiss him. He pushed her aside.

"What are you so high and mighty about?" she asked. He didn't answer. They sat at the kitchen table and talked a little about the children. Mostly, they were silent.

Gene got up to leave after an hour. "Will you walk me to the bus?"

"Yes."

They walked along the dirt path up to the main road in silence. He was waiting for her to apologize for betraying him, to beg his forgiveness and ask for him to come back to her. But she said nothing of the kind, and he began to wonder if he really did want her back.

"And how is your husband?" he said through gritted teeth.

"Just what do you mean by that?" she said. "I have only one husband and that man is not the one you're talking about. You're my husband, or at least you were. Don't play with me, Simas."

"Why did you do it? You knew what I was going through. The news hurt so much. Was it really that tough for you out here?"

"Just a damn minute! Have you forgotten what you told me when we parted in Potma? I walked out of there with nothing. You pushed me out of your life. You told me it was over!"

"Gene, I had no choice."

"You don't know how hard it was for me. They [the KGB] came and they came and they came, always demanding that I try to influence your behavior, even though I knew you were too stubborn to be influenced by anyone. They offered me a divorce. They offered me an executive job at the store. And believe me, Simas, I was tempted. I think in many ways it was harder for me than for you."

"I know it was hard for you," he said, "but do you think I went to prison just to make things harder for you? When will you finally understand? You probably think I was a fool for speaking out and protesting. You always have."

"Well," Gene said, on the verge of tears. "Why don't you try to weigh my pain against your pain, and if it's a matter of who was hurt more, you decide. Just remember, I came here today. I came to you. And you let me know that you consider me a stranger."

She hurried off toward the bus station. He marched back to the house.

I got back to the house and just stared into space. I had blown it. I had lost her. I wanted her back, and I could have had her if I had just bent a little. I had been so cold. I closed my eyes and tried to ask Jonas Kadzionis and Shimon Grilius, my confidants from Perm, what I should do.

They asked me if I still wanted her.

I said I did. I told them that my dream was to take my whole family to America. I couldn't go without my wife and children.

"All right," they said. "You want her. So what's stopping you from telling her that?"

"I guess it's just my pride and ego, a feeling that she insulted me deeply by living with that man," I answered. "And if she was capable of living with that man, I wonder whether I know her at all. Maybe she has changed and we wouldn't be happy together anymore. I mean, could she really have cared that much if she ran into the arms of another man?"

"I thought we went through all this in prison, Simas," I could hear Shimon saying. "You left her all alone when you went to the camps. It was natural for her to turn to someone else. The real question is whether you still care about her."

"Oh, I care. I'm just not sure how much, if any, of our old love is still there."

"There's only one way to find out, isn't there?" they said.

"You're right. I'll go to her in Klaipeda."

Then Jonas and Shimon disappeared from my head, and I was alone with my thoughts. I remembered the old days in the seamen's barracks in Klaipeda, when we were just married, when we were so poor we didn't even have a bed. We only had one another, and we were happy. I had to go back to her. But why had I showed her so little feeling on our first meeting? Had camp life really dehumanized me that much? How did I become so cold, so proud, so sure of myself? I was going to have to show her that I was still a human being.

Three days later, Simas rang the bell of the apartment in Klaipeda that he and Gene had sought for years, then shared for only weeks. Gene came to the door. He kissed her on the cheek.

"Let's go for a walk," she said.

"Gene," he said as they walked. "I want you to forgive me for the other day. I didn't say what I really wanted to say. But please understand. I'm still not sure I can choose the right words to say what I mean. . . . Gene, will you come back to me?''

"That's totally up to you,'' she said, as if she did not much care one way or the other.

"What about him? Does he live with you?''

"No. There are times when he comes here. We began to have problems before you came back and he hasn't slept here since your return. Your being here makes him a stranger.''

"I want you back, Gene, but I'm not going to live in that apartment. If I see that guy, I don't know what I'll do to him. I know you're going to think this is a stupid question, but does he work for the KGB?''

"He's too dumb for something like that,'' she answered in a tone that said the question was stupid.

"You think I'm paranoid, but I'm serious. The KGB hasn't forgotten me. They're all over Griskabudis. We can't be too careful.'' He paused. The next question was the big one. "Gene, my mother already has an American passport. I'll be able to get one, too, or so I've been told. Before I go ahead with that, I want to know whether you will go with me.''

"I think so.''

"Are you sure?''

"Do you have any idea what life is like over there?''

"Whatever it's like, they don't have Siberia,'' he said. "I'm not trying to sell you a fairy tale. But it's a nation of immigrants, and we should be able to get along. I'm a healthy man. We'll learn the language. Anyway, there are many Lithuanians there already.''

"It'll be tough on the children,'' she said.

"It'll be tough on all of us for a year or two or three or four, but eventually we'll be all right. I'll use whatever strength I have left to get those kids the comforts they need and to make sure that truth, not lies, touches their hearts. Don't worry and don't be afraid. We can do it together.''

"And what about you, Simas? Are you going to continue to shoot your mouth off all the time? I want a husband, not a politician. The children need a father, not a prisoner.''

"Gene, I can't promise you I'll be quiet. I have seen too much. I

211

have spent the last four years in the best classroom in the world, and I must carry forth what I have learned. It is my duty.'' He paused and swallowed hard. ''Will you come with me?''

''All right.''

When Simas was released from Vladimir, American diplomats in Moscow were told that the Kudirka family's request to emigrate to the United States would be granted, although it might take time ''to work out all procedures.'' Based on that assurance, the United States had decided to take a low-key approach.

''During the time that the Soviet bureaucracy moves methodically through this case,'' Ambassador Walter J. Stoessel, Jr., cabled Washington, ''we would hesitate to take any action which would appear to be pressuring the Soviets unnecessarily. . . .'' Kissinger agreed, cabling back that Stoessel was to ''take no, repeat no, immediate action.'' Advisories went out to departmental spokesmen in both Moscow and Washington telling them to respond to all press queries on the Kudirka case with answers like ''I have no information on that.''

The strategy worked, and by mid-October the Soviets had approved the family's emigration. But now a new problem arose that had nothing whatsoever to do with Soviet–American relations: Where in the United States was Simas going to arrive—New York or Chicago? Without his knowing it, Simas had become the prize in a struggle for power and prestige within the Lithuanian-American community itself, and the arrival site had become the major point of contention.

What had happened to Simas on the *Vigilant* in 1970 had been the biggest thing to happen to the one million Lithuanians in the United States, as a group, since the Communist takeover of their motherland in 1944. During the postwar years, Lithuanian-Americans had grown used to the fact that their ethnic concerns were ignored by the rest of America, that they were often dismissed as right-wing fanatics with unpronounceable names and thick accents. They had resigned themselves to the reality that the American people, on the whole, did not share their priorities. But the Kudirka case was different; the right of oppressed peoples to seek sanctuary in the United States was not just a Lithuanian issue. Simas's case provided a unique opportunity to bring the plight of Lithuania and the other captive nations of Eastern Europe to the attention of all Americans.

So the stakes in terms of the publicity that would come with Simas's landing were high, and several ethnic organizations were battling for the spotlight and control of his arrival. The Lithuanian-American Council, based in Chicago, and the Lithuanian-American Community, based in Philadelphia, were the main combatants. The dispute seemed petty to the diplomats who had obtained Simas's release. But it was anything but petty to the two groups. Both wanted Simas, and both sent prepaid tickets to Moscow for the family's trip out. The Council's tickets were for Moscow to Chicago; the Community's, for Moscow to New York.

Neither organization could make a solid claim that it, and it alone, had been responsible for Simas's release and thus deserved the prize of first look at him. In essence, the Kudirka case had been the work of individuals, not organizations. But in the view of those individuals—the Paegles and Daiva Kezys—the Community had played a greater role than the Council. To be sure, the Council, under its president Dr. C. Kazys Bobelis, had done substantial lobbying on Simas's behalf in Washington. But only the Community, under S. Algimantas Gecys and Ausra Zerr, had encouraged Daiva and Grazina in pursuing the citizenship claims. The Community had even paid much of Daiva's expenses, since she was a member of the Community's Public Affairs Council. (The Paegles, who belonged to neither group, chose to spend nearly $3,000 of their own money for the transatlantic calls they made to Lithuania throughout 1974.)

On October 18, Daiva and Grazina learned that the State Department had decided to have Simas fly to Chicago on the Council's tickets. They were furious, and so was their friend on Capitol Hill, Bob Hanrahan.

Hanrahan dashed off a letter that afternoon to President Ford, who, Hanrahan suspected, had not known the repercussions within the ethnic community of a Chicago arrival:

I feel it is very unfair for congressmen (and senators) who would not even assist in early efforts, to now step forward and insist on having a hand in the arrangements for the Kudirkas when they arrive in America, and to claim all the credit for obtaining his release.

Individual citizens of Lithuanian descent have spent hundreds of dollars of their own money for phone calls to the Soviet Union, for mailing packages of clothing and other commodities to the Kudirkas to assist them in surviving in their bleak homeland, and assist them in obtaining some of the necessary papers. Now many others have stepped forward to welcome the Kudirkas, when in reality they would furnish no money to help pay for the phone calls and packages, because they could get no publicity at that time.

At the State Department, Dyess, who had already been assigned to escort the Kudirkas to the United States, was disturbed by the dispute. It threatened to sour his happy ending. He was eager to work out some sort of compromise. His first idea was to bring Grazina Paegle along as a translator, which would at least give her some time alone with the Kudirkas before they got to Chicago. But the Council, on hearing the plan, insisted that its own representative be included on the flight from Moscow as well. Meanwhile, Grazina, growing angrier by the day, called her senator, Clifford Case of New Jersey, and Daiva called Javits of New York. Both senators contacted the White House and demanded to know what was going on.

In a few days the dispute was resolved. Dyess would go to Moscow in the company of a State Department translator and no one else. And the Chicago-versus-New York decision would be left up to Simas.

On Monday October 28, in response to an urgent telegram, Simas entered the American embassy in Moscow. There Leonard Willems, the same man who had handled Mrs. Sulskis's paperwork, examined Simas's papers, asked him some questions, and had him sign some forms. After an hour, Willems pulled out a little blue book with an American seal on the front, stamped it, and handed it to Simas.

"This is your American passport," Willems said. "With this you belong here. Welcome to American soil." He stood up and reached across his desk to shake Simas's hand.

"Oh, thank you," Simas said in English, smiling broadly and shaking Willems's hand again and again. "Thank you, thank you." Then they made arrangements for the family's departure from the Soviet Union. The five of them—Simas, Gene, Lolita, Evaldas, and Mrs. Sulskis—would leave Moscow on the morning of November 5 via Aeroflot to Frankfurt. From Frankfurt they would fly Pan American nonstop to the United States.

That night he went to a Moscow apartment to meet the dissidents who had helped his mother so much. He accepted congratulations from Kovalev, Tverdokhlebov, and the others on his American passport and answered their questions about life in the labor camps. Who was in Perm Camp Thirty-six when he left? Were conditions improving or worsening? How is Bukovsky? Did you get the message from Sakharov last year? What prompted your protests? What caused your transfers from Potma to Perm, and from Perm to Vladimir? How many times did you try to get messages out to us? They ate sardines and tiny sandwiches and drank toasts of champagne, wine, whiskey, and cognac from paper cups and glass jars.

"The day you come back to Moscow, we'll meet you at the station," Kovalev said. "We'll put you up, get you to the embassy, and see you off. We'll make sure you get on that plane."

Simas flew back to Klaipeda the next day. Four days later the entire family was in Griskabudis with suitcases packed.

On their last night in Lithuania, he led Gene through a driving rain to the church in the center of the village. The old, octagonal church was dark except for the glow of two candles at the altar, and empty except for Simas and Gene, another couple, the old sexton, and the priest in his white vestments. Simas, in a simple black suit, and Gene, in her best pink dress, walked down the aisle and knelt before the altar.

215

The priest read a prayer and then turned to Simas. "Do you take this woman to be your wife?"

"I do."

"Do you take this man to be your husband?"

"I do."

The priest talked of loving and cherishing, supporting and defending. Simas started to cry. He had always wanted to be married in a church, particularly in this church, where he had grown up. He had come here, next to the cemetery where his grandparents were buried, to reassert his commitment to his wife on the eve of their journey. They had been through a lot together—and separately. They would need great strength to face the new crises that life in a new country was certain to bring. This was no performance for the benefit of his mother, gossipy neighbors, or the children. None of them even knew it was happening. This was their moment and theirs alone.

The priest placed Gene's hand over Simas's and asked the sexton for the rings. "With these rings, I bind you together as man and wife in the name of God. Let no power tear you asunder, till death do you part."

Simas kissed the cross the priest held in his hand, and Gene did the same. Then they kissed each other, thanked the priest, and walked back out into the rainy night.

Their train arrived in Moscow on the morning of November 4. Kovalev and several other dissidents met them at the station, as promised. Gene, Mrs. Sulskis, the children, and the dissidents piled into one taxi and went to the apartment where Simas had stayed the week before. Simas and Kovalev got into another taxi and went to the American embassy. Willems was waiting outside to escort them in.

Once inside, Simas was introduced to the two men who would accompany him on the journey: Dyess and Algis Rimas, one of the two State Department employees, out of a total of 6,000, who spoke Lithuanian. Dyess asked what items the family would be taking out with them. Simas listed the items—some clothes, books,

Erratum: Please note that in the photograph section following page 118, pages 6-7 and 4-5 are transposed.

photographs, pieces of amber, towels and tablecloths (gifts for the Paegles), and an egg-based cake that looked like a mountain of peanut brittle.

"That's all?" Dyess asked through Rimas's translation.

"Yes."

"Wonderful."

"Do you think there will be a big problem?"

"Relax. There won't be any problem. Anyway, it's our problem, not yours. This time tomorrow you'll be over the Atlantic. But there are two important matters I must discuss with you now." He sounded nervous. "When you arrive in the United States, there is to be no big press conference or celebration. It has to be that way. It has to be very quiet. Is that understood?"

Simas nodded, although he could not understand why the American government would want to silence him.

"The point is," Willems said, "we don't want to make the Soviets sorry we let you out." Willems then showed him a long list of persons who had been refused Soviet exit visas to join relatives in America. "We don't want to ruin their chances."

"That's right," Dyess agreed. "Now, there is a possibility that one or two correspondents may approach you in the Moscow airport tomorrow. I would be very grateful if you gave them no interview or comments. And please, don't see any correspondents tonight. You will have plenty of time for that later."

Simas nodded again.

"There is one other problem. We have two sets of airplane tickets for you. You have many friends in the United States. One group wants you to go to Chicago. The other wants you in New York. You'll have to decide. Where do you want to go?"

"It doesn't matter to me," Simas replied innocently, not knowing how important the site of his landing had become to Lithuanian-American leaders in the United States. "I just want to get out."

"You have the final choice," Dyess said. "You should know this much. In New York there will be very few Lithuanians. In Chicago there are thousands of them. It's really the Lithuanian capital of the United States."

Simas was confused. He didn't really care where he went, although he thought his mother would like to go to wherever Grazina was. He asked if he could call Grazina and ask her advice. Dyess had the call put through to New Jersey.

"Good evening, Grazina," Simas began. "I am at the American embassy. I am being put in a position to make a choice about airplane tickets, between New York and Chicago. I sense that the preference on the officials' part would be Chicago, although I think we would rather go to New York, if that's closer to you."

"Simas, what are you doing?" Grazina cried. "You have to come here. Don't you want to live with us? I can't really explain exactly what's going on with these tickets. But we want you here in New York."

"Good," he said. "That's the way it will be."

He hung up and turned to Dyess. "I would prefer to go to New York if I have a choice because we know Grazina there. She is expecting us."

"That's fine with me. New York it is."

The plane left right on time, and as it started to move I felt the tightness inside my chest snap. I had broken with the Soviet Union. It really was happening. It wasn't just a dream. I had been stripped of my past, the good and the bad. Everything that had been my life for forty-four years was gone, outside the airplane. I did not even know where I would sleep that night, or what I would do when I woke up the next morning.

The engines revved up for takeoff, and in their whine I heard the yells and groans of the prisoners in the labor camps, fighting and screaming for life. I felt that I was going to scream too. I put my hand over my mouth to stop myself. I had expected to die with them. Now, in the life that was about to begin for me, I would have to be their spokesman. On my last night in Moscow, the dissidents had told me how important it was that I use whatever fame I had to present their case to the world. And who was I? A nobody, a peasant boy from Lithuania, not a real dissident. I couldn't change the world. I would do what I could.

The plane was airborne now, and I was remembering a story I

had heard in the camps. The prisoners in Siberia used to be put to work chopping down trees and loading them into riverboats. According to the story, they would sometimes chop off their hands and hide the hands among the logs, hoping that someone in the outside world would take notice and ask questions. I felt a little like a chopped-off hand, although I hoped I would be a little more effective. I did have a tongue—not an educated, polished tongue, but a tongue that would speak words that came from the heart.

When the plane landed in Frankfurt, I felt as high as I'd ever felt in my life. At long last I had fulfilled the dream of getting to a foreign port. We waited in the airport for about an hour and then boarded Pan American Flight 73 to New York.

As soon as I walked onto that plane, I figured it had to be some sort of special flight arranged to give me and my family an overly favorable view of America. Unlike Soviet planes, this one had a carpet on the floor, a wide variety of magazines and newspapers, and a fresh, clean smell to it. When the plane took off and the seat belt signs went out, the stewardess came around and passed out gray plastic contraptions that looked like doctors' stethoscopes. She showed me how to put one on and then stuck the end of it into a hole in the armrest. All of a sudden, an orchestra was playing inside my head. And every time I flipped the little dial I got different music. I was in ecstasy. Then they served lunch. They gave me a choice between chicken and meat. The portions were so big that I thought the meal they gave me was to be shared by all five of us. All the little side items were so nicely packaged. For dessert I could choose whatever flavor of ice cream I wanted. The Americans were obviously trying to brainwash me!

I got the attention of Algis Rimas, the translator.

"Is this a special flight or something?" I asked.

"What do you mean, special? . . . No, it's a normal flight."

"You mean the next plane from Frankfurt to America will be exactly like this?"

"No, not exactly . . ."

"Aha!" I said, thinking now I would hear the truth.

"They may serve steak instead of chicken."

I wondered what a "steak" could possibly be. My stomach was

fuller than it had ever been before. The stewardess asked if everything was all right, and I just giggled. How could anything be wrong? And then, to top it all, they showed this beautiful color movie. . . .

At the Soviet desk of the State Department in Washington, Richard Combs received a terse cable from Frankfurt. "Pan Am 73. No press yet." That told him everything he needed to know.

In southeast Chicago, Congressman Robert Hanrahan was preparing to address the annual Election Day luncheon of the Roseland Kiwanis Club, the final episode in his unsuccessful campaign for reelection. But the votes were not counted yet and the congressman was not yet depressed when the telephone beeper went off in his coat pocket just after noon. He went to the pay telephone by the club bar, called his campaign headquarters, and found a message to call the White House. He called.

"Bob, this is the President," Gerald Ford said. "Kudirka's in the air, and he's arriving in New York this afternoon. I know how much you've worked on this, and I wanted to keep you informed."

"Thank you, Mr. President."

"And Bob, good luck today."

"Thanks again."

At Chicago's O'Hare Airport, the television cameras were in place to record Simas's arrival. No one had told the television people that Simas was going to New York.

In Queens, Daiva Kezys got the news—Simas would arrive at John F. Kennedy Airport at 3:00 P.M.

Before the movie was over, Dyess asked me to come sit with him.

"Simas," he said through the translator, "suppose there are correspondents at the airport who walk up to you and ask you questions. What are you going to say to them?"

"I don't know. It depends on the questions."

"Well, think about it so it doesn't come out too vitriolic," Dyess said.

"I don't understand."

"Well, as we told you before, there are other people like you still back there in the U.S.S.R. What you say may make things rough for them."

"What if I just say that I want to thank America for bringing me here?"

"Perfect—limit yourself to that, and you'll be fine."

There was an announcement over the public address system. We were approaching New York. Rimas helped me change my watch to New York time. Then the plane dropped out of the clouds and touched down on the runway.

"Let everyone else get off the plane first," Dyess said. He must have seen the way my face tensed up when he said that. "Don't worry. There are just a few formalities."

The plane emptied, and our group waited, then walked off into the airport building. It couldn't have taken us five minutes to get through immigration. I couldn't believe how easy it was. I had been sure that the Central Intelligence Agency would interrogate me before letting me enter the country. But there were no interrogators. The airport was so attractive, and the officials so pleasant and polite. I thought that this must be the façade America puts on for foreign travelers. I vowed to visit an American prison soon, so I could see the bowels of this society as well.

We kept walking down a carpeted hallway. Then we passed some long counters and signed some forms, and Rimas told us we had just gone through customs. They hadn't even opened our suitcases! Dyess, who had gone ahead, came back to tell us that there weren't any reporters or photographers waiting outside. That made him happy.

I was walking toward a set of frosted doors, the last doors between my past and my future. The doors flew open, and 150 people, all of whom I had never seen before, were waving and shouting my name.

"Simas! Simas!"

It was over.

Epilogue

Nothing in his experience, either before the jump or after, had prepared Simas for life in the United States, particularly the life of a minor celebrity. The adjustment turned out to be more difficult than he had anticipated, and he found that some of the problems he had tried to leave in Lithuania had followed him across the Atlantic.

At first, his life here was an endless whirl of press conferences, speeches, and airports. He appeared before groups of Lithuanian-Americans, fishermen, and human rights activists of every stripe. He traveled to Boston, Hartford, Waterbury, New York, Philadelphia, Baltimore, Washington, Miami, St. Petersburg, Cleveland, Detroit, Chicago, St. Louis, Omaha, Minneapolis, Phoenix, Los Angeles, Ottawa, Toronto, and Montreal. He dined with senators and congressmen, received the keys to a dozen cities, and was received as a hero on board the *Vigilant,* at anchor in New Bedford, four years to the day after the jump.

But it all began to sour soon after the five members of the Kudirka family—Simas, Gene, the two children, and his mother—moved in with the Paegles in New Jersey. Because of their inability to understand English they were totally dependent on the Paegles for legal and financial advice. Simas signed over to the Paegles control of the publishing rights to his life story as well as indirectly giving them access to a bank account containing funds raised for the Kudirkas by well-wishers. The Paegles controlled the places the Kudirkas went and the people they saw, and friction between the two families was inevitable. In July 1975 the Kudirkas moved to the Bronx, New York. The dispute with the Paegles was finally settled by a consent decree filed in the Superior Court of New Jersey in June 1977. The Paegles admitted receiving $4,800 from the bank account, but denied having taken it illegally. Simas asked that they be allowed to keep the money as reimbursement for their expenses in helping him win his freedom. The court also invalidated all the contracts Simas had signed that benefited the Paegles.

The explosion in his personal life might not have hit him so hard if there had been any sort of professional life to divert him. But unlike so many of the Soviet dissidents who emigrate or are exiled to the United States, he was not an intellectual for whom a prestigious university would be proud to create a slot. He was a radio operator, and nothing more, and lacking command of the English language, he was not even a radio operator. He did find work as a part-time house painter, which kept him busy for a few months, while still giving him time to work on this book and a television movie and stay active in the human rights cause. In his free time, he made speeches on behalf of the presidential campaign of Senator Jackson, his hero from Perm, until Jackson withdrew from the race.

Eventually, he came upon a solution to his unemployment. In partnership with Daiva and Romas Kezys, with whom he remained friendly, he bought a sixty-five-unit apartment building in the Bronx, which he and Gene managed and maintained. By mid-1977, his life had settled into something approaching a routine, and he said he was happy. He still could not get over the freedom of speech he enjoyed as an American. On his first speaking tour, he had criticized then-Secretary of State Kissinger viciously, using phrases he had learned from the Perm "literati," but no government agent knocked on his hotel room door the next morning or brought him in for questioning. He got a thrill every time he passed a newsstand and saw the variety of newspapers and magazines offered there. He valued the fact that in his own home, or anywhere else, he could speak his mind without fear.

He was disappointed, however, by what he sensed as a lack of moral responsibility in American society. That void, he felt, was reflected in the way the government approached the human rights issue, although that may have changed under President Carter. As a government, Simas said, we mouth principles when it is convenient and ignore them when it is not. He could not understand why the United States should ever be reluctant to speak up for men and women whose only crimes were what they wrote or said. True, he conceded, the Soviet Union does not kill dissenters the way some other countries do or the way the Soviet Union itself did twenty-five years ago; but imprisonment or exile is a harsh punishment for a man who loves freedom, and loves his country as well.

He could not understand why Americans worry that a strong stand on human rights jeopardizes détente. If it does, he told whoever would listen, then détente is not worth having; for if the Soviets do not respect human rights, how can we expect them to respect any agreement they make with us. There are principles on which compromise is not possible.

As he came to terms with the strengths and weaknesses of American society, though, he appeared to be suffering from an affliction common to men who have risked their lives for a cause and then must content themselves with daily rations of stopped-up drains and broken windows. At times he felt that his life was meaningless, certainly less meaningful than when he had stood at the forefront of the protest movement in the labor camps. Every day had meaning then. There were times during his first three years in the United States, particularly in the early months, when he would have preferred to have been in Perm with Jonas Kadzionis and the other men he left behind. At other times, he felt guilty about the material comforts and the freedom he enjoyed here. And he felt guilty about the fact that Kovalev and Tverdokhlebov, the dissidents who had helped him so much, were doing time in Perm themselves.

This book, of course, is a chance for him to give his life new meaning. On his last night in the Soviet Union, he promised the dissidents that he would speak out, despite his own doubts about his ability to tell the facts about labor camps, isolation cells, death trains, and psychiatric tortures. With this book, perhaps, he has kept his commitment to those still at sea.